A PARADISE
OF SMALL HOUSES

A PARADISE
OF SMALL HOUSES

The Evolution, Devolution,
and Potential Rebirth
of Urban Housing

IIIIIIIIIIIIIIIIII

MAX PODEMSKI

BEACON PRESS
BOSTON

BEACON PRESS
Boston, Massachusetts
www.beacon.org

Beacon Press books
are published under the auspices of
the Unitarian Universalist Association of Congregations.

27 26 25 24   8 7 6 5 4 3 2 1

This book is printed on acid-free paper that meets the uncoated paper
ANSI/NISO specifications for permanence as revised in 1992.

Text design and composition by Kim Arney

Library of Congress Cataloguing-in-Publication Data is available for this title.
Hardcover ISBN: 978-0-8070-0778-5
E-book ISBN: 978-0-8070-0779-2
Audiobook: 978-0-8070-1636-7

For my mom

CONTENTS

A PARADISE
OF SMALL HOUSES

The House on Morrison

My grandparents' house was on 43rd Avenue and Morrison Street in Southeast Portland, Oregon. The interior design was reminiscent of a Polish Baroque palace as imagined by Liberace: a shag carpet covered the floor of the living room with three-inch yellow and red strands, like spaghetti in marinara sauce. The shelves were lined with purple and gold German glassware and silver goblets. An oil portrait of my aunt, which my family referred to as the "Mona Paula," peered down from over the fireplace, painted by an admirer of hers. As a child, when I came to visit I would search for the big bag of mini Crunch Bars that I knew my grandmother kept somewhere in the house. After scouring the drawers of the oak and marble furniture, sometimes all I would come up with were silver dollars and gold Krugerrands that she hid in case she had to flee in the middle of the night.

My grandparents were born in the 1910s in the shtetels of southern Poland. My grandfather, Max, came from a very poor family, and when he was six was sent to work in one of the giant textile factories in the large city of Lodz. With virtually no formal education, he never learned to read. However, he became a master tailor, wore colorful three-piece suits, and had a refined sensibility. My grandmother, Anna, was the daughter of a baker and spoke five languages. However, in English she was prone to malapropisms and would refer to a chest of drawers as "chester drawers."

Instead of saying urban renewal she would say "Irving renewal," perhaps in confusion with the name of a Portland street.

After surviving Auschwitz, my grandparents married in Lodz and started to rebuild their lives. However, they were soon forced to flee Poland in 1951 with their two children, my father and aunt, after Polish partisans began murdering Jews. After stints in Israel and a displaced persons camp in Hanover, Germany, they came through Ellis Island and ended up in the Pacific Northwest. By cleaning houses and working in clothing stores, every few years they moved a little farther from the Jewish immigrant enclave of South Portland where they'd first landed. In 1962 they built the house on Morrison Street.

The house they built—a squat brick duplex with a long, low-slung roof resembling an army barrack—was aggressively plain, especially when compared with the small Arts and Crafts bungalows that surrounded it. However, it contained subtly ingenious features. The entrance to my grandparents' unit faced Morrison Street, and the entrance to the second unit was off 43rd. Each had two bedrooms; there was also a third bedroom sandwiched between the apartments with doors leading into both, in case one ever needed to be enlarged. To make extra money, they would rent out the second unit, and later in life my grandmother even rented out the basement to a German man named Diedrich who kept a Volkswagen topped by a canoe in the driveway.

As I grew up, my interest shifted from finding candy bars to studying cities. I studied urban planning in Los Angeles, Denmark, Brazil, and New York. I worked for an environmental justice organization to repurpose a blighted flood control channel and dangerous alleys into parks and public spaces and developed policies for the City of Los Angeles to alleviate the crippling housing crisis. However, over time I learned that planners and policymakers have not had even a fraction of the impact on the urban form of neighborhoods that people like my grandparents have.

Our nation's cities are by and large the work of immigrant and working-class people who scraped together funds and built a small home for themselves, sometimes with an extra unit or two for rental income. The result of this work is often discordant, messy, and—for anyone who has tried to navigate a vehicle through the winding streets of central Boston or renovate an old Victorian house—poorly suited to contemporary times.

However, it has also resulted in rich and vibrant neighborhoods that are today some of the most beloved in the entire country. Yet although the simple houses and apartment buildings that compose our communities have played a monumental role in shaping our nation's cities, the average person knows very little about them. This book is an attempt to tell the story of these buildings and, through them, tell the broader story of the American city.

ıı ıı ıı ıı ıı ıı ıı ıı ıı ıı ıı

In nearly every town and city across the United States there is an old house that has been preserved for posterity as a historic artifact and opened for the public to visit. In Brownville, Nebraska, population 142, the former home of a Civil War–era captain sits on broad manicured grounds with a heavily ornamented façade resembling a dollhouse. In Los Angeles, ornate Victorian homes have been rescued from demolition and transported to a slender lot on the shoulder of the Pasadena Freeway. Men costumed in top hats and women in giant hoop dresses walk the grounds. In both settings, the formal rooms are decorated with period decor: details like a rag doll on a child's bed or an enormous wood cauldron in the kitchen are meant to give a window into how people here once lived. It is this type of structure that forms the popular conception of housing in the United States. However, the reality is that most Americans were not wealthy enough to live in lavish and expansive homes, or even ones designed by a trained architect. In rural areas, they were built by the inhabitants themselves with the assistance of a few neighbors, using local materials and simple construction methods adapted from ancient practices. These homes, with their thatch roofs and mud or stone façades sheltering one to three multipurpose rooms, often looked like natural outcroppings of the landscape.

In cities, communities of local builders took on the job of constructing housing. These urban homes, like their rural counterparts, were based on ancient floor plans and composed of multipurpose rooms. They were often built at a modest and affordable scale, created livable and hospitable interior spaces with access to light and open space, and were flexibly designed to adapt to social and demographic trends. Such buildings are largely the product of immigrants who financed, developed, and lived in them. It is not the gingerbread mansions of tourist-brochure lore but these common everyday houses that represent our nation's most enduring architectural achievement. However, urban housing also represents the nation's deep inequity where Black people and other people of color were and continue to be left off the ladder of economic opportunity.

|||||||||||||||||||||||

Just a few years after its founding in the late seventeenth century, the terrace house of England was brought to colonial Philadelphia and adapted into the row house. This small home, attached via its side walls to a series of identical neighbors, was well-suited to the crowded city and also offered each household a greater sense of privacy and independence than an apartment offered. This incredibly versatile building type could be adapted still further depending on the occupant, from a rich magnate's limestone townhouse to the poorest workers' tiny one-room version called a trinity that required a ladder to ascend to the upper floors.

In nineteenth-century New Orleans, refugees of the Haitian Revolution settled on the outskirts of the city, where they built shotgun-style houses—long and narrow structures in which each room led directly to the next. This type of home had originally been introduced to the Caribbean by enslaved people from Africa, where it took on influences from the dwelling styles of the Arawak people as well as neoclassical architecture from Europe. Its unique climate-adaptive features and innovative frame construction led the shotgun house to become the dominant housing type in New Orleans and eventually spread across the country.

In Chicago, which grew from a provisional outpost into one of the world's largest cities in the few decades between the Civil War and turn of the century, builders invented an entirely new construction method: the balloon frame, which made it possible for a simple workers cottage to be erected in a matter of days. Their lightweight construction allowed the cottages to be lifted onto timber piers to add additional floors, moved around on a lot, or even rolled across a neighborhood to make room for larger buildings. Due to gradual adaptations to the workers cottage, over time the "pine jungles" that they comprised on the periphery of nineteenth-century Chicago became dense urban neighborhoods by the early twentieth.

The period from 1900 to World War II saw the modernization of urban housing in the United States, which up to this point had been essentially medieval. Now new forms, from the triple-deckers of New England to the bungalow courts of the West Coast, filled American cities with modern, open homes that still spoke to regional customs and cultures. Instead of one or two multipurpose rooms that served as settings for everything from cooking to sleeping, these new housing types introduced individualized rooms for different activities. Household drudgery was replaced by modern appliances that were conveniently located in purpose-built kitchens. Instead of fetid outhouses, bathrooms were brought inside and contained the new holy trinity of a porcelain sink, toilet, and bathtub.

ıııııııııııııııııııı

Despite this rich history, if schoolchildren are taught anything about working-class urban housing it is the reform movement that emerged in the late nineteenth century to ban it. During that period, known as the Progressive Era, American cities saw a new influx of immigrants who—unlike the existing population of Protestants from Northern Europe—were largely Catholics and Jews, as well as other ethnicities and religions from around the globe. A reform movement arose to campaign against the types of homes that many of these new arrivals lived in: dense, multifamily urban housing. The movement's stance was built on the moral argument that such dwellings robbed their inhabitants of dignity. Apartments in particular were seen as transitory buildings that granted their residents anonymity and the temptation to sin. While many such buildings of the time were indeed overcrowded and in need of improvement, the reform movement was also fueled by nativism, racism, and classism. To this day, urban housing is still largely seen as a second-rate dwelling for the destitute. In the minds of Progressive reformers, the only proper dwelling was a single-family home, owned by its inhabitants, which, they claimed, tied a person to their community and forced them to be morally upstanding.

By the early twentieth century, the tenements and teeming slums had largely been eradicated. Improved wages and transportation allowed working-class white people to leave inner-city neighborhoods. Yet the movement against dense urban housing continued—with each passing decade, new limitations were imposed city by city. Restrictions requiring buildings to be set back from both the street and neighboring buildings were designed to ensconce homes in greenery, yet also made it impossible to build traditional row homes or small apartment buildings. In the 1930s, parking spaces began to be mandated in new housing, which turned front porches and stoops into garage doors. By the 1950s, these regulations had largely usurped the creativity of the builder as the main driver of housing design. In Los Angeles, rectangular, stucco-clad dingbat apartment buildings, which were almost entirely driven by the need to provide parking, proliferated. In Houston, entire neighborhoods of skinny townhouses were built that meet the street not with a front door but a long driveway. Yet from a national perspective, even these types of dense housing are outliers. By the close of the twentieth century, zoning codes enacted by cities and towns across the country stipulated that the only residential structure that could be built was the detached single-family home. These laws were a triumph of the housing reform movement, enshrining the biases of nineteenth-century reforms into law.

However, by the 1990s the culture shifted. After decades of movies and TV shows that had portrayed cites as apocalyptic wastelands ridden with psychotic taxi drivers and home invasions by mohawked punks, shows like *Friends*, *Felicity*, and *Sex and the City* depicted them as filled with attractive young white people grabbing coffee and cosmos. By this time, several generations had grown up in the suburbs, without their parents' memories of urban pollution, crime, and overcrowded housing. To them, cities were not threatening or dangerous places, but adult playgrounds filled with opportunity. By the 2000s many cities were growing faster than their suburbs for the first time in a century.[1] In 1950, Boston had a population of over 800,000 people but in the succeeding decades that was reduced by 29 percent.[2] However, since 1980, the city has added 110,000 new residents.[3] Portland has nearly doubled its population from 360,000 in 1980 to 650,000 today.[4] New York City has grown from 7 million in 1980 to 8.8 million today, absorbing a population greater than the entire city of Philadelphia.[5]

The growth of cities over the last thirty years represents a realignment of the American Dream. Owning a home is still a fundamental value, but the community in which it resides has become increasingly important. Today, houses in walkable urban environments are by far the most expensive in the country, with a value 40 to 200 percent higher than comparable ones in the suburbs.[6] Urban neighborhoods are also preferred among businesses, with commercial office space in walkable areas having an average price-per-square-foot 74 percent higher than suburban business parks.[7]

As people move back into cities, however, they confront the zoning codes that ban any new construction of dense urban housing. It is this mismatch that is at the root of the nation's severe housing crisis. Since the 1990s, housing costs have tripled in the US, and in 70 percent of the country, the cost of buying a home is out of reach for the average American. A worker making minimum wage cannot afford to rent a two-bedroom apartment of any size in any state without financial assistance.[8] The nationwide affordability crisis became even more pronounced during the Covid-19 pandemic. From December 2019 to June 2022, home prices went up 45 percent and rents by nearly 20 percent. At the same time, the amount of new housing construction fell, with one economist telling the *New York Times* in December of 2022, "We're sitting right now at the worst housing affordability we've seen in several decades."[9]

As central cities have suddenly become desirable places to live, neighborhoods in these areas—from the South End in Boston to the Mission District of San Francisco—have transformed from working-class to luxury. In order to accommodate the well-off population moving into these areas, the interiors of formerly working-class buildings are being reconfigured into mansions. In the Wicker Park neighborhood of Chicago, apartment flats in three-story buildings are converted into a single 6,000-square-foot home with entire walls made of glass.*

In Los Angeles, a 1920s Echo Park bungalow court, situated in a neighborhood once famous for being the location of the film *Mi Vida Loca*, was converted into a "curated co-living community" by a developer from London.[10] In New York, many nineteenth-century brownstone row homes were subdivided into apartments or even rooming houses soon after they were built. Now, as a new gilded class descends on Manhattan and Brooklyn, these beloved structures are not only being turned back into single-family homes—international billionaires are also demolishing the interiors and doubling the square footage, leaving only the façades intact.[11] As this

---

*See, for example, this remodeled building in Chicago: Zillow, "1935 W Schiller St, Chicago, IL 60622," accessed November 11, 2019, https://www.zillow.com/homedetails/1935-W-Schiller-St-Chicago-IL-60622/158773104_zpid/.

occurs, the longtime residents who once rented and sometimes owned these traditionally dense and affordable forms of urban housing are being displaced to make room for the affluent.

In cities on the West Coast, the worst off of these displaced families end up in the tent cities that have sprouted on sidewalks and empty lots. The inability to build new housing has resulted in Los Angeles County lacking an estimated half a million units of housing.[12] Almost every available space, from freeway underpasses to flood control channels, has become an encampment that accommodates some of the sixty thousand people who are estimated to be unhoused. In 2017, a hot plate in an encampment in a gully next to the 405 freeway sparked a massive brush fire, forcing mansion-dwellers like Rupert Murdoch and Gwyneth Paltrow in the adjacent Brentwood neighborhood above to evacuate.[13] The urban resurgence that began in the 1990s is beginning to look more like a new urban crisis.

ııııııııııııııııı

Throughout much of the nineteenth and twentieth centuries, the United States excelled at building high-quality housing that was attainable to working people. The buildings that came out of that era continue to be a crucial source of affordable urban housing today. However, these buildings have other benefits that reach far beyond the affordability crisis. Residents of the dense, centrally located neighborhoods where traditional urban housing predominates rely on walking, biking, and mass transit to get around at much higher rates than those who live in lower density, more sprawling areas. The result is that people living in places like New York City have an average carbon footprint that is less than 30 percent that of the typical American's.[14] For this reason, scientists say that building denser cities is more effective at combating climate change than installing solar panels on every home or retrofitting every building.[15]

In the United States, the most important factor influencing your educational path, your economic success, or even your health is where you live—your zip code carries even more weight than your genetic code.[16] But the most economically productive places in the country are increasingly concentrated in just a handful of metropolitan regions that also happen to have the highest housing costs. Whereas fifty or a hundred years ago the rich and poor were separated by a few neighborhoods, they are now divided by hundreds of miles. And whereas affordable urban dwellings once allowed working-class families to establish themselves in opportunity-rich cities, soaring housing costs have eroded any such footholds.[17] The immense potential of dense urban housing to battle climate change and reduce economic inequality would be considered a panacea by most. Yet this silver bullet does not need to be invented in an MIT lab or a Silicon Valley office park—it lies in the old neighborhoods of every city. Instead of looking at these structures as artifacts of a different era, we must seek to relearn their lessons.

The houses discussed in this book were chosen not because they are unique but because they are ubiquitous and represent types that can be found in neighborhoods across the country. Each structure is emblematic of a particular moment in our nation's urban development, and the book is organized chronologically, with each chapter building off the last. However, a reader can also feel free to skip around to the sections that most interest them. The text is further bolstered by drawings, photos, and diagrams. Houses are not merely utilitarian structures—they are deeply shaped by the unique cultures of their cities and have then gone on to shape those cultures in turn. So while scholarly articles, turn-of-the-century sociological studies, interviews, books, and contemporaneous news accounts were used for research, so were films, literature, music, and art. Most importantly, I spent time in each city and house discussed to discern how people have historically lived in these spaces, how they are used today, and how they shape the broader environment around them.

CHAPTER 1

Philadelphia Row House

A Paradise of Small Houses

O n top of Philadelphia's City Hall stands an enormous bronze statue of William Penn, a visionary who set out to create a new type of city: a place where a diverse group of people would coalesce around a common set of ideals, and equality and health were embedded into its very design. From his perch five hundred feet in the air, Penn looks out over the city he founded over three hundred years ago. Yet past the glittering skyscrapers, lying before him is not quite the utopia he imagined but instead a vast plain of squat brick buildings: tens of thousands of narrow, brick row homes lined up side by side, constituting nearly 70 percent of the city's housing stock. They come in every conceivable style and configuration. In the old colonial core, tiny homes dating as far back as the eighteenth century, with dormered windows jutting out from the sloped roofs, line cobblestoned alleys. Near stately Rittenhouse Square, the row houses become opulent mansions clad in granite and brownstone. Radiating out from Center City, even more variations of the row house line the city's straight, gridded streets for miles in every direction.

The row house traces its roots to Northern Europe, but Philadelphia— considered to be the birthplace of America—adapted the structure into one uniquely suited to the United States. Their compact, single-family structure allowed for private property and individual expression despite the crowded urban environment, thus giving even working families the opportunity to be homeowners. Local builders became experts at manipulating the city's narrow lots to create well-appointed and commodious homes. The Founding Fathers saw their columns, carefully ordered façades, and other neoclassical details as linking the nation to the ancient republics of Greece and Rome. As the Philadelphia row home was exported across the nation, it helped shape the country's very notion, both physically and symbolically, of what a house should be.

                    |||||||||||||||||||

Utopian communities often bring to mind images of dusty people worshiping crystals in geodesic domes, or bearded hippies in hemp chokers living in huts rubbed down with elk manure. However, left out of this discussion is perhaps one of the most successful utopias ever conceived—Philadelphia. As the son of an admiral, William Penn had been groomed to be part of Britain's ruling elite from an early age. However, he lasted only two years at Oxford and shortly after had a religious awakening, renouncing his upbringing to join the radical Religious Society of Friends. His conversion to Quakerism made him a permanent outsider in Anglican England. He became notorious for his diatribes calling for more civil liberties and was arrested several times for instigating a riot. Yet despite this background, due to a debt owed to his father, in 1681 King Charles II of England granted Penn a charter for forty-five thousand square miles of land in the American colonies.[1]

Penn had been indelibly shaped by the inequality of Europe, where the aristocracy luxuriated in gardens and palaces while the rest of the population lived in squalid conditions, especially in urban centers. Cities like London were a suffocating warren of densely packed, crudely built wooden structures enveloping narrow, chamber pot–soaked streets. These conditions had led to the Great Fire of London in 1666, when Penn was twenty-two years old. The city had been almost entirely destroyed, with the lead roof of St. Paul's Cathedral melting into molten rivulets that ran into the gutters. It was an event that both traumatized and radicalized him.

Penn saw his land grant not as a way to gain wealth, but as an opportunity to test out a holy experiment based on democratic and communal values.[2] The capital city of his colony would be a refutation of the European city—a refuge for poor craftspeople, farmers, and religious minorities.[3] Thomas Holme, a surveyor hired by Penn, chose a well-drained narrow strip of land on which to build the capital, bound by the Delaware River to the east and the Schuylkill River to the west. Penn entered into a purchase agreement with the Lenape people, who had inhabited this area along the Delaware for centuries, reserving the land they lived on for their use.* However, Penn's view of equality did not extend to African Americans, with slavery existing in the city until the nineteenth century.

On this space between the two rivers, Holme plotted a grid of numbered streets running north to south along the Delaware, bisected by two main streets: Broad, running north to south, and Market, running east to west. In each quadrant of the city, Holme placed large public squares, with the largest one in the center.[4] Penn wanted his capital to be more like an agglomeration of country estates than like the crowded and congested urban centers he knew back home. He instructed Holme to lay out the city so that each house could have "ground on each side for gardens, or orchards, or field, that it may be a green country town, that will always be wholesome and never burn."[5] Instead of buildings being jammed so close that it was unclear where one ended and another began, the city's large blocks were divided into half-acre lots, over four times the size of the standard single-family home lot found in most American cities today.

This type of utilitarian street grid, with single-family homes nestled into large lots, has become the basic template of US urban development. It is a scheme that dates back to the Bronze Age and has been found in places ranging from the Indus Valley to Mexico. However, at the time that Philadelphia was being planned, it had fallen out of fashion, and Penn's decision to lay out the city in this way reflected his utopian vision. During the same period in which English architect Christopher Wren was

---

* Walter Licht et al., "The Original People and Their Land: The Lenape, Pre-History to the 18th Century," West Philadelphia Collaborative History (n.d.), retrieved January 22, 2023, https://collaborativehistory.gse.upenn.edu/stories/original-people-and-their-land-lenape -pre-history-18th-century; the scholar Pekka Hämäläinen argues that Penn's relations with Indigenous people were not pure altruism but a pragmatic decision based on the geopolitical power among Native tribes during this era. Almost immediately after Penn's death, his heirs reneged on this agreement under the notorious walking treaty where 750,000 acres were taken from the Lenape.

proposing to replace London's medieval warren of streets—now ravaged by the Great Fire—with radial streets that framed palaces, public spaces, and grand monuments, Penn's grid was meant to avoid these hierarchies and make all places in the city more or less equal. He hoped this would promote equality and a common understanding among the city's residents. The radical and visionary plan for Philadelphia became a powerful marketing tool for the new city. It was advertised across England, inspiring colonists to journey across the ocean to Penn's capital, Philadelphia—the City of Brotherly Love.

While Penn envisioned Philadelphia as an egalitarian utopia, the site that Thomas Holme had selected along two large rivers was ideal for commerce. The city soon became one of the most important colonial ports, where a robust community of merchants traded with Europe, the Southern colonies, and the Caribbean. Just eight years after its founding in 1682, Philadelphia's twenty-two shopkeepers and 119 craftspeople were considered to be the most skilled in all the American colonies.[6] Yet Penn was never truly able to see his city blossom due to being called back to England to join the court of King James II.[7] In total he only spent four years in Philadelphia, and without his tight grip, the inhabitants of the thriving colonial port ran roughshod over his dream of a country town.

IIIIIIIIIIIIIIIIIII

Penn's visionary plan was out of step with a basic reality of the time. In the seventeenth century, the main mode of transportation was one's own body. Philadelphia was therefore, like all other pre-nineteenth-century settlements, a walking city. Development did not sprawl across the grid in large estates, which would have necessitated long, arduous trips in order to accomplish everyday tasks. Instead, homes and businesses clustered into just a few blocks around the Delaware River wharfs. By 1689, the forty-three half-acre lots Holme had plotted along the Delaware had been subdivided into seventy much smaller parcels. Alleys were cut through the large blocks, with the single half-acre lot along each being subdivided into as many as twenty additional parcels. By the first decade of the nineteenth century, over ten alleys had been cut from Front Street to Second Street.[8]

One of these alleys had been created in 1703 when two blacksmiths named Arthur Wells and John Gilbert opened a cart path through their adjoining properties. The 15-foot-wide Elfreth's Alley, as it became known, quickly filled with diminutive wooden 800-square-foot stand-alone homes packed side by side. The interiors of these houses utilized medieval floor plans that colonists brought with them from England. They consisted of a *hall*—a more public room that faced the street and was the setting for daily chores like cooking and making soap and yarn—and a slightly smaller back *parlor*, which was a more private, formal space for resting or entertaining guests. While larger homes would have additional rooms on the upper floors, the tiniest of these homes were called *huts* and had sleeping areas lofted above the parlor, accessed by a ladder.

Along narrow lanes like Elfreth's, all classes and social strata huddled together. Wealthy merchants and doctors lived next door to town criers and skinners. The economy at the time revolved around small family-sized firms, and each tiny home would often double as a place of business. The front hall would become a storefront, a workshop for an artisan, or an office for a businessperson. Even the wealthiest merchants lived above their counting houses next to the docks on Water Street.[9] The mixed nature of the city made it a lively environment. Merchants would place their wares on display outdoors and people would mingle in the street. Over one hundred taverns operated in the city, which facilitated communication, business, and the city's social life, with beer being sometimes used as currency.[10]

However, life in colonial Philadelphia was not an endless spring break flotilla party. The city's compactness made it susceptible to the disease and fire that Penn had so desperately wanted to avoid. Trash and animal manure piled up along the narrow alleys, and when fires occurred it was common for neighbors to form human chains to pass water buckets to put them out. Yet the city was also incredibly dynamic. Penn's views about equality and religious freedom had imbued the city with a culture of entrepreneurial innovation where ideas were freely exchanged. Philadelphia became one of the main intellectual centers of the colonies, and in places like City Tavern, which stood a block from the river, public debates and lectures helped foment and hasten the American Revolution.

||||||||||||||||||

Penn had envisioned Philadelphia as a city of the future, yet in the late seventeenth century, its architecture was essentially medieval. The wood shacks that composed the city's housing, with their hall-and-parlor floor plans, epitomized the centuries-old practices that had been brought to the colonies directly from Europe. Building materials were culled from local sources, such as timber, thatch, and clay, and the resulting structures often blended in with the natural landscape. These dwellings embodied *vernacular architecture*, which the professor and folklorist Henry Glassie defines as buildings that exhibit "the knowledge that people develop during lives of environmental engagement."[11]

However, a movement that sought alternatives to these age-old practices had been percolating in Europe since the Italian Renaissance of the fifteenth century. Inspired by the texts and ruins left behind by ancient Rome and Greece, cities like Florence and Venice became showcases for an architecture that gave aesthetic principles the same importance as environmental ones. Instead of façades that were primarily intended to protect the inhabitants from intruders or weather, they were carefully arranged based on proportion and symmetry. Decorative bands divided each floor of the building, and a cornice was placed at the roofline. Elaborate ornamentation, including Greek and Roman columns, was used to delineate windows and doors. On a vernacular building, a person with knowledge of the local environment and culture could intuit the practical purpose of each structural element. However, to even begin to understand these Renaissance buildings, one needed a more esoteric and privileged knowledge of classical architecture.

By the seventeenth century, the Renaissance architecture of Italy had made its way to England. On the outskirts of British cities, parks or squares inspired by Italian piazzas were constructed. Around these, designers envisioned grand palaces with unified, classical design schemes. However, the nobility—perhaps with the feces-soaked petri dishes that had constituted most British cities still fresh in their minds—largely preferred estates in the country.[12] And so a new type of residential architecture started to rise along these squares: the terrace house.

This type of narrow house—divided from its neighbors on either side by a shared party wall—had long been popular in Belgium, the Netherlands, and other Northern European countries. It is believed that British aristocrats were exposed to this type of home when they fled to Holland after Puritans executed the king and took over the British government in the mid-seventeenth century under Oliver Cromwell.[13] The houses that began to appear in England around the new squares and public spaces had exteriors that were unified across multiple units into a single grand façade ornamented with cornices and long rows of columns. The entire structure was placed onto a podium, with a terrace in front of the colonnade. Instead of appearing as multiple dwellings, the overall effect of these monumental structures was of a palace.

These homes, which became known as *terrace houses*, proved to be extremely popular in Britain, and wealthy urbanites came to favor them over detached villas. By the eighteenth century, grand developments, such as the Royal Crescent in Bath, started to flank squares and public spaces across the country. During the Industrial Revolution, mass-production technologies allowed developers to build standardized terrace houses for the middle and working classes outside booming cities like Manchester, Liverpool, and Birmingham.[14] The terrace house came to be the standard urban dwelling of the United Kingdom, with even the home of the prime minister at 10 Downing Street in London being a narrow, gray-brick structure.

||||||||||||||||||||

The elegant terrace houses of England were contrasted by the feculent appearance of many American cities. Upon one of his first visits back to Philadelphia after returning to England, William Penn was disgusted by the pigs proudly trotting down the mud-logged streets and the bedraggled collection of homes that included log cabins and caves dug out of the riverbank. In response, Penn ordered a brick factory be constructed, and thanks to the region's amenable soils, by 1690 the city boasted four brickmakers and ten bricklayers.[15]

As the leading port and intellectual center of the American colonies, Philadelphia received and absorbed the architectural ideas coming out of England. One of the first structures in the city to demonstrate the classical design of Europe was the Slate Roof House, built just north of City Tavern in 1687 by a Quaker merchant named Samuel Carpenter. This home was not made from wood, nor did it have the steeply pitched roof or overhanging second-floor "pents" associated with the medieval style—instead, it had a flat façade made of brick produced by one of the city's factories. Its tall chimneys, dormered roof, and windows and doors were carefully arranged in the Georgian style, a more refined version of Renaissance architecture that had emerged in England. With its attention to proportions such as the height of each room and the spacing of the windows, the Georgian style proved ideal not just for grand palaces but also for much smaller buildings.[16] In 1691, a ten-home complex built at Front and Dock Streets took the features of the Slate Roof House and distilled them into an economically and spatially efficient form.[17] This complex, called Budd's Long Row, was the first terrace house development to be built in the United States.

Row houses, as they became known in the US, quickly took hold in Philadelphia and were soon occupied by every class and social strata in the city. Along the wide main arteries like Market Street, traders and merchants built large row homes to show off their wealth and refinement. These homes, which still stand in some parts of the city, rise to three stories and, like the Slate Roof House, have a dormered roof and tall chimneys. Their façades are made from pressed brick, which have very small seams, making them look like one solid piece of stone. They are further adorned with neoclassical detailing—decorative cornices, windows shutters, and elaborate door frames, all of which vary depending on the social status of the owner. The layout of these large row homes modified the traditional hall-and-parlor scheme by applying the Georgian principles of formality and privacy. The two rooms, which were previously of different sizes, now had the same dimensions. In larger homes, instead of entering the front room directly, one would first enter a hallway running along the party wall with the entrance to the ground-floor rooms leading off it. This was almost identical to the upper-class terrace houses of England and became known as the *London house plan* (see image 4).[18]

Though imposing, these large row homes were still confined to skinny lots, constrained by the spatial limitations of the walking city. Visitors to Philadelphia, especially from the Southern colonies, would comment on the lack of space. By the early nineteenth century, kitchens became a way to both enlarge and distinguish row homes. Using the long lots, kitchens would be contained in a narrow structure appended to the back of the house called an *el*. For the wealthiest families, the el would also have a dining room and a second floor containing servants' quarters (see image 3).

On lesser streets, middle-class artisans and merchants would occupy two-story row homes with a dormered roof that sheltered a small attic room called a *garret*, containing rooms for children or servants. The neoclassical detailing would often be reduced to a simple cornice and arched doorway. For the more well-off, the kitchen would be contained in a small el, but in most houses, it would be in the basement and accessed from an outside hatch that allowed people to bring coal, firewood, and other messy items inside without having to walk them through their main living space. The shutter doors leading to these basements are still a prominent feature along Elfreth's Alley and in other older sections of the city.

The interiors of these more modest homes had the two-room Georgian plan, but because they were on narrower lots, they lacked a hallway. The front parlor acted as a living room and the back room as a formal dining area. In some cases, the wall dividing the rooms featured a large French door that could be opened in order to combine them into one large space for entertaining. Instead of the standard flight of stairs, the upper stories were accessed by an incredibly compact spiral stairwell, often so narrow and steep that a handle, similar to one that would be used to open a cupboard, was attached to the wall to help people climb them. The style of these staircases diverged from those found in England or Europe and, along with the kitchen el, are one of the true innovations of the Philadelphia row house: their compact nature maximizes the building's vertical space while leaving enough room for a decently sized living area.

The lowest class of housing was found along the narrow alleys and the small dead-end passages, called courts, that went into the interiors of the city blocks. Here, a slender type of row house predominated, one that rose to three stories in height with only one 10-by-12-foot room on each floor. These homes were nicknamed "father, son, and holy ghost," which was shortened to trinity—the name they are commonly known by today. Trinities became home to the city's poorest residents, who were often mariners, low-level artisans, and laborers, with each of the small rooms sometimes rented out to a different family. Many of these residents would bring their own mattress to avoid sleeping on the floor and becoming a buffet for the infamous vermin known to inhabit many of these court homes. However, these accommodations were still better than those of the most destitute, who slept under the tables at grog shops and oyster houses.

IIIIIIIIIIIIIIIIII

The home of Philadelphia's most famous citizen, Benjamin Franklin, illustrates the development of row homes in the city. In the mid-eighteenth century, Franklin left his rented house in the crowded walking city and built a detached single-family home nestled into a garden on the edge of town. As Franklin grew more prominent, he added a new wing with a dining room and library, and three large Georgian row homes used as rental properties were built along Market Street at the front of the property. By the time of Franklin's death in 1790, the city had enveloped his estate. His heirs cut a small court named Orianna Street through the property, demolished his large house, and built in its place speculative row homes that served as rental units for the general public.[19]

By the time of the American Revolution, Philadelphia had become the largest city in the colonies and the fourth-largest in the English-speaking world. What once was a crude settlement of rural shacks had been transformed into an elegant city of brick row homes. The once-muddy streets were paved with flagstone sidewalks with posts to protect pedestrians from traffic. Not everyone embraced the Philadelphia style—foreigners found the city's straight streets and uniform buildings odd, with one diplomat saying it was too much like a chessboard to be beautiful.[20]

But the young nation took pride in Philadelphia's orderly appearance. During meetings of the Continental Congress, Thomas Jefferson slept and worked in a row home along Market Street. He saw the city's classical architecture as connecting the country to a lineage stretching back to the democracies of ancient Greece and Rome. After the Revolution, the English Georgian style became known in America as the Federal style. This patriotic architecture was most visible in the brick-fronted, dormered-roof row houses, which came to dominate the cities of the Northeast in the eighteenth and early nineteenth centuries.[21] The gridded streets and identical houses were thought to convey the nation's values of equality, property ownership, and the common good. Penn's vision had seemingly been realized. However, the true nature of Philadelphia's urban environment was often hidden along alleys and courts. Just behind the stately homes on the main boulevards lurked the rickety wood huts and trinities that housed over two-thirds of the population.[22]

||||||||||||||||||

As Philadelphia grew, the construction of row houses became one of the city's main economic drivers. Between 1790 and 1850 alone, over fifty-two thousand homes were built.[23] However, the nation's first architecture school would not be founded until 1868, at the Massachusetts Institute of Technology. Moreover, the title of *architect* was only used by a select few self-taught elites whose practice consisted almost entirely of grand civic buildings and large mansions. Housing remained almost entirely the realm of builders with no formal education. Their training consisted only of a teenage apprenticeship followed by a few years spent as journeymen, wandering the colonies providing day labor for various craftspeople. Yet despite this, the builders of Philadelphia developed innovations such as the kitchen el and the tiny spiral staircases. They became masters in manipulating the tight confines of narrow lots and party walls to create light-filled and well-proportioned homes. With their tall ceilings and windows on multiple sides of rooms, even the tiny trinities still feel spacious today.

The city's tight-knit building culture resulted in design approaches being shared and replicated, and a remarkable uniformity exists across the row homes built during the eighteenth and early nineteenth centuries. Entire blocks have similar cornices, window treatments, and rooflines, even when built at different times by different builders. This consistency was further facilitated by the use of pattern books, which acted as how-to manuals and contained everything from architectural styles and floor plans to technical specifications. Indeed, the rise of classical design during the Renaissance is credited to a pattern book called *Ten Books on Architecture*. This ancient text, written by a Roman architect and engineer named Vitruvius, was rescued from the dusty shelf of a Swiss monastery by a Florentine papal aide in 1414.[24]

The most commonly used pattern books in the United States were often less illustrious—one of the most popular for US row houses in the early nineteenth century was a British publication called *Mechanick Exercises*. Although the title makes it seem as if it was written by a child learning to read and write, it was published by Joseph Moxon and purported to be able to teach someone to build a house without any experience as a journeyman or apprentice.[25] British pattern books like Moxon's led to the proliferation of the row house in Philadelphia and then across the US. This resulted in common features across the homes, such as the widespread utilization of the London house plan layout and Georgian design schemes.

The Philadelphia row house became so admired that the city's builders spread it up and down the East Coast. As this occurred, the standardized elements of the row house were tempered to different cultural and geographic constraints. By the mid-nineteenth century, unique variations of the row home could be found across the country, designed for local preferences and using local materials. In Baltimore, marble quarried just north of the city adorned elegant Italianate façades with brilliant white stoops, windowsills, and decorative friezes popping out of deep-red brick exteriors. In Washington, DC, row homes were set back from the street with a small garden in front and a bay window capped with a small turret. The stark difference between row homes in Baltimore and Washington, just forty miles apart, demonstrates the hyperlocal building cultures that emerged during this time.

In 1810, an American architect named Robert Mills attempted to wrest control of the row house from the builder and elevate it to high design. Mills was from Charleston, South Carolina, and moved to Philadelphia after having trained under Thomas Jefferson and Benjamin Henry Latrobe, designer of the US Capitol. Up to this point, the vast majority of row house developments in the city had not advanced much since Budd's Long Row and merely repeated the same identical façade on each home. In a project called Franklin Row, Mills integrated the fronts of ten row houses into a grand and unified design. The basic elements of the Philadelphia row house—the arched doorway, chimney, and dormered roof—were refined by creating a pattern on the brick façade and using tripartite windows that framed one large window with two smaller ones.[26] Instead of being identical, the façades of each house varied slightly from the others to create a cohesive design.

However, such ambitious row house architecture would not be common for many more decades. The egalitarian values of the United States in the postcolonial period mandated that homes be relatively subdued and that grand architectural gestures be reserved for large civic buildings. Mills would go on to design the Washington Monument and the Treasury Building in Washington, DC, creating few other residential buildings.

Even after architecture emerged as a profession in the US, for decades its practitioners looked down on common housing, seeing it as the realm of "ignorant mechanics."[27] Yet that Mills would even attempt a project like Franklin Row shows how deeply ingrained the row home had become in the building culture of Philadelphia by the early nineteenth century.

IIIIIIIIIIIIIIIIIIIII

In the years after the American Revolution, Philadelphia was such a powerful center that in 1808 Congress considered moving the capital back there from Washington, DC, a proposal that was only defeated after several days of vigorous debate.[28] Yet as trade became more important in the nineteenth century, Philadelphia's inland river port, which often froze during the winter, was becoming outmoded compared to the deep open-water harbors of Baltimore and New York. Philadelphia's civic leaders, faced with the prospect of becoming a backwater, lobbied the state legislature to invest in vital infrastructure that would bring the city into the industrial age: canals, railroads, and dams. These investments vaulted Philadelphia into one of the leading industrial centers in the nation, nicknamed "the workshop of the world."

The life of a local artisan named Matthias Baldwin parallels the city's rise as an industrial metropolis. Born in 1795, at age sixteen Baldwin apprenticed as a jeweler, later becoming a master with a small workshop on an alley off Walnut Street.[29] By the time of Baldwin's death in 1866, this workshop had grown into the Baldwin Locomotive Works, with a plan that comprised over thirty buildings on nineteen acres of land. This was evidence of how far the city's economy had advanced, from small artisans crafting twisted pipes and warped leather boots to firms creating some of the most cutting-edge technology of the time.

Due to its sheer size, the Baldwin Locomotive Works was not located in the city proper of Philadelphia but in what was then a separate jurisdiction called Spring Garden, northwest of Penn's grid. The building industry in the city had previously consisted of small teams of builders constructing one to two homes a year, but with the new factories like the Locomotive Works came a need for much larger developments. This was aided by infrastructure improvements such as the omnibus, introduced in New York, Boston, and Philadelphia in the 1830s. These horse-drawn carriages ran on fixed routes and transported workers from the periphery into the central city. The era of the walking city was over—development now spilled out from Philadelphia's confines along the Delaware River to envelop the green fields surrounding it.

In 1849, a developer named Joseph Montgomery built thirty-two row houses right next to the Baldwin factory. Teams of subcontractors used an assembly-line approach: they first erected all of the party walls separating each row home from another, then all of the chimneys, then scaffolding for the roofs, and finally the interiors. Previously, smaller components such as window sashes, shutters, and doorways had to be fabricated by the builders themselves, usually during the winter, with the actual houses built during warmer months. But by the time Montgomery started work, these components were mass-produced in factories.[30]

Although these new neighborhoods of the nineteenth century were built on virgin land outside Penn's grid, they still mimicked the old fabric of the walking city. Penn had mandated that implementation of a standardized network of roads take precedent over private property. This resulted in the continuation of the original street grid as the city expanded.[31] Montgomery's development consisted of homes in a range of sizes, and following the precedent established in the old colonial city, he placed the larger, more well-appointed homes measuring 15 feet wide and 28 feet deep on the broad main streets.[32] These homes eschewed the classical detail of the Federal-style houses—instead, they had plain brick façades, white cornices, and arched doorways and were meant for merchants and businesspeople who would ride the omnibus into the central city for work.

On a narrow alley directly behind the large merchant houses, Montgomery built much smaller, one-room-per-floor trinities whose only ornaments consisted of austere cornices and simple rectangular window frames. These homes were meant for working-class residents who could not afford the twelve-cent fare to ride on the omnibus and so needed to be within walking distance of their place of employment. Such workers included domestics who served in the development's larger homes as well as employees of the Baldwin factory. These examples from Montgomery's development show the continued tradition of placing different sizes of homes along roads according to their width as Philadelphia expanded beyond the walking city.

In cities like New York and Boston, the omnibus caused the rich to retreat to separate enclaves while the poor clustered in teeming slums. But in Philadelphia, because of the variety of housing types that were included in the city's new developments, the mixed-income nature of the walking city remained. Even today, tiny trinities sit directly across from new luxury high-rise apartments in Center City. This type of mixing was considered acceptable because in Philadelphia the social status of an area was not tied to the neighborhood, or even the block, but to the outermost homes lining a particular street. (This was also a concept that had been brought to the city from England, where it had become common for small apartments for servants, called *mews*, to be constructed over the stables behind the large terrace houses that were the public face of the area.) This quirk meant that wealthy residents in Philadelphia would remain in the heart of the city even as it industrialized. Around Rittenhouse Square, for instance, the elite built monumental row houses constructed of sandstone, granite, and marble with beautiful gardens filled with grapevines, roses, and honeysuckles. During this time, Philadelphia had one of the most established upper-class societies in the country, with a block of row houses on Chestnut Street considered the peak of the American aristocracy. However, directly behind the neighborhood's large stately homes were tiny trinities, which housed the linen weavers who worked in the nearby factories along the Schuylkill River (see image 3).[33]

Montgomery's development and the other new neighborhoods growing around the factories outside the old walking city quickly became self-contained ecosystems with churches, schools, and business districts. With a large percentage of the population now commuting to factories or offices, by the mid-nineteenth century it was no longer common for homes to double as workshops and stores as they had during colonial times. However, developers retained some of these qualities by creating small retail spaces on the corners of blocks to house businesses serving the immediate neighborhood, like taverns, grocers, and—particularly during the twentieth-century Great Migration—storefront churches. These corner stores resulted in Philadelphia having a peculiar retail layout to this day. Instead of stores and restaurants only being clustered along one main drag, they remain scattered throughout otherwise entirely residential neighborhoods.[34] On the main streets it became common for the bottom floors of row homes to be converted into small workshops and storefronts. Just as in the walking city, the proprietor would often live directly above.

ıııııııııııııııııı

With the row homes pressed closely to the sidewalk, Philadelphia's streets and alleys became much more than places to simply drive or walk down. As late as the 1950s, merchants would ply their wares and services door to door along alleyways and residential streets, including knife sharpening, kosher shochtim butchering live chickens, and horse-drawn aquariums where one could buy fresh fish. Some families would collect the manure from the horses that pulled these mobile storefronts to fertilize their gardens. Each block and neighborhood developed unique street games like half-ball and buck buck, relying on landmarks such as mailboxes, fire hydrants, or the front steps of a row house.

The city's vibrant street culture endures to this day. During the warm summer months, Philadelphians set up chairs, patio furniture, barbecues, and smokers directly along the sidewalk. Children scoop water from buckets and run through sprinklers underneath beach umbrellas set up in front of schools and daycares. In contemporary South Philadelphia sits a tiny court called Beck Street. If one notices it at all, it might simply be mistaken for a service alley, as it is full of garbage cans for the cafés and shops along South 2nd Street. However, as you walk through the narrow passage, you notice that the street has been closed off with posts. Lights have been strung from house to house, illuminating a shared little piazza that the residents have filled with tables, chairs, and plants. Brooms and other household items are left leaning against the small homes. Compared to the large houses that make up most of America, Philadelphia's row homes and trinities are tiny. Yet their small spaces force people out of their homes and into the public realm. Through this, people become not just neighbors but also part of deeply rooted communities.

ıııııııııııııııııı

In 1854, the city of Philadelphia, which was still composed entirely of Holme's original grid, merged with Spring Garden and the broader county, growing the city to a total area of nearly 130 square miles. Compared to the small urban scale of the colonial period, the new city borders were difficult to comprehend and were criticized for being ridiculously expansive, encompassing fields, pastures, and entire towns that had developed miles from the city core.[35] Yet as pokey horse-drawn omnibuses were replaced by much faster electric streetcars as well as elevated trains, subways, and commuter rail lines, the rural land around Philadelphia—and other large American cities—rapidly filled in.

However, in a country that had fancied itself an agrarian nation of gentleman farmers, the phalanx of identical row homes that marched like a Napoleonic army across the countryside beyond large industrial cities was seen as a particularly egregious type of blight. The marble friezes below the cornice of a Baltimore row house were lost on a European critic who only saw an "exceedingly unattractive" city where every building looked the same.[36] To a writer for the *Washington Post*, the richly carved facades of brownstone row homes in Brooklyn were not romantic or naturalistic but "pretentious, mere shells."[37] Philadelphia had gone from being handsome, but exceedingly regular, to just being "droll and tepid," as described by essayist Agnes Repplier.[38]

To these critics, the row house was not charming or quaint but a manifestation of greed: a product of rapacious developers gobbling up land and erasing any contours of the landscape under a relentless grid of streets. This antipathy against speculative urban housing had deep historical roots. The inventor of the two-room London house plan that had become so popular in the US was a British developer named Nicholas Barbon. Described by one of his contemporaries, the lawyer and biographer Roger North, as an "exquisite mob master," Barbon was infamous for defying laws and even royal decrees so that he could build his developments in the aftermath of the Great Fire of London. He illegally knocked down buildings and engaged in physical altercations with those who objected to his projects, including a group of lawyers who were angry that their view of the countryside was being destroyed.[39]

The terrace houses that Barbon and other British developers produced were further criticized for being shoddy and cheap. Property developer George Downing saw his work merely as a path to wealth and power, and to achieve this he built the most inexpensive product possible. His development along Downing Street in London had mortar lines drawn onto the façades of each home to give the appearance of evenly spaced bricks. British prime minister Winston Churchill said that the terrace house at 10 Downing Street and its neighbors were "shaky and lightly built by the profiteering contractor whose name they bear."[40]

Yet although the row house had been shrouded in ignominy virtually since its inception, these narrow houses represented something extraordinary both for the time and today. It was a modest but well-appointed home that even a working-class laborer could afford. The access provided by Philadelphia's 264-mile transit network of horse-drawn streetcars and commuter trains, which by 1880 was the largest in the world, made constructing row houses relatively cheap. A developer could buy five acres located within a half hour of City Hall for as low as $70,000 (the equivalent of a little more than $2 million in 2023), where they would then erect nearly two hundred homes.[41]

While American cities at the turn of the twentieth century were marked by intractable urban slums, Baltimore and Philadelphia, due to their abundance of relatively cheap row houses, had the lowest rates of overcrowding in the country. Philadelphia in particular became an international model for housing and was nicknamed the "city of homes." One of its typical row houses was even exhibited as a model dwelling in the famous White City of the 1893 World's Columbian Exposition in Chicago. New York housing reformers Lawrence Veiller and Jacob Riis praised Philadelphia as a city "where the tenement problem was practically unknown," and a writer for *Harper's Magazine* described it as a "paradise of small houses."[42]

The housing successes of Philadelphia and Baltimore were due not only to an abundance of land and ambitious row house developers but also to unique financial innovations. Ground rent, a practice originally created in the seventeenth century to allow noblemen to develop their land without selling it, was widely utilized in Philadelphia and Baltimore and helped spur the development of row houses. Wealthy property owners, many of whom traced their holdings to land grants from William Penn, would advance money to builders who would develop homes on their property. These builders would then sell the homes directly to consumers or back to the landowner, who would then lease them out. In Philadelphia, row home owners would pay a ground rent—around 6 percent of the total cost of the land—as an annual fee. This system made it cost effective for builders as well as consumers, who were able to purchase just the home and not the land underneath.

The affordability allowed by ground rents was further bolstered by the creation of a new type of lending institution. Sitting at 12th and Market in downtown Philadelphia is a five-hundred-foot-tall skyscraper composed of limestone piers framing large windows and topped by a large sign reading PSFS. Although this building, completed in 1932, is considered the first modernist skyscraper in the US, the firm that commissioned it, the Philadelphia Savings Fund Society, dates back considerably further. The Society was founded in 1816 as the nation's very first savings and loan. By the 1870s savings and loans had been established across the nation; however, Philadelphia, with over four hundred, had by far the most.[43] These institutions allowed working-class people to pool their funds then get a home mortgage at a modest interest rate. Anyone earning up to $25 in a week was considered a potential homeowner.[44] During the turn of the twentieth century, wages maxed out at $12 a week in a place like the Baldwin Locomotive Works, and, on the lower end, were $7 for someone working in a textile factory. However, if a family had multiple earners, it was possible to purchase a 16-by-31-foot two-story brick row house for $300 down.

By 1930, over half of the populations of Philadelphia and Baltimore owned their homes. However, this pathway into the middle class was not open to everyone. Since Philadelphia's founding, its neighborhoods had been not just economically diverse, with trinities sitting next to mansions, but also ethnically diverse. Various immigrants as well as a large population of African Americans lived together along the city's alleys and courts. However, as their white neighbors began to leave the crowded inner wards of the city for new homes in the early twentieth century, Black residents found themselves increasingly segregated into overcrowded and dilapidated areas of the city. Many savings and loans would not extend financing for African Americans who sought to live in newer and less crowded white areas. Although savings and loans did exist in Black neighborhoods, segregation meant there were fewer homes to choose from, and they were often more expensive than ones available to a white family.[45] In his sociological study of African Americans in Philadelphia in 1899, W. E. B. Du Bois wrote, "Here is a people receiving a little lower wages than usual for less desirable work and compelled in order to do that work to live in a little less pleasant quarters than most people and pay for them somewhat higher rents."[46] Denying an entire community the important wealth-building asset of homeownership would have lasting repercussions in Philadelphia and other American cities.

llllllllllllllllllll

In 1879, a sixteen-year-old boy named Henry Ford walked the nine miles from his family's farm to Detroit. Interested in mechanics from a young age, he longed to invent a device that would improve mobility for people living far from trains in small towns and rural farms. By 1903 he had founded the Ford Motor Company, one of hundreds of car manufacturers that had been established around that time in Detroit. The first model the company produced was a two-seater with an eight-horsepower engine. However, Ford, ever seeking to create a cheaper and more reliable car, released a new model every few months, each of which was assigned a different letter of the alphabet. On June 16, 1908, the Model T was introduced. It had a four-cylinder, twenty-horsepower engine, could go forty miles an hour, and was reliable and simple to fix. Whereas every other car of the time was over $2,000, the Model T was $850—well within reach of a working person—and the price would continue to decrease. By 1926, Ford produced nineteen thousand Model Ts a day, with other auto manufacturers producing tens of thousands of different types of vehicles.

The row home's long and narrow shape had been premised on the fact that people needed to live close to their jobs and to transit. While these structures allowed people to attain ownership of a simple home in a crowded city, the trade-off was access to light. Because two sides of the building were party walls, windows could only be placed on the front and back of the building, a predicament that bedeviled all row houses from the tiny trinities to large mansions. (In post–Civil War New York, as spacious light-filled apartments became in vogue, young residents would derisively refer to people still living in gloomy brownstones as "cave-dwellers."[47])

Yet with the advent of widespread car ownership, people became freed of the spatial configurations that necessitated compact urban buildings like the row house. Detached single-family homes became accessible not just to gentlemen farmers but also to a clerk who could now drive downtown for work and be home for dinner. In contrast to row homes and apartments, these structures had windows on all four sides and looked out onto a lawn instead of a concrete court with neighbors washing their unmentionables. By World War I, half a million people lived in the three suburban Pennsylvania counties surrounding the city.[48] The once-prodigious borders of Philadelphia now seemed like an overflowing girdle.

By the 1910s and '20s, urban developers were no longer competing to have the closest development to a streetcar but rather with single-family homes in the suburbs. In response, the row house went through yet another metamorphosis. These new homes were substantially larger than previous versions, being 20 feet wide and 36 feet deep. Instead of flat, highly urban façades, they had architectural styles associated with rustic and rural settings. Brick was replaced with stucco and topped with a mansard roof made from Spanish-style tile or shingles in the style of an old English cottage. Instead of a stairway leading directly to the sidewalk, these homes had a large porch and were buffered from the street by a small lawn. Inside, the ancient hall-and-parlor layout had been brought up to modern standards, with separate rooms for dining and living, a bathroom, and bedrooms.

The broader width of the buildings and the configuration on the lot allowed developers to incorporate more windows, and they were marketed as "day lighters." Vast quantities were built in far Northeast and West Philadelphia as well as in Baltimore and Washington, DC. As the automobile became increasingly popular, many day lighters became untethered from mass transit, which had been the traditional instigator of row house development dating back to the horse-drawn omnibus.

Yet the term *day lighter* was a very feeble attempt for the row house to compete with the suburbs. In this new era of single-family homes, advertising the fact that a row house had more windows would be today's equivalent of motels with fading signs touting cable TV. Suburban developers trying to lure middle-class residents out of the city ran ads describing row homes as "tunnels." In 1918, the city of Baltimore annexed a large area on the fringe of the city and stipulated that no row houses could be built there.[49] The row house, which was once celebrated as a patriotic symbol of the nation, began to be seen as a second-class dwelling and was abandoned by the very cities that had initially embraced them the most.

|||||||||||||||||||

After World War II, the remaining row houses of Philadelphia's walking city sat derelict and forlorn, like broken antiques stuffed in the corner of a secondhand store. All around them were massive government-funded public works projects of postwar renewal: elevated freeways, modernist towers, and windswept parking lots. Many of the old nineteenth-century row houses looked as if they hadn't been touched since carriages rolled along cobblestone streets. Their once-elegant façades were crooked and deteriorated and many served as flophouses. Other still lacked heating or indoor plumbing and were abandoned. In the half century after World War II, cities across the country hemorrhaged population, with Philadelphia losing half a million people. To planners and city officials, the diminutive row houses and other forms of workers' housing were embarrassing relics of the past, standing in the way of modernization.

Yet to a small contingent of countercultural bohemians, the old houses of the urban core were much preferable to sterile apartment towers or suburban tract homes. The beret-topped hipsters and reefer-curious professionals of the 1950s saw these buildings as romantic vestiges of the past. In the core of Philadelphia—as well as in Brooklyn Heights in New York and Federal Hill in Baltimore—old row houses started to sport fresh coats of paint. In the windows, filthy lace curtains were replaced with the faces of well-fed children sporting voluminous bowl cuts. Old storefronts were converted into smoky cafés where Chianti was sipped from goblets to the sound of bongos and spoken word poetry. As dilapidated buildings were purchased by these affluent newcomers, the poorer residents who once occupied them were displaced. In the 1960s in Philadelphia's historically working-class and African American Seventh Ward, the Black population fell by 55 percent, while the white population grew by 67 percent. The oldest portion of the Ward near the Delaware River was later rebranded Society Hill. In 1964, a British sociologist coined the term *gentrification* to describe the nascent movement of educated professionals back into cities.

The back-to-the-city movement soon become a national phenomenon, stretching from New Orleans to San Francisco. The seeds planted by this movement and other urban revitalization efforts have turned Penn's original grid, now known as Center City Philadelphia, into one of the most desirable areas in the region. Nine out of the top ten most expensive neighborhoods in Philadelphia are either inside Penn's original grid or directly adjacent to it.[50] Tiny trinities have been converted into luxury pieds-à-terre, some selling for as much as $800,000. The lineage of narrow row homes has endowed Philadelphia with a human scale that is missing from the vast majority of North American cities. A key criterion cited by urban designers and planners to define a walkable and dynamic neighborhood is one where a new type of activity is happening every fifteen to twenty feet.[51] This is almost the exact scale of the row house, and the narrow tree-lined streets of the city's inner neighborhoods are jam-packed with cafés, bars, bookstores, and shops.

The current desire among young urbanites to live in vibrant, walkable, centrally located areas like Center City Philadelphia has made row homes fashionable again. Part of the appeal is that they can easily be adapted to contemporary tastes. Traditionally, row houses were constructed by putting joists between two party walls, meaning that none of the internal walls are load-bearing. This enables the interiors to be reconfigured: multiroom Victorian-era floor plans are overhauled into airy lofts, while the back is made into a giant window facing a garden. Behind an exterior from the nineteenth century, the interior can be an open, high-tech space of white walls, black leather furniture, and steel appliances. The resurgence of the row house is yet another amazing chapter in the incredible evolution of these buildings.

Yet the recent infusion of wealth has not been evenly distributed. In 1970, Philadelphia was still very much the city of homes, with nearly three-quarters of residents considered middle class. Around a small pocket of poverty in the ancient areas around Center City, the vast sprawl of the outer streetcar neighborhoods was economically solid and stable. Today this has flipped, with the central neighborhoods of Philadelphia being the wealthiest and whitest and the periphery being the poorest, housing the bulk of the Black and Latin American populations.[52] The row house no longer represents a middle-class ideal but is instead a symbol of inequality: one in Center City is incredibly expensive, while an almost identical version a few miles away in North or West Philadelphia sits abandoned. This is the legacy of racist policies that have denied generations of African American residents homeownership opportunities and starved their neighborhoods of investment.

The Philadelphia row house is emblematic of housing in America, at once a marker of the country's promise and of its gnawing challenges. The blocks of tidy row houses that sprawled across the cities of the Northeast in the early twentieth century epitomized a country where an immigrant laborer could become a homeowner and where rich and poor lived next to one another in roughly similar houses. Today, Philadelphia's glittering core and dilapidated periphery illustrate the nation's deep inequality and segregation, where access to opportunity is often based on the color of your skin. Contradictions that have become emblematic of housing in the United States.

CHAPTER 2

New York City Tenement

The Lowest Depth

In a country that defines itself by the single-family home, the sheer crush of humanity in New York truly distinguishes the city from any other. With twenty-nine thousand people per square mile, the city is more than twice as dense as Chicago and over three times as dense as Los Angeles.[1] The borough of Manhattan has nearly seventy thousand people per square mile, with some zip codes reaching as high as two hundred thousand. In older sections of the island below Houston Street, the rigid grid dissolves into a web of narrow streets enveloped by the heavily ornamented façades of centuries-old buildings. Neighborhoods like the Lower East Side or Greenwich Village can feel more like a medieval European town or a Moroccan casbah than an American city. On a warm summer night, a walk down Orchard or MacDougal Streets can be like jostling through a massive house party, with people spilling out onto the street from tiny bars and restaurants.

The symbol of New York that represents its astounding density is the skyscraper. However, the precedent for these steel and glass edifices filled with plutocrats and multinational corporations is a type of apartment building built by and for immigrants. As millions of people came into the city from around the globe in the nineteenth century, builders stacked tiny apartments on top of one another seven stories high on narrow lots.

This resulted in one of the most compact dwellings the world has ever known: the tenement. The term originates from an Anglo-French word referring to something that is rented, and it was once used to describe all multifamily apartment buildings in the US. At the turn of the twentieth century, during the height of the tenement, the density of Manhattan's Lower East Side surpassed that of contemporary megacities like Dhaka or Lagos.* In its time, the tenement was considered so inhumane that the fight to abolish it became one of the defining legacies of the Progressive Era. If the Philadelphia row house embodied the nation's values of egalitarianism and homeownership, the tenement came to symbolize the unbridled capitalist greed that has also characterized the country.

IIIIIIIIIIIIIIIIIIII

The unparalleled density of Manhattan traces its origins to the Commissioners' Plan of 1811, one of the most radical urban schemes ever envisioned. The plan reimagined what was then a provincial outpost of winding streets and wood houses as a hyper-compact city. During the colonial era, New York had been marked by haphazard development in which private interest outweighed the public good. The narrow and sometimes clipped streets were interrupted by buildings intruding into the road. By the turn of the nineteenth century, the need for a more orderly approach to growth became clear, and in 1807, the state appointed three commissioners to create a plan for the city's streets.

As opposed to Williams Penn's vision for Philadelphia as "a green country towne," the plan the commissioners came up with aimed to wring out every square inch of Manhattan for productive use. There would be no grand boulevards forming stars or ovals, as in the plan developed a few decades earlier for Washington, DC, and even existing geographical features of the island, like streams and hills, were obliterated.[2] In their place would be a relentless grid of roughly 200-by-600-foot blocks.

---

* The densest neighborhood in the world is Lalbagh Thana in Dhaka, Bangladesh, with 168,000 people per square kilometer ("The Most Densely Populated Neighborhoods in the World," World Atlas, https://www.worldatlas.com/articles/the-most-dense-neighborhoods -in-the-world.html, accessed June 26, 2023). In 1900, parts of the 10th Ward of the Lower East Side had 268,000 per square kilometer ("Housing Density: From Tenements to Towers," Skyscraper.org, https://skyscraper.org/housing-density/history/, accessed June 26, 2023).

In another reality, the Commissioners' Plan might just have been another fever dream of the Industrial Revolution, when visionaries foresaw ever more ambitious and spectacular technological innovations. However, in 1825, the construction of the Erie Canal drastically increased New York's importance in trade. Between 1821 and 1835, the population of every ward in the city tripled or quadrupled.[3] New York was growing so fast that by 1835 the Street Committee opened all gridded blocks up to 42nd Street.[4] The Commissioners' Plan now looked providential: with its rational subdivision of land, the plan had created an efficient framework for the rapid development of the city. By 1860, New York had leapt past Philadelphia and Boston as the country's unrivaled economic center, with 62 percent of the nation's foreign trade going through its port.[5]

Unlike Philadelphia, where rich and poor would occupy the same block well into the twentieth century, the Manhattan grid perpetuated an extreme stratification between classes. As streets were opened, the wealthy retreated out of the congested colonial-era walking city at the southern tip of Manhattan and went north up the spine of the island. In mere decades, the city's most fashionable neighborhood moved progressively north from the Battery near New York Harbor to Great Jones Street, then to Union Square, and finally bordering Central Park.[6] As soon as the rich had moved their last mahogany snuffbox and oil portrait out of the row homes and large houses in Lower Manhattan, the buildings would be divided into multiple units for rent. This often led to the rapid degradation of the surrounding neighborhood as the wealthy fled the invading rabble. In just a few years, once-elegant districts became filthy slums.

Whereas Philadelphia and Baltimore had open fields to expand onto, Manhattan was hemmed in by wide rivers, which would not be easily crossed until the opening of the Brooklyn Bridge in 1883. New York's urban fabric was largely composed of squat, Federal-style row houses, which proved ill-equipped to handle the multitudes of people streaming into the city.[7] In 1850, Philadelphia, with a population of 121,000, had 23,600 more houses than New York, with its population of 700,000. As a result, New York had an average of nearly fourteen people per residential building, compared to just six in Philadelphia.[8] In the worst slum districts, the overcrowding was unimaginable. One of the city's few surviving row houses from this period is the James Brown House on Spring Street near the Hudson River. Today the ground floor is home to the Ear Inn, one of the city's oldest bars, which describes itself as "a dump with dignity."[9] This small brick building looks like a vestige of the past pressed amidst the crystalline towers and hulking industrial buildings of modern Manhattan. However, in the early 1800s, a two-story dormer-roofed structure like the James Brown House could have eleven families occupying it. Based on Manhattan's current average occupancy rate, this is more people than the twelve-story condominium building that sits next to the house today.

Due to the row houses' utter inability to accommodate New York's immense need for housing, builders were forced to innovate far denser building types, and they had little place to go but up. The traditional dimension of lots in the city, which was codified in the Commissioners' Plan, is 25 feet by 100 feet, which had been based on the width of a house that could be built with hand and animal labor in 1640, around the time the city was founded.[10] The city's row houses often occupied less than half of their 100-foot-deep lots, leaving a large patch of precious open space behind the home. On such spaces, which may at one point have housed the tulip gardens of a Dutch Burgher, some of the first purpose-built apartments in the United States were constructed. These back structures were basically the early nineteenth-century version of a backyard granny flat. However, instead of being painted in edgy Oaxacan blue and storing dad's guitars, they often looked like overgrown outhouses. Shoddily built outdoor stairways provided access to each floor, and additional floors were often added to the back buildings over time, with some rising as high as five stories.[11]

These back buildings flew in the face of almost all social mores relating to housing during this time. In the early nineteenth century, placing multiple families under one roof was socially unacceptable to the point of being considered unpatriotic. America thought of itself as a country of landowners who lived in single-family homes, preferably in the country. This was an ideal that had been forged in the row houses of Philadelphia and articulated by the Founding Fathers. Thomas Jefferson, for example, thought all Americans should be farmers with the exception of masons, carpenters, and smiths.[12] At least the back buildings were able to conceal their shame behind a single-family home. Yet as the need for housing became ever more dire in New York, the taboo was eventually broken. In

1824, a multifamily apartment building was built at the front of the lot in full view of the public at 65 Mott Street in present-day Chinatown.[13]

Although the apartment building would soon be viewed as a foreign intrusion on the city's landscape due to its association with immigrants, the building type was actually a natural evolution of the row house. Throughout the colonial period it had been common for the owners of large homes to sublet rooms out to boarders. However, this was not the typical landlord–tenant relationship and there was an intimacy between the owner, often an older widow, and the tenant, usually a young man or woman. Instead of awkwardly nodding to one another in the hallway or leaving each other passive-aggressive notes, they functioned more as a family and shared meals and chores.[14] As freestanding metal stoves for cooking and heating water were introduced in the mid-nineteenth century, it was no longer necessary for boarders to share kitchen facilities. Due to this innovation, large houses started to be divided into individual apartments.[15]

Developers began to design large row houses with their eventual subdivision in mind. By the 1820s, four- and five-story Greek Revival row homes with red-brick façades and white columns around the doorways had gained favor over diminutive Federal-style row homes. Their sidehall London house plans allowed the two rooms on each floor to be made into a separate apartment with the hallway linking them (see image 7). In some cases, a New York row home would serve a single family for just a decade before being turned into an apartment building, concealed behind the elegant façade of a more socially acceptable single-family home.

Because it was a purpose-built multifamily apartment directly in public view, 65 Mott Street was something entirely new. However, it also tried to disguise itself as something more familiar. As opposed to the tumbledown appearance of the back buildings, 65 Mott took the form of a warped Georgian row house on steroids. It had a cornice and pressed brick exterior yet rose to seven stories, nearly twice the height of the tallest row house (see image 5). Whereas the authentic Georgian style emphasized carefully balanced proportions regulating the height of each floor and the spacing of openings, the windows of 65 Mott were crowded onto the façade like pepperoni on a pizza. The typical steep front staircase, called a stoop—a vestige of the building traditions of Dutch colonists—was replaced by a storefront containing a distillery.

While the exterior of 65 Mott was bizarre and gargantuan, the interior floor plan was an even bigger aberration. Next to the distillery was a long hallway connecting to a narrow, winding staircase, providing access on each floor to four two-room apartments, each measuring 200 square feet. Combined with the five-story back building behind it, 65 Mott created over thirty apartments on a lot that previously only had a single home.[16] It was the first of a type of building that would come to be known as a *tenement*, a word used to describe nearly all multifamily apartment buildings in the US up until around the turn of the twentieth century. At first they were hailed as an efficient and economical solution to New York's housing crisis. Similar to the way a tiny-home community or converted shipping-crate apartments would be described today, newspapers of the time wrote that tenements provided modest accommodations for the working class "without respect for show."[17] However, while the outsides of the tenements may have looked respectable—especially compared to the overstuffed row houses, which often tilted to one side like a witch's house in a fairy tale—the interiors were nearly uninhabitable. The hall-and-parlor scheme was again adapted for use in the tenement, sometimes with a third additional bedroom tucked behind the two front rooms. However, due to the long, narrow lots, only the room facing an outside wall would have a window, leaving the back rooms in perpetual darkness. Units facing the rear of the structure had windows but got very little light because they were often only twelve feet away from the back building. Two sinks and sixteen toilets served the entire building.[18] Interior staircases and hallways were also entirely devoid of natural light, and tenants and social workers would tell stories of tripping over small children and passed-out drunk people while trying to access a unit.[19]

Apartments within the tenement would be rented out by a landlord, and tenants would often sublease rooms within their units, resulting in each housing multiple families. A tenement like 65 Mott Street could therefore house over two hundred people—four times as many as the converted row homes. Even the dank cellars would be rented out as dwellings for the most impoverished. With multiple families cramming into the 200-square-foot apartments, people would sleep on tables and chairs or in bunk beds. Whereas the tiny trinities in Philadelphia had tall ceiling and windows to make them feel voluminous, tenement apartments felt suffocating even when empty—the paucity of windows made them not just dark but also stiflingly hot. When packed with warm human bodies during summer months, disease would burn through the buildings like wildfires. Between 1850 and 1860, seven out of every ten children in the city under the age of two died, and more New Yorkers passed away each year than were born.[20]

Blame for the poor conditions inside tenements was placed on the 25-by-100-foot lots, which were not only narrow but—due to the miserly Commissioners' Plan—were also laid out back to back without even an alley dividing them. While generously sized for a row house, they offered an extremely inadaptable configuration for purpose-built multifamily housing. The challenge of designing properly lit and ventilated apartments on these long and narrow lots would vex architects and policymakers for decades. Housing reformer Robert W. De Forest said in 1902, "If Dante were today writing his 'inferno,' the lowest depth would be reserved for those men who invented the twenty-five-foot lot and imposed it on so many American cities."[21]

⸽⸽⸽⸽⸽⸽⸽⸽⸽⸽⸽⸽⸽⸽⸽⸽⸽⸽

By the time of the Civil War, two very different cities occupied the tight confines of Manhattan Island. Along Fifth Avenue an average of twelve families per block lived in increasingly large and elaborate row homes.[22] In these fashionable districts emerging Uptown, the brick exteriors of the Federalist and neoclassical houses had been replaced by brownstone. This soft, locally sourced stone was carved into ornamental façades and was often accompanied by beautiful wrought-iron railings and gates. As opposed to brick, which shows the mason's hand in mechanical repetition, brownstone has the unbroken quality of a rock face, as if a structure was built out of an escarpment like the ancient edifices of Petra. The interiors were equally well appointed, with parquet flooring and ceilings adorned in crown molding. Many considered New York's upper-class housing and neighborhoods to be the most elegant in the country.[23]

Meanwhile, along the East River and in the older sections of the city south of 14th Street, an average of seven hundred people lived on each block.[24] The barely habitable tenements had become New York's default dwelling, housing 480,000 people out of a total population of 700,000.[25] The city's fifteen thousand tenements constituted teeming and increasingly foreign slums, which were considered the filthiest places in the country.[26] New York's tenement district radiated out from the notorious neighborhood of Five Points, where the present-day Civic Center is. The neighborhood had first been built around and then on top of Collect Pond, which had provided the city's water supply during colonial times. After homes started sinking into the damp soil, causing yellow fever to rage through the area, upper-class families quickly fled. Five Points soon became a slum as its closely packed wood houses were subdivided for apartments and as former industrial buildings were taken over by squatters. These converted factories and warehouses, known as a rookery, were where the poorest and most destitute sought shelter. They had nicknames that sounded like places Oscar the Grouch would go on date night, such as Rag Pickers' Den and Rotten Row. The most infamous was the Old Brewery, originally built in 1792; by 1837 it was considered too dilapidated to continue to be used to brew beer and was converted into housing. It was rumored to contain over one thousand people, many in windowless cellars. The largest room, known as the Den of Thieves, housed up to seventy-five people whose living space consisted of rag piles on the floor.[27] One of the reasons that tenements were celebrated at first was because of exactly this type of low-class housing.

As New York's population boomed and the rich fled the older sections of the city, the slums of Five Points metastasized to encompass a huge swath of Lower Manhattan. North of Five Points near 65 Mott Street, where Columbus Park is currently located, was Mulberry Bend, one of the mostly densely populated blocks in the world. To the southeast along the East River was Cherry Hill, a once upper-class neighborhood where George Washington had lived. By 1880, the columns and cornices of the neighborhood's once-elegant row homes had rotted away, and the interiors became hideouts for bandits and criminals. Cherry Hill became one of the most squalid districts in the city, famous for its alley inhabited by a gang of blind beggars. To the northeast was the neighborhood that would become synonymous with the tenement, the Lower East Side. Once a mixed-use neighborhood of workshops and modest homes for artisans, by the nineteenth century its wood houses had been replaced by towering tenements.[28] The back houses and crooked streets of Lower Manhattan formed a warren of hidden passages where saloons, pushcarts, and gangs jostled against the crowds of people escaping their suffocating apartments.

Like a deranged Victorian-era amusement park, they often had names like Bone Alley, Bottle Alley, and Bandits' Roost.[29]

These neighborhoods were distinct from the orderly Uptown brownstones not only physically but also socially. By the early 1800s, New York had become the main port of entry for the Irish fleeing the potato famine and Germans escaping war and political instability. These immigrants would disembark boats along the East River and walk a few blocks inland to Five Points or the Lower East Side and find housing. By 1855, the area now known as the East Village was home to a concentration of German residents that was the largest in the world outside of Vienna and Berlin, and by the late nineteenth century, New York had more Irish people than Dublin.[30]

As massive as the wave of Irish and German immigrants was, it was small compared to the waves to come. By the late nineteenth century, dozens of cultures crammed next to each other in just a handful of blocks. Mulberry Bend was dominated by Italians, Five Points had become Chinatown, Greenwich Village was known as Little Africa, and the Lower East Side became home to hundreds of thousands of Jews from Eastern Europe.

Although slum areas existed in other cities, nothing matched the scale, density, and diversity of New York. In the mid-1800s three-quarters of the US population lived in rural areas or small towns, primarily composed of Northern European Protestants. Comparatively, the overstuffed slums of New York were so exotic that they became tourist attractions and were hyperbolically detailed in popular guidebooks.[31] Just as today packs of lads walk the streets of Las Vegas and New Orleans on raucous stag parties, people would travel to Lower Manhattan to gawk at what the journalist Jacob Riis described as the "queer conglomerate mass of heterogeneous elements."[32] Once tourists arrived, there were countless "hooks and snares" to occupy them, from underground opium parlors to the exotic pushcart rag sellers to the bars of the Bowery, some of which allowed their patrons to suck beer from a keg for as long as they could hold their breath in exchange for a small fee.

IIIIIIIIIIIIIIIIIII

With the upper class enjoying tea parties in lavish townhomes while the poor crushed into human sandwiches in overstuffed tenements just a few blocks away, New York was one of the most inequitable cities in the world in the nineteenth century. As more immigrants arrived with each passing day and housing conditions became increasingly dire, the problems of the slums became hard to ignore. In 1849, a cholera epidemic that began in a cellar dwelling swept through the city, killing five thousand people. This catastrophe was just one of a series of epidemics, fires, and riots emanating from the slums.[33] This succession of disasters convinced at least a portion of the city's elite that something needed to be done to improve New York's housing.

While the upper classes were physically separated from the tenements, they were still inextricably linked to them. Due to a land grant from the queen in 1705, the elite Episcopalian institution Trinity Church owned a sizable chunk of Lower Manhattan. This made the church, which counted many of the city's power brokers as members, the largest landlord of tenements in the city by the turn of the twentieth century. Many of New York's wealthiest citizens had an even more direct stake in the slums. The furrier turned real estate magnate John Jacob Astor owned thousands of tenements, due to his extensive land holdings. By 1880, Astor's heirs were receiving $5 million a year from tenements.[34] However, because the tenements had been developed through the ground rent system, Astor, Trinity Church, and other members of the city's elite had an arm's-length separation from the deplorable conditions in their buildings.[35] This saved them from some of the embarrassment and scorn directed at other developers, such as Barbon and Downing.

The charitable and religious groups seeking to improve the city's housing often moved in the same upper-crust circles as the powerful men who profited from the tenements. Reformers therefore needed to walk a careful balance of improving conditions while not inhibiting profits. Their primary aim was to show builders how to create structures with better sanitation and light, but that were still lucrative for landlords. One of the first of these model tenements, Gotham Court, was built in 1850 in Cherry Hill. The building was long and narrow and provided unheard-of amenities for the working class, including running water in each unit. However, Gotham Court garnered only a 5 percent return compared to the typical 10 to 30 percent return of normal tenements.[36] The building was soon sold to speculators, and conditions rapidly deteriorated. For decades after that, the building was considered one of the worst slums in the city.[37]

While the elite could withstand the epidemics and fires, the Draft Riots of 1863 were a breaking point. The Irish inhabitants of Five Points and other nearby slums wreaked havoc for several days in one of the most violent episodes of civil unrest in US history. Angered by their conscription into the Civil War, they murdered Black residents in the streets and lit African American orphanages on fire before marching Uptown, where they set fire to Protestant churches and the mansions of abolitionists.* While triggered by the Civil War, the Draft Riots were considered a referendum on the city's housing and galvanized a much larger effort to enact policies that would improve it.[38] In the aftermath of the riots, a series of laws were passed in the city requiring permits to be issued for the construction of new buildings, stricter construction standards, and that at least one toilet be provided for every twenty residents. However, New York's bureaucratic structure was weak and extremely corrupt, controlled by the notorious Tammany Hall political machine. This reality, coupled with a fierce pushback from the real estate industry, made any reforms largely illusory. Despite an 1860s law calling for more robust building standards, in 1884 a Westside tenement collapsed because of a faulty mortar mixture, killing several workers. A study done that same year found that only 30 percent of tenements had any toilets at all.[39]

In 1878, the magazine *Plumber and Sanitary Engineer* hosted a design competition to create a better tenement in terms of light, ventilation, and sanitation. However, the catch was that it had to be economically feasible, contain the same number of units as a traditional tenement, and be built on a standard New York City 25-by-100-foot lot. The winner was an architect named James Ware, whose design placed a small indentation on the side of the building that would result in light and air shafts servicing each apartment. The city's Tenement House Act of 1879 codified Ware's design into law by banning the construction of new back buildings and limiting the amount of space a tenement could take up on a lot to no more than 65 percent.[40]

The dumbbell-shaped tenements proliferated across the city (see image 7), but Ware's air shafts quickly transformed from a beacon of light

---

* The 2002 film *Gangs of New York* is largely set in the Old Brewery and depicts the Draft Riots as well as the evolution of Five Points in the nineteenth century.

to a portal to hell. The light wells, often no wider than a coffin, conveyed noise and odors throughout the building, filled up with trash and bird excrement, and became a breeding ground for rodents. Once the noisy, rat-filled indentations had been sufficiently stuffed with trash and sewage, they would then catch on fire, with the light well acting as a chimney.[41]

To many Americans, however, the problems of the slums were not just due to poor planning or venal developers but also to moral failings of their inhabitants. Apartments were tinged with a sort of sexual taboo, emanating from the fact that women had to live under the same roof as men who were not members of their family. This sin was thought to lead to other illicit behavior, such as drinking and sloth. A guidebook from 1872 said of the tenements, "There can be no such thing as shielding the young from improper outside influences. They have every opportunity to become thoroughly corrupted without leaving the house. Decency is impossible."[42]

The tenements of New York were unfavorably contrasted with the row houses of Philadelphia. Reformers felt that the density of New York allowed a "man's identity (to be) lost in a crowded tenement district"—they did not have to uphold a high moral character because they could live anonymously in a crowd. The single-family row homes of Philadelphia, on the other hand, were considered a path to self-improvement, rooting people in a community and allowing them to regulate their lives with separate rooms for sleeping, eating, and spending time with their families. This was thought to make Philadelphians steady, thrifty, with a character that was "subject to comment."[43]

With the physical improvement of New York's housing proving to be difficult, reformers pivoted to a shorter-term goal of mentoring tenement dwellers on proper behavior. This was often done in a harsh and forceful way because most reformers, as well as the broader society, viewed the poor's plight as resulting from their own actions. America was seen as the land of opportunity, a place where a lack of success could not be attributed to anything but one's own wickedness or sloth. While reformers were largely culled from the ranks of upper-class, American-born Protestants, tenement dwellers were almost entirely immigrants, including large numbers of Catholics and Jews. Reformers saw these people as inherently inferior, almost childlike, and in desperate need of guidance to surmount their circumstances. In order to correct bad habits, the poor needed to go through a cleansing process involving abstinence and strict moral instruction. One program sent inner-city children West to live with families on farms and in small towns. However, this often resulted in them simply being used as slave labor on farms and ranches. The reformers' approach was summarized by the head of the New York State Board of Charities, Josephine Shaw Lowell, who said: "All charity must raise and elevate the moral nature, even if the process is as painful as plucking out an eye."[44]

In her quest to uplift morals, Lowell organized a team of all-female sanitary squads, accompanied by a police officer, to visit tenement dwellers in their apartments. Like parents making an impromptu visit to their child's dorm room, the sanitary squads would perform nighttime raids, frantically sorting through residents' bedding and possessions searching for a bottle of whisky, a tawdry comic—any evidence of loose morals. If they were not satisfied with what they found, they had the power to fine landlords and even condemn buildings.

However, for many other reformers, the ultimate goal was not moralizing to the poor, but rather eradicating tenements and multifamily housing for the lower classes altogether. They considered any structure that was not "private and individual" to be substandard. The model tenements of the 1850s were considered merely a pit stop on the resident's journey to eventually living in a bucolic country cottage. In later housing and policy proposals created by the reformer Lawrence Veiller, multifamily buildings were categorized as being "class C," to be discouraged.[45] As Jacob Riis put it, "A shanty is better than a flat in a cheap tenement any day."[46]

IIIIIIIIIIIIIIIIII

While reform efforts largely failed to improve the quality of tenements, they did succeed in bringing increasing ignominy to the structures. By the late 1880s, much of the city's elite had publicly divested from directly constructing tenements or acting as their landlords.[47] This ushered in a new era of tenements that were largely built by and for immigrants. However, New York had unique conditions that made development much more challenging than in other cities. In Philadelphia, the terms of ground rents were in perpetuity, and in Baltimore they were ninety years, after which ownership reverted to the renter.[48] In New York, ground rents were as short as twenty years, after which they reverted to the landowner.

The lending capital for housing in New York presented another challenge. In 1888, Philadelphia had 450 savings and loans, which gave even hourly wage factory workers the opportunity to buy a house. By contrast, New York and the then-independent city of Brooklyn only had forty-eight savings and loans, despite having twice the population of Philadelphia.[49] Instead, a more informal network of lenders started to develop. The tight ethnic communities of Lower Manhattan had their own economies composed of saloons, grocers, and butchers. Many of these businesses played multiple roles as notaries and lawyers as well as agencies for employment, steamships, and real estate. Eventually some of these enterprises became full-fledged banks.[50] The short-term and mercenary lending practices of these financial institutions, however, made their loans incredibly risky propositions for investors who, by the post–Civil War era, were almost entirely immigrants. The combination of ground rents and lending capital meant that New York developers needed to generate as much profit as they could within a relatively short window. This resulted in many focusing not on single-family homes but on highly dense, revenue-generating tenements that they could build as fast and as cheaply as possible.

Yet despite these challenges, many took the risk. For Eastern European Jews in particular, who had escaped a tenuous existence in the shtetels that dotted the band across Eastern Europe known as the Pale of Settlement, property ownership was a powerful symbol of security. Many toiled for decades in sweatshops or operated pushcarts on the crowded streets of what was known as Jew Town on the Lower East Side to save enough to construct their own building. This community ultimately developed nearly half of all tenements in both the Lower East Side as well as those in the North End of Boston.[51] Some of these immigrant enterprises turned into powerful institutions. Joseph Durst, an immigrant from Austria, parlayed his wealth made as a dressmaker into a real estate empire that went on to develop One World Trade Center.[52] The owners of Rockefeller Center are descended from Julius Tishman, who used revenue from his department store to build a Lower East Side tenement.[53]

Yet for every successful developer, many poor immigrants sank their life savings into structures only to be financially ruined. Because of the terms of the loans, the most successful borrowers were the ones who could build and sell their tenements as quickly and as cheaply as possible.

Part of what made reform efforts so difficult in New York was that this need for speed made it imperative for investors to cut construction time and costs by any means necessary. Tenement developers became known as *skin builders* because their buildings were skin deep, lasting only long enough to find a purchaser before falling apart. The builders would find the cheapest materials possible, then do the lowest quality work, which was called *lumping*. They used three-day paint, which looked good for a little while before deteriorating. It was also a fire hazard and could "burn as fast as a man could run."[54]

If the tenement did not collapse before construction was completed, it would then be sold to an individual or pool of investors. A tenement could be bought with a down payment of $1,000 to $3,000 and monthly payments as low as $5. These investors would then contract out the management of the building to a leaseholder who was responsible for renting out the building. The leaseholder usually lived in the tenement they managed and performed duties ranging from finding tenants to collecting rent to acting as a handyman. In exchange they would receive a small allowance out of the building's total gross rent income, which incentivized them to keep the tenement fully occupied. Acting as a leaseholder was often the first step to becoming a tenement developer. If they quickly filled their buildings and turned a profit, they would then invest in their own building.[55]

While in Philadelphia the immigrant village stretched across a street, alley, or court, in New York it was compressed into a single building. The developer would often be related to the leaseholder, who would in turn rent out the apartments to additional family members. This made each building like a self-contained community displaced from Sicily, Galicia, or County Cork onto the streets of Lower Manhattan. The film director Martin Scorsese, in a radio interview with Terry Gross, recalled his experience growing up in a tenement in Little Italy:

> My parents grew up in those apartments on Elizabeth Street, which are very chic now and cost a lot of money, but they were born in them, and they were living in them with 12 to 14 people. Luckily, we were only . . . four people down the block on 253 Elizabeth—my brother, myself, my mother and father. But the doors were open. Other people, the neighbors next door were . . . pretty much living with you. My uncle was living

downstairs with his two kids and his wife and the dog. And, you know, my father's uncle ran the building. He was an old Italian guy who was really scary. He lived on the ground floor.[56]

||||||||||||||||||

While immigrant ownership of tenements did not improve the conditions inside, it did precipitate a renaissance in their design. In 1886, a tenement was built at 375 Broome Street that still rises along the narrow streets of Little Italy as if it was on the Champs-Élysée. Each window is capped with triangles, semicircles, crowned figures surrounded by laurels, and Stars of David. Beneath the elaborate cornice sits a bust of the developer peering over his creation, a Jewish immigrant named Wolf Baum.

By the turn of the twentieth century, the classical architecture of the Renaissance had filtered its way through Northern Italy, England, and Philadelphia to crescendo in jubilant ornamentation on the streets of Lower Manhattan. Pedestrians craned their necks to take in the elaborate doorframes, window caps festooned with laurels, various combinations of Roman and Greek columns, keystones, and multiple belt courses that were increasingly layered onto the façades of tenements like frosting on a wedding cake.

Up to this point, American culture, which valued frugality, had had an uneasy relationship with architectural ornamentation. In the early nineteenth century, Robert Mills's refined row homes in Philadelphia were considered too ostentatious, even for the wealthy. But by the Civil War, these norms began to change as robber barons erected monumental palaces along Fifth Avenue. In 1882, Cornelius Vanderbilt built what is still one of the largest private homes ever constructed in the city on Fifth Avenue. Like a chateau for a manic duke, it was so overloaded with turrets and stonework that it looked as if it would implode under its sheer weight.

Yet sensibilities had not changed so much that slapping winged angels and Roman columns on tenements—regarded as misery receptacles for the dregs of society—would be seen as anything other than an incredible act of subversion. The tenements of the late nineteenth century were therefore an artistic provocation, mixing high and low in a way that would not be seen again until Andy Warhol's soup cans three-quarters of a century later. But to the immigrant developers who had quite literally crawled out of the slums to claim a stake in America, the tenements were proud symbols of their socioeconomic ascendance.[57]

The builders of decorated tenements were emboldened by a broader acceptance of multifamily housing in New York. Richard Morris Hunt was one of the nation's first architects to be trained at the École des Beaux-Arts in France. Inspired by the elegant Parisian apartments constructed as part of Baron Georges-Eugène Haussmann's renovations, in 1869 he designed the Stuyvesant Apartments in Gramercy Park. However, the building held little appeal to anyone other than young affluent bohemians who wanted an alternative to a large row house, which had to be maintained and staffed.[58]

But by the late 1800s, with technological innovations such as elevators, electricity, and telephones, luxury apartment buildings in cities like Boston and New York became the preferred abode of the upper classes. While Hunt had had to conceal the true nature of the Stuyvesant by having its façade mimic a series of row houses, new apartment buildings started to unabashedly embrace a monumental and opulent appearance. The Dakota, completed in 1884, rose on the then-undeveloped West Side fringe of Central Park and housed sixty-five entirely unique apartments under a monumental gabled roof. It was complemented by other equally elaborate structures up and down Broadway and Park Avenue.* These buildings were so extravagant and elegant that they remain some of the city's most coveted addresses, and the Dakota has been home to many celebrities including Judy Garland, Leonard Bernstein, and Bono. One famous resident, John Lennon, was assassinated under its arched, cathedral-like main entrance.

The explosion in ornamentation was also due to the factories that appeared after the Civil War, which mass-produced architectural decorations such as galvanized iron, terra-cotta, and brick. These products were then marketed in catalogues at affordable prices. Suddenly, the detailing found on the apartment buildings lining Broadway or on the mansions along Fifth Avenue could be replicated on a tenement in the Lower East Side. Tenement construction had always been defined by tight and highly leveraged budgets, necessitating lumping and skinning, but by the turn of the twentieth century developers were encrusting their buildings in

---

* One of these buildings, The Belnord, built in 1908, is prominently featured in the television show *Only Murders in the Building*.

affordable ornamentations. This was about more than just the owner's pride. By the late nineteenth century, tenements were not just the lowest class of housing, but also a product that needed to be marketed with an aspirational appeal. Even the interior hallways were decorated with pressed tin ceilings, tile floors, and oil paintings depicting idyllic country houses. However, the interior floor plans were often identical to earlier, less ornamented buildings.

As Zachary J. Violette writes in his thesis on decorated tenements during this period, the goal of these building "was nothing short of a rebuff of the slum stereotype, a physical demonstration of not only improving housing conditions these communities were making themselves, but also an assertion of their desire and ability to use the material goods of American architectural culture in their own terms."[59]

|||||||||||||||||||||

By the turn of the twentieth century, New York City had eighty thousand tenements housing over 60 percent of the population. The buildings lined the north/south avenues of Manhattan, and a massive tenement district stretched along the length of the East River from the Brooklyn Bridge to Harlem. An 1894 report by the state legislature found that New York was the densest city in the world, surpassing Paris, London, and Bombay, with the Lower East Side being the most densely populated place on the planet.[60] Tenements had also infiltrated the outer boroughs of the Bronx, Brooklyn, and Queens, which, along with Staten Island, had been consolidated with Manhattan via public referendum in 1898 to form one enormous city.

While other American cities relied on the British model of detached single-family homes and row houses, New York's built environment was more similar to continental Europe. The upper class increasingly lived in palatial Parisian-style apartments, while the lower classes lived in structures more similar to the large apartment buildings in Berlin or Naples. Compared to the rest of the nation, New York's urban form was quite literally foreign. To this day, its vertical density makes it unlike any other city in the English-speaking world.

With the publication in 1890 of *How the Other Half Lives* by the muckraking journalist Jacob Riis, the conditions of New York's slums were publicized to a national and international audience. Riis was a Danish immigrant who had experienced the cruelty of the city's streets firsthand. After first arriving in New York, he sought refuge in a police barracks where a locket containing a photo of his lost love was stolen and where his dog, which he was made to leave outside, was killed.[61] His book viscerally documented the conditions in the alleys and claustrophobic apartments of Lower Manhattan. Using the recently invented technology of night photography, Riis was able to show children huddled in gutters and men sleeping virtually on top of each other in tiny rooms.

How the Other Half Lives was a national sensation. The book's massive success also elevated housing as a pressing issue for elected officials in New York. This included the city's young police commissioner, the rising political star Theodore Roosevelt. Roosevelt was descended from an old New York Dutch family known as the Knickerbockers and was raised in a brownstone off Fifth Avenue. He was exposed to conditions in the slums during midnight tours with Riis and asked him to provide a list of the sixteen worst slum districts in the city. Roosevelt took action accordingly, and by the 1890s Gotham Court had been demolished, Mulberry Bend had been turned into Columbus Park, and Five Points had been cleared for what is now the Civic Center.[62]

Roosevelt would go on to be elected governor in 1899, and two years later he signed into law the 1901 Tenement House Act, which made the tenement, as it had been known, illegal to build in the state of New York. The Act was heavily influenced by reformer Lawrence Veiller and required that every apartment have a toilet, that rooms be no smaller than 70 square feet and have outside light, and that courtyards be at least 12 feet by 25 feet. What made these regulations different from the litany of previous failed reform efforts was that the 1901 Act also established a tenement house bureau to enforce it. Instead of a ruddy faced, half-drunk, Tammany Hall apparatchik, this bureau would be headed by Veiller himself.[63]

One of the most substantial effects of the 1901 Tenement House Act was that it broke the curse of the 25-by-100-foot lot by making it illegal to build any large apartment building with a footprint smaller than 40 by 100 feet. The substantially larger New Law tenements were typically 50 feet wide with four to six units per floor, whereas the older dumbbell tenements created under the 1879 law had crammed the same number of units in a 25-foot-wide building.[64] The wider New Law buildings meant structures had to expand beyond the dumbbell shape and take on new configurations that would result in well-lit and spacious apartments. However, this also made them much more expensive to construct and it no longer became feasible for a pushcart operator to build a tenement with money saved from selling kishkes. Tenement construction would now be left to well-established, well-financed builders who would build three—and sometimes up to twelve—buildings at a time.

Although developing a tenement became out of reach for the middle class, the rising wages of the early 1900s made the rents in New Law buildings accessible even to the working classes. The dramatically expanded subway system provided speedy and affordable access from Manhattan to the outer fringes of the five boroughs.[65] By the 1920s, block upon block of large, well-appointed New Law tenements were being built in places like the Bronx and the upper tip of Manhattan. Instead of the two-room railroad layouts typical of older tenements, the apartments in these buildings had spacious floor plans, some of which included dining rooms, kitchens, and multiple bedrooms, all with windows facing a street or courtyard. Laying out these spacious plans while also working within the strictures of the city's complex building codes and tight urban lots was extremely challenging. The architect Rosario Candela, who designed some of the city's most elegant apartments in the 1920s, parlayed his spatial abilities into cryptography during World War II.[66]

The New Law buildings traded in the busts, columns, and decorative friezes found on the fronts of older tenements for a more refined aesthetic. They had architecturally cohesive styles ranging from Gothic to streamlined modern. In some cases the interiors rivaled and even surpassed the buildings of the wealthy in terms of light and air. The stretch of apartment buildings that appeared along the Grand Concourse in the Bronx from the 1910s to the '30s became known as the "Park Avenue of the middle class."[67]

Yet as immigrants and their children left for better housing in the fast-developing fringes of the city, new and more restrictive immigration laws meant there was no wave of fresh arrivals to replace them in the tenement districts. In 1929, the New York State Board of Housing estimated that in the area bounded by the East River, the Brooklyn Bridge, Centre Street, the Bowery, and East 4th Street there were thirteen thousand vacancies out of seventy-nine thousand apartments.[68] New regulations also made many old tenements in this area functionally uninhabitable, with the Multiple Dwellings Law of 1929 being the knockout blow. This law required landlords to carve out space for a bathroom in every apartment—not just in new buildings but also in existing ones. Rather than undergo costly upgrades, many property owners chose to simply board up their old tenements, only leasing out the ground floor as retail space.[69] After the passage of the Multiple Dwellings Law, the number of abandoned units on the Lower East Side rose 700 percent.[70]

IIIIIIIIIIIIIIIIIIIII

In 1993, the musician Iggy Pop gave a tour of his Lower East Side neighborhood to Dutch documentarian Bram van Splunteren.[71] As captured in grainy '90s video quality, graffiti-covered tenements in various states of abandonment are interspersed with vacant lots, some of which play host to ad hoc flea markets. By this point, artists, musicians, and intellectuals had become drawn to grittier neighborhoods—places like the Mission District in San Francisco, Venice Beach in Los Angeles, and Lower Manhattan, which for most of their existence had been working-class areas defined by low rent, often dilapidated apartments, and boarding houses. Unlike the first mid-century wave of back-to-the-city hipsters, who had sought to restore old brownstones and row homes in areas like Greenwich Village and Park Slope, this wave reveled in the immaculate dilapidation of their surroundings. To them these buildings represented a type of authenticity lacking in more sanitized and affluent areas. During the tour, Iggy Pop shows van Splunteren where he used to "score drugs," admires the "really nice graffiti to look at," and points out the "funky buildings" before ducking into a bakery and ordering pastries in a flat, Midwestern-accented Spanish.

Iggy Pop's East Village tour came at the latter half of an astounding artistic flourishing in Lower Manhattan, whose music and art scene birthed artists like Talking Heads, Keith Haring, and Jean-Michel Basquiat. In the '70s and '80s, movements like street art and punk music were avant-garde and considered an expression of the deeply marginalized inner-city neighborhoods that had been abandoned by much of society. Yet by the '90's, many of the artists that were part of the Downtown scene had become household names; Keith Haring's work, for example, started to appear in children's cartoons and on T-shirts. Their cultural ascendance corresponded with a broader acceptance of places like Lower Manhattan and other urban neighborhoods. Today, instead of finding squatters siphoning power into abandoned buildings or GG Allin busting out of the Mudd Club covered in feces, the streets of the Lower East Side are filled with European tourists and NYU students searching for brunch. The vacant lots and abandoned buildings that once made certain parts of the neighborhood feel like post-war Dresden have sprouted luxury apartments and hotels.

Remarkably, much of the old urban fabric remains intact. The city's first tenement, 65 Mott Street, still stands. Wolf Baum's bust still looks down on Broome Street, but instead of a glue factory or taxidermist on the ground floor, it now houses a dimly lit bar and a bakery custom-designed for Tinder dates. While the exteriors remain largely untouched, the once-primitive interiors have been completely redone. The original four-unit layout on each floor of the Mott Street and Broome Street buildings has been reduced to a single unit per floor, with rent going as high as $5,000 a month.

The tenement still constitutes a majority of the dense patchwork of buildings in Lower Manhattan. They now are often mixed use, with some having two stories of retail on the ground floor. Combined with their narrow width and density, they have resulted in the area becoming the most walkable, vibrant, and transit-oriented neighborhood in the entire country. As these qualities have gone from markers of poverty to commodities valued by businesses and the professional class, New York has grown wealthier and more populous than at any point in history. These attributes have also made the city one of the most sustainable in the nation, with average carbon emissions among New Yorkers being three times less than the national average.[72] The city's tenement stock, rather than leading to a moral plague as predicted by reformers, has helped New York thrive in the twenty-first century.

New York's resurgence today is in part due to the policies championed by the housing reformers well over a century ago. An International Building Code now ensures that the dark prison-cell apartment of the nineteenth century cannot legally be built anywhere in the country. The barbaric housing conditions and resulting fires, riots, and plagues have largely been eradicated, creating much more livable urban environments. Lesser known but of equal importance is the work of tenants themselves, who were often female immigrants. Through mass rent strikes and tenant mobilizations, their efforts resulted in many important reforms in New York City, including written leases and rent control.[73]

Yet at its core, the housing reform movement at the turn of the twentieth century was an effort to define housing in America. Reformers wanted the country to be not one of dense cities and renters like in Europe, but of single-family homes and property owners. They cast dense multifamily housing as anathema to the nation's values: "Class C, to be discouraged." The reform movement was largely successful in this endeavor, with their views being codified in zoning and building codes that favored single-family homes.

However, just as a large home nestled into a verdant lawn was not an option for all at the turn of the twentieth century, so remains the case today. Ironically, the inability of many land-use systems to allow for dense housing is creating overcrowded conditions reminiscent of the nineteenth century in the nation's largest and most expensive cities. In 2017, two dozen people were found living in the basement of a laundromat in a working-class section of San Francisco. Like a modern-day Old Brewery, the space had illegally been divided into cubicles, many of which had no access to outside light, with all inhabitants sharing a single bathroom.[74] In New York, it is estimated that 9 percent of all households are overcrowded. In parts of Queens and the Bronx, which have replaced the Lower East Side as destinations for immigrants entering the city, it is common for multiple families to cram into apartments as small as 500 square feet.

Though centered in New York, the housing reform movement was nationwide. While the laws created in the early twentieth century were in response to the tenement, the actual proliferation of the building was mostly limited to New York. Yet the structure still looms large over debates around housing, as can be seen in the ambiguous usage of the word *tenement*. In the 1920s, the Chicago housing reformer Edith Abbott described how the term has come to not so much describe a type of building, but rather a condition: "the tenement carries with it the idea of extreme deterioration and poverty. People in the tenements are for the most part people of very small incomes, and destitute people of all nationalities and races."[75]

The word has now taken on a dual meaning. It is used to refer to pre-twentieth-century working-class New York City apartment buildings while also becoming an epithet used to describe dense housing across the country, either because of a building's characteristics or the people who inhabit it. This usage exemplifies how multifamily housing is seen as a threat to a neighborhood's physical and social character. When the construction of a new apartment building is proposed, neighbors often worry as much about who will live there as how it looks. As the housing and climate crises compel policymakers to encourage dense forms of housing, these decades-old prejudices have been revived. This is all a legacy of reformers' battles over the tenements, which turned housing in the United States from a utilitarian shelter into a moral litmus test.

CHAPTER 3

New Orleans Shotgun

A Talking Place

L ocated in a massive swamp along the banks of a great river prone to violent and sudden shifts in direction, New Orleans is one of the most precariously situated cities in the world. Yet even a glance at a primitive seventeenth-century map shows the incredible strategic importance of this location. To the north, the Mississippi River gives access to the fertile interior of North America, and to the south, the Gulf of Mexico connects to the bounty of the Caribbean.

This location made New Orleans a unique crossroads, and the city's architecture reflects not only its geography and climate, but also its unique cultural sphere. Whereas the row houses of the Northeast were directly imported from the urban confines of London, the shotgun houses that line the streets of New Orleans are descended from rural dwellings designed for the plantations of Haiti. The housing type marks a branching off from the closely packed brick dwellings of the Northeast to the more open and provisional structures of the interior and the West.

The precise origins of the shotgun's distinctive features as compared to other American homes—its narrow footprint, broad porch, and peculiar layout of interconnected rooms—have befuddled architectural historians for decades. This has resulted in the home being considered nothing more than a hastily thrown-together shack. Yet the shotgun's unique qualities make it a link in the African diaspora from the Yoruba people of West Africa to the Caribbean to the American South. The shotgun is a testament to the ways in which a house is not just a utilitarian shelter, but also an expression of cultural values.

IIIIIIIIIIIIIIIIIIII

Four thousand years ago, around the same time that the Indus civilization was flourishing on the Indian subcontinent, the land that is now New Orleans was formed by silt carried down the Mississippi River. This natural levee, fifteen feet tall at its highest point and two miles across at its widest, was essentially a small island in the midst of a vast cypress swamp. At any moment, the Mississippi could shift dramatically, resulting in a crevasse or breach that could return this landmass back to the sea.[1] Yet although precarious, this piece of land was particularly well located. Bayou St. John gave it access to Lake Pontchartrain and provided a substantial shortcut to the Gulf of Mexico, especially when compared to going directly up the mouth of the Mississippi.[2] For centuries the Bayogoula people inhabited this levee, traveling up and down the river and using the bayou to get food from the lake.

Throughout the sixteenth and seventeenth centuries, the colonial powers in the Caribbean—France, Spain, and England—had heard rumors of a great river that gave access from the gulf into North America. However, the weaving waterways at the mouth of the Mississippi made it difficult to find. In 1536, a Spanish expedition in search of the river was taken by currents to Texas, forcing them to trek on foot two thousand miles overland; they eventually ended up on the Pacific Coast of Mexico. Over one hundred years later, in the late seventeenth century, a group of French explorers set out from Quebec and, via the Great Lakes, traveled down the Mississippi until they smelled the salt water of the Gulf of Mexico. As recalled by a member of the expedition, there, "with all possible solemnity, we performed the ceremony of planting the cross and raising the arms of France."[3]

However, settling this hostile land proved difficult, and it would be four more decades before a French military engineer named Adrien de Pauger laid out New Orleans in 1721. His plan reflected the great potential of this site, with sixty-six blocks stretching for a mile along the Mississippi and half a mile inland. Flanking the city were large protective walls, and in the center, next to the river, was a military marching ground. Around this open space that would later become Jackson Square, imposing government and civic buildings were placed, including St. Louis Cathedral.[4] New Orleans was meant to unfurl in front of passing ships arriving after weeks on open seas and in malarial swamps, signaling the might of the French empire—even on the far side of the world.

Yet in the early eighteenth century, New Orleans was still very much a rustic outpost constantly dealing with outbreaks of disease and flooding. The city's architecture was marked by openness to the outdoors, with houses elevated one story into the air on brick or wood plinths to maximize airflow underneath. A steeply pitched roof designed to withstand high winds and torrential downpours extended over a broad front porch. This gallery wrapped around the home, functioning both as a hallway and an outdoor room, with tall French doors connecting it to the interior. This high degree of permeability between indoor and outdoor was meant to make life semi-habitable in the city's hot and swampy climate. These features are a stark contrast to the row houses of Philadelphia, which appear to be almost fortified in comparison.

The uniqueness of New Orleans's early homes is due to them being derived not from any European housing type, as with the row home, but from a Caribbean dwelling called a *bohío*. This small, rectangular, pitched-roof structure, elevated above the ground with an outdoor gallery, had been developed by the Arawak people of the Caribbean. Early colonists adopted the bohío as a provisional structure when first settling on the islands. As the settlements became more established, the colonists' bohíos retained the climate-sensitive features but used a European floor plan that modified the typical hall-and-parlor scheme with smaller, closet-sized rooms called *cabinets*, separated by a semi-open space called a *loggia*. This style of architecture prioritized maximizing airflow through broad openings and outdoor spaces. By 1720, these homes could be found on plantations and in towns across the French sugar colonies of the Caribbean, as well as in New Orleans.[5] These plantation houses set a precedent for architecture in the city for centuries to come.*

---

* The Pitot House on Bayou St. John is an intact example of one of these plantation houses.

The hybrid qualities of the plantation houses, which adapted various cultural traditions to local conditions and technology, came to be emblematic of Creole architecture. *Creole* is originally a Portuguese term used to describe someone born in the French or Spanish colonies, including residents of New Orleans before its annexation into the United States, which is also how this term is used in this chapter. Many scholars, however, define *Creole* more broadly as a process of adaptation to local cultural or environmental conditions, through which an object, practice, or language becomes "creolized." This spirit of innovation and improvisation is an integral element of the architecture as well as the broader culture of New Orleans.[6]

IIIIIIIIIIIIIIIIII

By the turn of the nineteenth century, New Orleans, though just eighty years old, had already been a part of two different colonial empires. After being established by the French, it was unceremoniously handed off to Spain in the 1760s, then returned to France four decades later for a brief period. Despite the city being passed around like a rotten crepe, the transition between these two empires was relatively easy, with both countries sharing broad cultural similarities. New Orleans was also much more connected, both culturally and economically, to the Caribbean for it to matter much which distant European power officially controlled it.[7]

By the turn of the nineteenth century, the French emperor Napoleon realized that with his conquests in Europe and the rebellion of enslaved people in the colony of Saint-Domingue, he could no longer hold his colonies in continental North America. US president Thomas Jefferson seized on this opportunity to add the important trading post of New Orleans to his young nation. However, his representatives were shocked when France decided to also throw in a large chunk of French-controlled North America. With the Louisiana Purchase in 1803, New Orleans was no longer a distant colonial outpost and instead instantly became the seventh-largest city in the United States.

Almost immediately, entrepreneurial Americans poured into the city. However, with the majority of these newcomers being Northeastern Yankees, they quickly found themselves out of their element in the swampy, Latin confines of New Orleans. Their ability to communicate with the locals was impeded by a language barrier, with the majority of Creoles speaking French and both sides refusing to learn each other's tongue. This was further compounded by the fact that when they were able to communicate, the brass tacks manner of the Americans clashed with the baroque and indirect style of the Creoles. They also had a vastly different conception of leisure time. Americans tended to be intensely focused on work and making money, perhaps reserving a few moments in the evening to have their children read them a Bible verse, while Creoles enjoyed wine-fueled balls and spent Sundays gambling and hunting.[8]

Due to these irreconcilable differences, New Orleans fractured itself into two. Just north of the original grid, the city's first *faubourg*, or suburb, was established. Officially called St. Mary, it quickly became known as the American section.[9] In turn, the original city laid out by Pauger became known as the French Quarter by Americans and as Vieux Carré, meaning "old city," by the Creoles. The Americans set to work on developing their sector into a Northeastern city transported to the Louisiana bayou and built red-brick commercial structures reminiscent of those in Philadelphia or New York. Carondelet Street, lined with cast-iron buildings, became the center of the cotton trade. In 1833, a row house development called Julia Row was built, with the façade and floor plan of its thirteen homes looking as if they had been lifted off the streets of Philadelphia.[10] The American transplants viewed this Anglo architecture as civilizing the city.[11]

Meanwhile, the Creoles did everything they could to ignore their new neighbors, as if their time under the American regime would soon pass like that under France or Spain. They still outnumbered Americans for most of the nineteenth century, and crossing Canal Street into the French Quarter was like entering another country. The French language dominated, and the Quarter was a distinct ecosystem with its own hotels, newspaper, and opera house.[12] Yet in the Creole tradition, they did note the new architecture that was rising across town. As New Orleans grew in wealth and population, the low-slung plantation houses, which had given the city the air of a rural Caribbean village, were replaced by larger and more substantial structures. The Creoles borrowed features of American-style row houses to create their own unique structure called the Creole townhouse. They maintained the Georgian floor plan common to London and Philadelphia but added several distinctive features. Large arched openings with French doors were added to the first floor.[13] Instead of austere brick, they were washed in stucco with wrought iron balconies attached to the façade. These balconies were the result of fire safety laws that had been established by the Spanish in 1784. The Creoles elevated them from utilitarian safety devices into elaborate works of art, with the wrought iron shaped into ornate patterns of flowers, leaves, and other motifs, crafted through the painstaking labor of enslaved people brought over from West Africa. These balconies functioned the same way that the gallery did on plantation houses—as an outdoor room. The grand townhomes and ornate balconies of the French Quarter rivaled New World capitals like Buenos Aires or Havana. In 1861, Baron Salomon de Rothschild wrote of the city, "In all my travels never have I seen anything which looks as much like Paris."[14]

As the Americans sweated in their stuffed collars across Canal Street, even they became susceptible to Creole architecture. This was partially because their attempts to build Northern structures in the city had been thwarted by the local conditions. These obstacles included not only the climate but also the local brick, which was incredibly porous and needed to be covered in stucco, which builders would paint a brick pattern on in a sad attempt to replicate the Northeastern style. Eventually Americans adapted their buildings to the city. The height of the floors on new buildings was raised to help carry out heat, and wrought iron balconies were put on new buildings and attached to older ones.[15] The climate-adaptive Creole architecture was starting to win over the Yankees just as it had the European settlers in the Caribbean. The divided city of New Orleans was starting to meld together, physically if not culturally.

||||||||||||||||||||

The annexation of New Orleans into the United States could have easily meant the end of its unique culture. With the Creole population beginning to adopt the customs and values of the broader American society, New Orleans could have ended up like any other large Southern city. Perhaps even the French Quarter would have been diminished or demolished. The only reminder of the New World Paris would be a dilapidated Creole townhouse marooned in a tarmacked parking lot, backlit by the lights of a Waffle House.

Yet in the same year that the Louisiana Purchase was completed, an unprecedented situation was unfolding just off the city's shores in the Caribbean, with massive consequences for New Orleans: the Haitian Revolution. The French colony, then called Saint-Domingue, was the world's sugar capital and therefore one of the wealthiest places on Earth in the eighteenth century. However, this wealth was created by the forced labor of enslaved Africans. This brutal system was so sadistic that the average enslaved person lived fewer than ten years after being brought to the island. Inspired by the French Revolution and its message of equality, enslaved Africans began an uprising in 1791. After a series of brutal battles, which resulted in much of the island erupting in flames, the French were driven out in 1803, leading to the creation of the world's first Black republic, renamed Haiti.[16]

Unlike the United States, with its sharp delineation between Black and white, in the French and Spanish colonies—including New Orleans—the racial hierarchy had a much greater degree of variants. Saint-Domingue had a robust community of over thirty thousand *gens de couleur libres*, or free people of color. These Black and mixed-race people had either been freed by their enslaver or had a white parent, which granted them freedom under colonial law. This population did have fewer rights than white people and had to defer to them. However, many of the free people of color were wealthy landowners and were highly educated, with some even being sent to study in France for a period of time.

The free people of color in Saint-Domingue had become deeply intertwined with the white elite, with some even enslaving others. Because of this, they were implicated in the Revolution and followed their white counterparts in fleeing the island for Cuba and other Caribbean colonies, bringing their enslaved people with them if they could. Eventually, many ended up in New Orleans. In 1809, fifty boats arrived there, bringing 1,887 whites, 2,112 enslaved people, and 2,060 free people of color into a city of 17,000. Altogether, nearly 12,000 refugees from Saint-Domingue would settle in New Orleans. The influx of the French-speaking Saint-Domingue refugees substantially reinvigorated the city's Creole culture. Between the booming American sector and the established Creole community, the city was the most ethnically and linguistically diverse in the country. The free people of color, combined with the large population of enslaved people, also made New Orleans a majority-Black city.[17]

|||||||||||||||||

Unlike the Americans, the Saint-Domingue refugees quickly melded with the existing Creole population, creating new faubourgs adjacent to the French Quarter. Treme, which some call the oldest Black neighborhood in the United States, was built north across Rampart Street, and Marigny was established south, down river. However, these new neighborhoods took on a very different character than the stucco townhomes of the French Quarter. The Saint-Domingue arrivals brought their own architectural typology in the form of long, narrow, lightweight homes. These buildings had distinct similarities to the city's plantation houses, most notably the broad front porch and overhanging gabled roof. However, their overall shape was entirely different. Instead of the wide hall-and-parlor floor plan, they were arranged in a long skinny rectangle consisting of four to six rooms linked together without a hallway, like the cars of a train. With this peculiar layout they became known as shotguns, both because of their long, narrow shape and also because it was believed that if you fired a gun through the front door, the bullet would exit through the back door without hitting any walls, a spatial pattern that was far different from the American standard.

For decades, architectural historians believed that the shotgun had evolved out of the plantation house. Both had originated from the Caribbean and traced their origin to the Indigenous bohío dwellings. However, whereas Europeans had taken the bohío and Westernized it by combining its climate-sensitive features with a European floor plan, enslaved people had Africanized it. The front porch was widened to four feet, and the overall dimensions were made long and narrow, resulting in a house called the *ti kay*. In the mid-1970s, scholar John Michael Vlach found that the Haitian ti kay has almost identical dimensions to the traditional Yoruba dwellings of Nigeria: ten feet wide by twenty feet long. Traditionally, both the bohío and West African dwellings were made from vernacular materials. Wattle, a lattice of wood sticks, was covered in daub, a combination of mud, clay, sand, and animal dung, to make the walls. The roof was made out of thatch. Over time, Black Caribbean artisans adapted modern European building methods to change the ti kay's construction from wattle and daub to a light wood-frame construction. This resulted in an incredibly adaptive structure that could be built quickly and, because it was on a raised foundation, picked up and rotated around plantations with the crops.[18]

The ti kay eventually became a standard housing type in Haiti and across the Caribbean, throughout all levels of society. Small provisional versions were built in rural areas, and more substantial iterations were built for wealthy free people of color in large cities such as Cap-Haitien and Port-au-Prince.

|||||||||||||||||||||

The shotgun arrived in New Orleans as the city was on the cusp of a massive expansion. In 1811, soon after the Saint-Domingue refugees began to arrive, the first steamship came down the Mississippi River. New Orleans became the main emporium for Midwestern commodities and Southern sugar and cotton, and it was one of the country's largest slave port, with 135,000 people being purchased there.[19] The city's dominance in trade made it one of the most important economic centers in the antebellum United States. By 1840 it was the third-biggest city in the country, with some predicting it would eventually become the largest.

As New Orleans boomed, it started to butt up against the geographic constraints of its location. The natural levee on which the city rested was hemmed in by the Mississippi River on one side and by a massive cypress swamp on the other. This resulted in New Orleans developing along the river in a crescent shape, with most growth heavily oriented upriver, or Uptown, past the American Sector. Uptown was favored because there the river formed an arch, making the natural levee there much wider than around the French Quarter downtown. Debris and refuse also flowed down the river, creating miniature garbage dumps along the banks. This resulted in the neighborhoods south of the French Quarter taking an additional sixty to eighty years to reach the urban density of the Uptown areas.[20] By 1847, the city measured five miles along the river and three-quarters of a mile wide, with a population of over one hundred thousand.[21]

Up and down the Mississippi and buffering New Orleans were plantations plotted in the French manner, forming wedges such that each property had access to the river and then narrowed as it extended into the back swamp. The plantations were separated from each other by canals dug to help drain away water.[22] As the city grew and expanded in the nineteenth century, real estate became more valuable than growing sugar or cotton, and the plantations were subdivided for new development. The canals were turned into wide main boulevards topped with 22- to 32-foot-wide landscaped medians that became known as the *neutral ground* (a phrase first coined in the 1830s to describe the median of Canal Street, which divided the Creole French Quarter from the American Sector). Today, major Uptown streets, such as Louisiana Avenue, Napoleon Avenue, and Washington Avenue, mimic the wedge-like shapes of these long-forgotten estates.

Pauger's French Quarter grid of narrow 30-foot-wide streets and 320-square-foot blocks was then extended onto the former plantations. The blocks were initially divided into lots that were 64 feet wide and 120 to 150 feet long. However, French law and custom mandated that each child receive an equal share of inheritance. This led to lots being subdivided, sometimes becoming as narrow as 16 feet.[23] The long and incredibly skinny parcels of land led to a gradual densification of the city, with new housing evolving from rural to more urban formats. Builders took the model of the old broad plantation houses and created new buildings that compressed and reoriented their features to conform to the city's narrow lots. This type of structure became known as a Creole cottage.[24]

Yet the Creole cottage, though abundant in older parts of the city, would not come to define New Orleans's housing stock. Many of the Saint-Domingue refugees were skilled artisans and, after arriving in the city, bought property and started building shotguns, both to live in and to lease as rental units.[25] Free people of color soon came to dominate the building trades in New Orleans, and by 1850 the city had 355 Black carpenters and 325 Black masons.[26] The light frame construction of the shotgun was not only faster to build, but also half as costly as the Creole cottage, which was built from heavy and expensive timber framing and ceiling joists.[27] This gave the shotgun structure a distinct advantage in a city whose population was doubling every decade during the antebellum period.

However, neither of these factors explains how the shotgun crossed racial and ethnic barriers to become the city's primary residential housing type. The diversity of housing found in the city in the mid-nineteenth century represented both ethnic divisions as well as competing urban visions. The Americans had moved on from row houses and started building large single-family homes farther Uptown. Evoking the country ideals of William Penn, this neighborhood was named the Garden District.[28] The narrow shotguns, with their peculiar layouts and claustrophobic lots, could have remained ghettoized in the Creole sections of the city. Yet by the turn of the twentieth century, the shotgun was found in every neighborhood and was inhabited by all races, ethnicities, and social classes. This was not only because it was cheap, easy to construct, and suited to the climate, but also due to the unique cultural conditions of antebellum New Orleans.

In the mid-nineteenth century, 63 percent of the free people of color in the city were women, while white men outnumbered white women two to one. The Spanish and French had left the city with the system of *plaçage*, or placement, where free women of color could form a romantic relationship with wealthy white men. In exchange, the women would receive a stipend and could claim an inheritance after the men died. It was also customary for the man to build the woman a house, particularly in the French Quarter or Treme. Like most things in New Orleans, plaçage is heavily romanticized and shrouded in myth, often involving elaborate balls where these relationships were arranged. The reality is that this system was often exploitative of desperate Saint-Domingue refugees trying to gain an economic foothold in a new city.[29]

Yet plaçage was usually a temporary situation and did result in a large group of property-owning free women of color.[30] Many of these women leveraged the homes they received from these relationships as a business enterprise and started specializing in boarding houses. These lodgings took the form of four-room shotguns with the first few rooms rented out to boarders—often white businessmen who'd just arrived in the city to seek their fortune—and the last being used as a living space for the owner. These accommodations gained a reputation for being the most luxurious lodgings in the city. Through these boarding houses, the shotgun was transmitted to the city's non-Creole population. The white businessmen came to associate the structures with a time in their youth when they were well cared for, and as these men ascended the business ranks, shotguns proliferated along the streets of the Garden District and other Uptown neighborhoods. But by crossing Canal Street, the building became Americanized. A hallway was added to connect the rooms, providing more formality and privacy. In some cases, an el extended off the back of the house to provide a grander entrance.[31]

Shotguns not only gained favor with the American merchant class but also became the housing of immigrant laborers. As in the cities of the

Northeast, large numbers of Germans and Irish poured into New Orleans beginning in the 1820s. Many settled in Uptown neighborhoods near the docks along the Mississippi, such as the Irish Channel, where they rented narrow shotguns lacking a hallway. This was not due to any affinity for Creole tradition but was—as with the trinity row house and the tenement—a space-saving measure. By the Civil War, the city's working-class housing increasingly took the form of doubles, which combined two shotguns under one gabled roof that were divided down the middle by a party wall (see image 8). Due to the demand for housing during this period, double shotguns eventually became more popular than single ones, especially among immigrants and African American migrants.

As the shotgun became New Orleans's default housing type, the façades adopted the latest American and European architectural trends. In the 1830s, many of the city's shotguns took on aspects of the Greek Revival style. The supports holding up the porch were turned into columns, and the triangle below the gabled roof became a pediment, making the shotgun look like a diminutive Greek temple. By the mid-nineteenth century, even working-class shotguns were layered in a level of decoration that anticipated turn-of-the-century New York tenements. Ornamental brackets connecting the front columns to the roof were intricately carved in different natural patterns, like the filigreed wrought iron balconies in the French Quarter. However, instead of being made by hand, they were produced by steam-powered sawmills and could be purchased from a catalogue. The decorative brackets became a calling card of the city's shotguns and also came to define an entire architectural genre that dominated the city between 1880 to 1910.[32]

From the street, many shotguns look like tiny, claustrophobic structures. However, similar to the trinity, builders made the interior seem bigger by creating high ceilings and floor-length windows. Walking through the house can induce a sense of déjà vu, with each room being the same size and nearly identical. Perhaps the biggest departure from the standard American home is that the kitchen and bathrooms are contained in the far back, forcing one to walk through the entire house, even intimate spaces like bedrooms, to reach them.

||||||||||||||||||

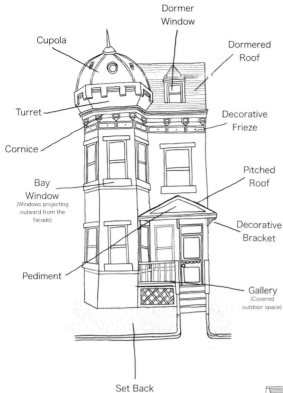

Cupola

Dormer Window

Dormered Roof

Turret

Cornice

Decorative Frieze

Pitched Roof

Bay Window
(Windows projecting outward from the facade)

Decorative Bracket

Pediment

Gallery
(Covered outdoor space)

Set Back

Image 1. This diagram of a fictional house can be referred to for the frequently used architectural terms throughout the book.

Image 2. A Philadelphia row house.

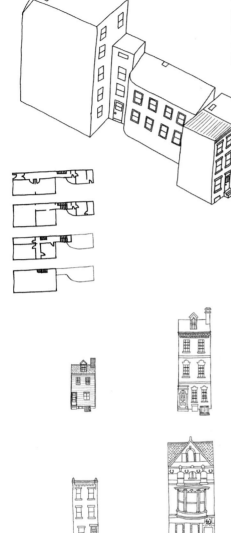

Image 3. Philadelphia builders were incredibly adept at manipulating narrow lots to create spacious and light-filled homes. Large row homes for the elite would incorporate back "els" that extended the home deep into the lot and contained dining rooms and parlors, as well as a kitchen and service areas. Small trinities for the working class, composed of a basement kitchen and a single room on three floors, would sometimes be built directly behind the homes of the wealthy.

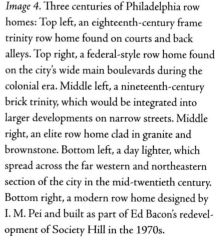

Image 4. Three centuries of Philadelphia row homes: Top left, an eighteenth-century frame trinity row home found on courts and back alleys. Top right, a federal-style row home found on the city's wide main boulevards during the colonial era. Middle left, a nineteenth-century brick trinity, which would be integrated into larger developments on narrow streets. Middle right, an elite row home clad in granite and brownstone. Bottom left, a day lighter, which spread across the far western and northeastern section of the city in the mid-twentieth century. Bottom right, a modern row home designed by I. M. Pei and built as part of Ed Bacon's redevelopment of Society Hill in the 1970s.

Image 5. In 1825, 65 Mott Street was the first tenement built in New York City. It was composed of thirty units in a front and back building and took the form of a stripped-down Georgian-style row home on steroids.

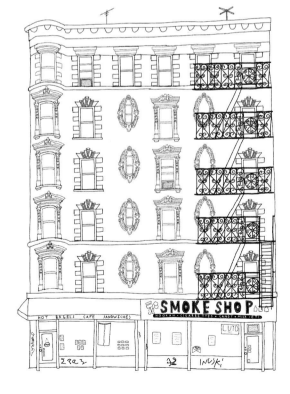

Image 6. After the Civil War, a competitive housing market led developers to drench their tenements in ornamentation, which transcended the common perception of the building as a misery receptacle for the dregs of society.

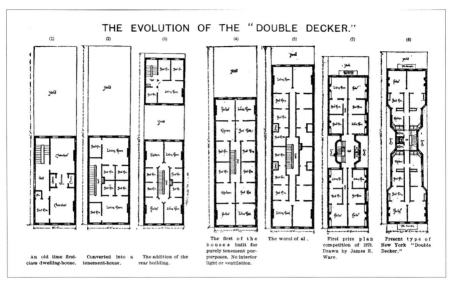

THE EVOLUTION OF THE "DOUBLE DECKER."

(1) An old time first-class dwelling-house.

(2) Converted into a tenement-house.

(3) The addition of the rear building.

(4) The first of the houses built for purely tenement purposes. No interior light or ventilation.

(5) The worst of al .

(7) First prize plan competition of 1879. Drawn by James E. Ware.

(6) Present type of New York "Double Decker."

Image 7. This diagram from an 1895 report on tenement house conditions shows the evolution of the tenement, from a subdivided upper-class house to the "dumbbell"-shaped buildings that resulted from an 1879 tenement reform law.

Image 8. A New Orleans double shotgun.

Image 9. The evolution of the shotgun: Upper left, a bohío house built by the Arawak people in the Caribbean. Upper middle, a traditional Yoruba dwelling. Upper right, a typical Caribbean plantation house. Middle left, a single shotgun. Middle middle, a single shotgun with a side hallway. Middle right, a double shotgun. Bottom left, a typical shotgun house found in the historic Third Ward of Houston. Bottom middle, a typical brick shotgun found in Louisville, Kentucky. Bottom right, a ti kay house, found in Haiti.

Image 10. A Chicago workers cottage.

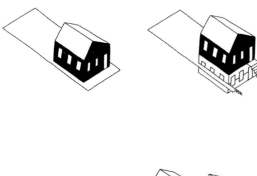
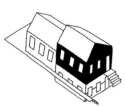

Image 11. Evolution of a workers cottage: Upper left, at first a small cottage would be built on a 25-by-125-foot lot. Upper right, the home would often be raised to create a second, semi-subterranean unit underneath, sometimes called a "Polish flat." Bottom left, additional structures would be appended to the back of the house. Bottom right, the original workers cottage, or "starter cottage," would be moved to the back of the lot to make room for a larger, multi-unit building at the front. Through these adaptations, over time, a lot containing one home could contain as many as ten.

Image 12. This aerial photo from 1901 shows Chicago's Near West Side set against a skyline of smokestacks and church steeples. The tiny pitched-roofed workers cottages in the foreground demonstrate a range of individual adaptations, resulting in each structure having varying heights and setbacks from the street, as well as back houses and various additions.

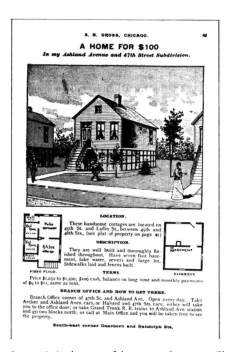

Image 13. At the turn of the twentieth century, Chicago became plastered in ads by the prolific developer S. E. Gross. The image on the left shows a workers cottage that included a semi-submerged flat. The image on the right shows how he targeted the city's immigrant population with ads written in various languages.

Image 14. A Portland bungalow.

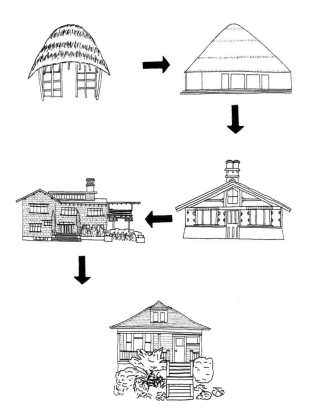

Image 15. The evolution of the Portland bungalow: Upper left, a traditional home found in Bengal, India. Upper right, a British officer's house, typical of those found on a colonial cantonment outside major Indian cities. Middle right, a bungalow built in a British seaside resort. Middle left, the Gamble House, a large Arts and Crafts style mansion. Bottom, a middle-class bungalow.

Image 16. Aerial photo of Levittown, 1959. Due to federal housing policy, after World War II, urban housing units went from being extensions of existing neighborhoods to being contained within entirely new planned communities on the periphery of the city. Developments like Levittown were a radical departure from traditional urban forms and contained standardized houses on their own large lots, set on curvilinear streets instead of a grid, and separated from buildings containing other uses, such as businesses and shops.

Image 17. An aerial view of downtown Portland, from 1955. The swing span of the Morrison Bridge connects the dense core of the downtown to the bungalows of the east side. The large green space in the upper-left-hand side of the image is Laurelhurst Park, surrounded by the curving streets of the exclusive Laurelhurst development. The wagon wheel of streets in the mid-right-hand side is Ladd's Addition. The farmland beyond would soon be developed with subdivisions as people left the inner core. By the 1980s, Harbor Drive along the river would be turned into a new park and the surface parking lot in the lower-right-hand corner would become Pioneer Courthouse Square, now known as Portland's living room.

Image 18. A Boston triple-decker.

Image 19. The evolution of a Boston streetcar suburb: Far left, old farm roads connect rural areas to the city. Middle left, as streetcars were built, developers would buy land along the tracts and subdivide them for large single-family homes and town homes. Middle right, the addition of crosstown streetcar lines allowed the working class to access the suburbs, and, in response, developers would further subdivide lots for smaller homes and triple-deckers. Far right, by the early twentieth century, once rural areas were now dense urban neighborhoods.

Image 20. The evolution of urban housing in Boston: Top, the two-room "London house plan" of a typical bow-fronted row home found in neighborhoods like the South End. Middle, the large elaborate floor plans of a town-home duplex, with separate stairways providing access to each unit, as well as third-floor servants' quarters. Bottom, the layout of a triple-decker, whose units could be over 1,000 square feet, with both a front and back porch and two separate stairways.

Image 21. A Los Angeles dingbat.

Image 22. Horatio West Court was designed by the architect Irving Gill in 1919 in Santa Monica, California. It is both an example of bungalow courts, which provided cheap, rental housing in the early twentieth century, and the emerging modernist style, with its stripped-down concrete walls painted white.

Image 23. Boulevard transformation: Top, as cars began to dominate the city's transportation system, Los Angeles's commercial boulevards became lined with strip malls, gas stations, and auto-body shops. Bottom, over time, however, these low-rise buildings were increasingly replaced with large podium apartment buildings such as those along Overland Boulevard, in the city's Palms neighborhood.

Image 24. Los Angeles architecture firms have been at the forefront of innovating new types of podium buildings. Westgate 1515, designed by Lorcan O'Herlihy Architects, uses open space to break up units and avoid long double-loaded corridors while engaging the public realm with storefronts, public space, and landscaping.

Image 25. 888 Beach Avenue, designed by James Cheng, pioneered the Vancouver Point tower by placing two narrow high-rises on a base made up of row homes.

Image 26. After being rezoned, austere, poured-concrete high-rises proliferated across the West End of Vancouver in the 1950s and '60s.

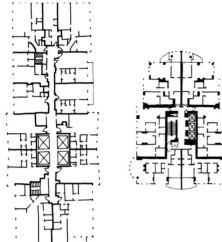

Image 27. Left, a typical floor plan of a high-rise or podium-style building in North America, with long double-loaded corridors and narrow units with few windows. Right, the slender floor plan of a point tower with fewer units but featuring more dynamic layouts that better integrate light and open space.

Image 28. Metrotown: The suburb of Burnaby, British Columbia, is one of the town centers designated by the Greater Vancouver Regional District. Since the 1980s, dozens of point towers have sprouted up around the city's SkyTrain stations, while suburban homes sit just a few blocks away. The skyline of downtown Vancouver can be seen in the background.

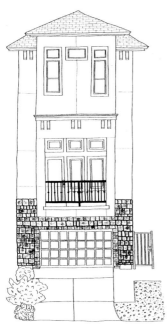

Image 29. A Houston town home.

Image 30. Three eras of Houston town homes: Top, after World War II, large developments of town homes were built outside the 610 loop in the city's expanding suburbs. These developments were like suburban subdivisions, except with attached homes and shared amenities such as pools and recreation centers. Middle, in the 1980s, experimental architecture firms built small developments like the Haddon Street Townhomes by Arcquitectonica in inner neighborhoods with each home being integrated into a cohesive design. Bottom, a new law passed in 1999 allowed lots to be subdivided into as small as 1,400 square feet, resulting in narrow homes separated by only a few feet.

Image 31. Built in 2018 by the architecture firm ISA, Tiny Tower reinterprets Philadelphia's trinity row homes as a modern dwelling.

Image 32. 3106 St. Thomas Street: By utilizing a tiny remnant lot, OJT architects produced a home that creates a modern and affordable house in an established, historic neighborhood.

New Orleans transformed the shotgun from a rural dwelling into an urban one. When situated on the city's narrow lots, they create a succession of minuscule façades along the streets, with only a few feet between each home. Yet despite its diminutive profile, the shotgun generously opens itself up to the street, with its broad porch and large windows and doors. This high degree of permeability turns the area around the home into a social space. Instead of simply being a route to get from one place to another, the streets of New Orleans function more like an outdoor living room.

Although its parades move down predetermined routes, Mardi Gras is more like a raucous citywide block party, with people carousing and drinking on nearly every corner. And on Sundays and after funerals, it is common for parades of roving brass bands to cause people to spontaneously spill out of their homes and dance and hang out in the street. On any given day, but especially during the hot and swampy summer months, residents may escape outside to chat with neighbors, practice musical instruments, or enjoy a cooler of beer. It is as if the long, train-like space of the homes pushes people outdoors.

New Orleans's vibrant street life is not only fostered by the physical qualities of the shotgun, but also by its cultural lineage. In the Yoruba culture, as well as in other West African traditions, the distinction be-tween the family unit and the broader community is blurred. This is expressed through the architecture, with the interiors of homes being only a little larger than their front porch. Life is meant to be lived outdoors in connection with the community, with buildings arranged around a large communal open space. Via enslaved Africans as well as the shotgun itself, this fusing of interior private space with exterior public space was transported to New Orleans.[33] The scholar bell hooks writes about how African Americans, whose extended families crowded into shotguns at the edges of rural Southern towns, saw the yard as a continuation of the living space. For a people that had been enslaved and oppressed, having control over a small garden or patch of dirt outside a shotgun was a form of resistance, a place where one could create a different reality. As hooks writes, this was a "liminal space where they can stretch the limits of desire and imagination."[34] In the paintings of the artist John Biggers, shotguns are depicted as temples, which can be interpreted as keepers of African American tradition. Biggers, who was one of the first people to elucidate the shotgun's connection to Africa, called the spaces around the home "talking places" where the community came together and shared lessons from the Bible.[35] By transporting the shotgun to New Orleans, the city's narrow streets became what the village square was in West Africa.

IIIIIIIIIIIIIIIIIII

In the early nineteenth century, New Orleans's remote location in the Deep South, far west of the Appalachian Mountains, made it a frontier town. The city became a natural point of debarkation for those traveling to even more remote locales in the vast expanse of land added by the Louisiana Purchase. One of the most pressing needs for these settlers was shelter, particularly structures that could be rapidly built without the aid of trained builders.

The shotgun's earliest iteration—as a lightweight, provisional structure meant to be rotated around plantations—proved well suited to meet this need. A cottage industry of creating prefabricated buildings emerged in New Orleans, with parts of houses loaded onto ships then floated up the Mississippi to be erected by pioneers. In the 1840s, the entrepreneur Samuel Denman marketed these prefabricated shotguns as having "Strength and Comfort, with Cheapness and Portability." The industry became so sophisticated that in 1849 an entire hotel was manufactured and sent in pieces from New Orleans to the gold rush town of San Francisco to be assembled.[36]

The biggest market for the prefabricated shotguns, however, was in New Orleans itself. The Louisiana Steam, Sash, Blind and Door Factory used steam-powered machines to create standardized building parts out of locally sourced cypress wood. By 1880, the factory was publishing a massive catalogue with hundreds of items for sale, including handrails, elaborate front doors, and decorative brackets, as well as complete designs for both single and double shotguns. The products were sent by barge and advertised as being easy enough for a "common hand" to build.[37]

The shotgun marks a turning point in the evolution of the nation's residential architecture. Housing no longer needed to be solid brick structures built by teams of trained artisans, but instead could be ordered from a catalogue and assembled in a week. Such housing types flourished in both rural and urban locations—anyplace that people needed to erect cheap and simple housing quickly. One-room shotguns built from white-washed siding and sheet-metal roofs were built on plantations across the South. They speckled the vast oil fields of Texas and Oklahoma and were used as rugged workers' housing on logging camps.[38] Shotgun beach cottages were built in Santa Monica, and more substantial brick variations were built along alleys in Washington, DC. The homes also migrated up the Mississippi and Ohio Rivers and now account for nearly 10 percent of the housing in Louisville, Kentucky, one of the few places outside of New Orleans to have created a unique architectural vocabulary around the shotgun.[39]

However, the highly evolved shotguns in New Orleans and Louisville were an exception, and most variations retained a provisional rural character, even in urban environments. Beginning in the 1910s, millions of Black people left the plantations and rural areas of the South and migrated to growing Southern cities, including Houston, Miami, and Atlanta, as part of the Great Migration. Blocks of bare-bones shotguns, lacking running water and without any of the ornamentation or artifice of those found in New Orleans, were speculatively built along unpaved roads in these cities to house these migrants.

In Miami, as many as 140 Black migrant families would cram onto a single block, packing into four-bedroom shotguns so close together the occupants could shake hands through the windows. They were almost all owned by absentee white landlords, with only 10 percent of occupants owning their homes.[40] By the mid-twentieth century, the worst slums in the nation were no longer the crowded tenements of the Northeast but instead the growing Black neighborhoods of Southern cities composed of these primitive shotguns.

ıııııııııııııııııııı

The bare-bones shotgun that proliferated in the urban ghettos and in the rural byways outside of New Orleans tinged the structure with a stigma of poverty. For many Americans today, they evoke the dilapidated shacks in the mid-twentieth-century photographs of Robert Frank and movies like *Deliverance* (1972). The house's deep association with African Americans compounded this stigma with racism, even though the vast majority of people had no idea of the home's provenance in Haiti and Africa.

In the early 1990s, Rick Lowe and six other fellow Houston-based artists attempted to subvert the common perception of the shotgun. At the time, the historically African American Third and Fourth Wards of Houston were filled with dilapidated and abandoned homes. The artists reclaimed a row of eight 600-square-foot shotguns that had originally been part of a thirty-house development built by Italian immigrant shop owners in the 1930s. After decades of housing generations of African Americans, by the '90s they sat abandoned and marooned in a sea of weed-strewn lots.[41]

This group of artists wanted to create a work out of these buildings to engage the current residents of the Third Ward. While most Houston residents and city officials considered the shotguns to be worthless pieces of blight, the artists knew that people in the community had a deep connection to the homes. They painstakingly restored each house and repurposed them as galleries in which to install temporary installations. This project has since grown into a nonprofit called Project Row Houses, a local term for this type of closely spaced shotgun home. The organization has taken on a broader mission that includes a youth program, as well as the development of new ground-up affordable housing.[42]

The core of Project Row Houses' work is rooted in the shotgun tradition of fostering community. The complex has no fences or partitions separating the individual homes, creating a broad open space on the interior of the block. For most homes in America, this type of interstitial space would only be used for occasional yard work and would mostly serve as a barrier denoting private property. Yet this space around these shotguns is enlivened at all times of the day via artists and community members mingling, the organization's youth group doing activities, or art patrons attending evening gallery openings. Project Row Houses has helped redefine the shotgun from a dwelling of last resort for the poorest in society to a community anchor, harkening back to the structure's roots in West Africa.

IIIIIIIIIIIIIIIIIIIII

By the turn of the twentieth century, a surge of recently emancipated African Americans from the rural South, as well as immigrants from Asia, Latin America, and Europe, arrived in New Orleans, transforming the city into an ethnic melting pot similar to the ports of the Northeast. Enclaves of Greeks and Jews, as well as a Chinatown, developed outside of the central business district. Creole families started to move out of the French Quarter as one hundred thousand Italians arrived beginning in the 1880s and divided old townhomes into tenements. However, unlike the cities of the North, sharply delineated ethnic ghettos were rare in New Orleans. Instead, these new immigrants mixed with the established population of Americans, Creoles, Germans, and Irish. This resulted in the city's distinctive accent, known by the onomatopoeic word *yat*, which is a mixture of Southern drawl, French-influenced vocabulary, and a New York subway conductor who sounds like Ray Romano after taking too many Percocets.

Ethnic and racial mixing had been a hallmark of life in New Orleans since the colonial period. Throughout the nineteenth century it was common for whites and free people of color to engage socially and in business. Enslaved people in the city often lived behind large houses and were given more autonomy than those on plantations. They interacted with non-Black working-class residents on the street, in bars, and in coffee shops.[43] They were also allowed to assemble on Sundays in Congo Square, with the music performed there leading to the rise of jazz around the turn of the twentieth century. The city's dense urban patchwork also reinforced social mixing. Uptown, the opulent homes along the wide main boulevard sat near the servants' and workers' small shotguns in the interior of the neighborhood, built on the narrow streets.[44]

While neighborhoods were mixed, the highest ground was reserved for the wealthy. Narrow bands of affluence existed on main boulevards, such as St. Charles Avenue Uptown and Esplanade Avenue downtown, both of which ran along natural ridges. Yet by moving just a few feet away, neighborhoods would become increasingly less desirable until inevitably reaching the water. The Mississippi docks ware a particularly noxious place, with work happening at all hours of the day. Bushels of wheat and bags of sugar, coffee, and other goods sat out in the open, piled up atop the levee; nearby residents would slash into the contents to replenish their pantries.[45] Bars, boarding houses, and brothels for sailors and longshoremen lined the surrounding streets in neighborhoods like the Irish Channel, Marigny, and Bywater, which were some of the poorest in the city.

Yet the Mississippi was the visible front of New Orleans and its economic lifeblood, and the chaos of the docks and goods piled high were a testament to the city's economic might. Meanwhile, the Backatown, on the opposite side of the city, was something to be hidden. This area bordered a large swamp where palmettos, large cypress trees draped in Spanish moss, and stalagmite-like tree stumps rose up from a black morass speckled with bright green algae. This was a beautiful but harsh environment where a seemingly solid piece of dirt could suck in a boot like a sinkhole, and alligators casually sunning themselves presented tripping hazards. Backatown became where necessary but undesirable places like factories and cemeteries, as well as Congo Square, were placed. The swamp and Mississippi River formed a hard border around New Orleans. In cities like Boston or New York it was possible, although expensive, to fill in the surrounding water to make new land, but making the New Orleans swamp suitable for development was much more difficult—the dense vegetation and massive cypress stumps would need to be removed before beginning the arduous task of draining out the fetid water.

Yet by the turn of the twentieth century, an invention by native son A. Baldwin Wood allowed New Orleans to transcend the muddy mire that surrounded it. Wood created a pump that could take in large quantities of debris-filled water, funnel it into canals, and flush it out into Lake Pontchartrain. By 1905, six pumps drained twenty-two thousand acres, the equivalent of fifty-two French Quarters. As Wood's system of pumps was expanded and improved, the city's landscape became one of the most engineered in the world. A system of pumps fed a web of concrete drainage canals carrying stormwater out of the city, and neighborhoods were enclosed by high earthen levees like the walls of a castle.

|||||||||||||||||||

The draining of the back swamp was a seismic shift in the city's spatial development. Before the pumps, 90 percent of the city's population lived on the natural levee, but by 1960 less than half of the city was on high ground. Aided by the electric streetcars introduced in the 1890s, which glided along the neutral ground of the wide main boulevards, families left the crowded wards along the Mississippi into the reclaimed swampland. As in Philadelphia, the pattern of the old city was largely extended into these new streetcar neighborhoods. The continuation of Pauger's grid and the division of blocks in long, narrow lots led to the area quickly developing with single and double shotguns. However, these new neighborhoods did not have the Old World charm of those built on the natural levee. Unlike the florid, bracket-style shotguns built along the river, homes in Backatown were often more rustic. Instead of grand columns, the supports holding up the gabled roof over the porch became tapered wooden posts resting on stucco pedestals, and plain painted wood supports replaced the ornately carved brackets.[46]

These relatively austere shotguns were inhabited by working-class African Americans, Creoles, and ethnic whites. In her 2019 memoir *The Yellow House*, Sarah M. Broom recalls the physical and social diversity of her grandparents' Backatown neighborhood. The narrow street they lived on was lined with single and double shotguns, and each side of the block was bookended by grocery stores, owned by whites, and bars, owned by Blacks. Though economically the city had become more stratified, different races still mixed: "[B]lack and poor lived in eyesight of rich and white, or white looking. . . . [A] different social world always lay around the corner."[47]

Yet while Backatown neighborhoods and much of New Orleans were integrated in the early twentieth century, the decades that followed would see increasing segregation. As soon as the post–Civil War Reconstruction ended and the federal troops enforcing the rights of African Americans were pulled, state legislatures across the South enacted restrictive laws curbing the rights of Black citizens. New Orleans's Creole residents, many of whom were mixed race, fell right on the fault lines of this racial bifurcation. In 1892, a light-skinned descendant of Saint-Domingue refugees named Homer Plessy decided to test these new laws and bought a racially restricted first-class ticket on a train from New Orleans to the neighboring town of Covington. After declaring that he was a Black man, he was immediately arrested, with the case eventually being referred to the Supreme Court. The 1896 ruling in *Plessy v. Ferguson* upheld the segregationist laws enacted across the nation. Even as streetcars and public transit systems were popping up in cities across the country, paving the way for spacious streetcar suburbs, the country's racial caste system, now formally legitimized by the Supreme Court, ensured that this mobility was only for the few.

By the mid-twentieth century, Backatown had become something new for New Orleans—a poor and homogenous Black ghetto. This area was also increasingly environmentally precarious and disaster prone. The draining of the swamp had resulted in the earth gradually sinking, sometimes as much as ten feet below the Mississippi River. By 2000, the topography of New Orleans was starting to resemble a bowl. The white-populated front of town and the lakefront neighborhoods on the natural and manmade levees formed the rim, and the Black Backatown was the basin.

IIIIIIIIIIIIIIIIIIII

For its entire history, the fate of New Orleans had been tied to the Mississippi River. Although volatile and foul, the river had brought immense wealth to the city, making it one of the great gateways of the Western world. However, as train lines expanded throughout the North during the Civil War, Midwestern goods—which had previously been sent by barge down the Mississippi or into the Gulf of Mexico to New Orleans—were able to bypass the city and go directly to their destinations on the coasts. With each passing decade, the city's economic stature gradually diminished. Once the hub of the South, by the late twentieth century New Orleans had been surpassed in population not only by Houston and Atlanta, but also by Charlotte and Orlando.

Yet New Orleans still had a historic charm and grandeur that its upstart Sunbelt rivals lacked, which was expressed in the city's architecture, cuisine, and music. With few other prospects, civic leaders parlayed the city's unique culture into a new commercial backbone: tourism. Along Canal Street, towering hotels blotted out the semi-vacant office buildings that had been constructed during an ill-fated oil boom in the '70s. A gargantuan convention center now stretches for nearly three-quarters of a mile along the Mississippi River. For centuries, the French Quarter had been a dense tapestry of various communities and cultures. This included longtime Creole residents, Sicilians, bohemians, artists, writers (including the playwright Tennessee Williams, who lived a few blocks from Jackson Square), and a thriving LGBTQ community. Yet by the latter half of the twentieth century, as the once-elegant clubs lining Bourbon Street became rowdy honky-tonks selling high-octane slushies out of street-facing windows, these facets were overtaken and the French Quarter turned into a Southern Las Vegas.[48]

With tourism now New Orleans's economic lifeblood, preserving the city's physical heritage became a huge concern. The groundwork for this had already been laid in the 1930s when the Vieux Carré Commission was established, becoming the first historic preservation body of its kind in the nation. With its broad authority to protect the built fabric of the French Quarter, this agency stopped a freeway from cutting the area off from the river and has prevented old buildings from being replaced by large hotels and tourist attractions.[49] Postwar, the preservation movement expanded beyond the French Quarter to encompass many of the city's historic neighborhoods. As bohemians and LGBTQ residents fled the daiquiri-fueled debauchery of the French Quarter, they renovated old shotguns and Creole cottages in working-class neighborhoods like the Marigny and Irish Channel. Interest in these historic homes was facilitated by the 1971 publication of the first of a five-volume set on the city's residential architecture by the nonprofit group Friends of the Cabildo (named for the historic New Orleans building that was once the seat of the Spanish colonial administration).* In most US cities this publication might have been greeted with stale cookies and coffee in the community room of a branch library. However, in New Orleans the books spurred regular columns in the city's newspaper on different house styles, which were breathlessly read by renovators.[50] By the early 2000s, the historic neighborhoods sitting atop the natural levee had been polished into an architectural showcase. In the French Quarter, horse-drawn carriages waited for passengers on cobblestone streets beneath beautiful wrought iron balconies bursting with flowers. Old streetcars teetered down St. Charles Avenue past the gleaming white columns of the neoclassical mansions and overhanging magnolia trees. Downtown, the jazz clubs and bars along Frenchmen Street in the Marigny recaptured some of the bohemian energy that had largely been erased from the French Quarter.

Yet just a few blocks past St. Charles Avenue or Rampart Street, the vast Backatown area suffered a level of physical and economic devastation that surpassed Rust Belt cities like Detroit. The population of the city's neighborhoods had fallen from eighteen thousand people per square mile

---

* The Cabildo is a structure flanking Jackson Square that was built in 1799 for the municipal government of the Spanish regime that controlled the city at that time.

to fewer than eight thousand, and the city had one of the highest numbers of abandoned properties in the nation. This was paired with some of the worst crime rates, school systems, and levels of poverty. Just as in the early nineteenth century, New Orleans had bifurcated into two separate cities. However, instead of being divided by language, it was now separated by race and geography. On the natural levee along the river sat the polished and renovated antebellum neighborhoods. This area represented 10 percent of the city's land area yet contained nearly half of the white population.[51] Immediately behind these neighborhoods on low-lying reclaimed swampland was the belt of increasingly dilapidated shotguns, which were 70 percent African American.

ııııııııııııııııııı

For decades, tourism had acted as a bandage concealing the deeper rot of poverty, mismanagement, and crime that plagued New Orleans. With Hurricane Katrina, the bandage was ripped off. The front page of the *New York Times* on August 31, 2005, showed a city submerged in water, with the skyscrapers of downtown poking up into the hazy sky. In what has been called the worst engineering disaster since Chernobyl, the system of constructed levees that had been built to protect the sinking city failed. Close to 80 percent of New Orleans flooded, triggering the largest human displacement in American history, with over one million people forced to leave their homes.[52] The hastily organized mass evacuation ordered a day before the storm was not comprehensive and left the poorest residents to fend for themselves. Aerial cameras captured horrific footage of people— including small children in diapers and elders in wheelchairs—stranded on rooftops and elevated freeways, baking in the brutal summer heat.

Like the Louisiana Purchase and A. Baldwin Wood's pump, Katrina was an epic event that fundamentally redrew the social and physical geography of the city. Tens of thousands of mostly Black New Orleanians lost their homes and scattered to Houston, Atlanta, and across the country. Of the one hundred seventy-five thousand African Americans who left New Orleans, only one hundred thousand have returned.[53] But Katrina also brought a new wave of people into the city. In the storm's aftermath, a slew of articles, books, and documentaries spurred a renewed appreciation of the city's immense cultural significance. This media coverage also placed the city on the radar of the type of educated young person who may have otherwise moved to Portland, Brooklyn, or Austin. The first wave of newcomers to the city was composed of what the geographer Richard Campanella has described as the Young Urban Rebuilding Professionals, or YURPs. These were largely young planners, architects, engineers, and nonprofit workers who came to help rebuild, many of whom chose to stay, attracting even more highly educated people into the city.[54]

Meanwhile, speculators and restorers swooped up damaged houses and other properties in the city's hollowed-out neighborhoods. Some still had an X spray-painted on the front by the Federal Emergency Management Agency (FEMA), delineating that rescue crews had inspected the home after the storm. The underlying structure of many of the old shotguns proved to be sound, with their native cypress wood construction withstanding years of neglect and the inundation of toxic stormwater. As renovation progressed, overgrown weeds were replaced with the brightly colored brackets and columns of restored shotguns, complete with the old-time gas lanterns hanging from the front porches. By the 2010s, the gentrification started to move past the Berlin Wall of Rampart and St. Charles, which had previously demarcated the tourist-friendly and largely white areas near the river from Backatown neighborhoods.

Yet these renovations often fundamentally altered certain essential qualities of the shotgun. Their permeability to the outdoors is severed with the interiors turned into air-conditioned inner sanctums protected by Ring doorbells and security systems. Sometimes fences are built, precluding traditional conversations across side yards. Even the floor plans have been altered, with the two units of the double shotgun being turned into a large single-family home with a more traditional layout. For this reason, in 2022 the Preservation Resource Center of New Orleans listed the shotgun as one of Nine Most Endangered Sites in the city, saying that "the shotgun plan is becoming lost as both interiors and exteriors are modified—no longer qualifying the home to be considered a true shotgun."[55] As the shotgun has been transformed, so has New Orleans. Many neighborhoods have become devoid of street life. In 2015, neighborhood advocates—mainly from gentrified areas like the Marigny—started lobbying for a noise ordinance, something unheard of in a city whose lifeblood is raucous street parties and live music.[56]

One would expect the city's preservation community and heritage guardians to rise up against this attack on the city's folkways. However, these traditions are those of the city's poor and working-class residents—a group that has historically been ignored by many scholars, particularly in architecture. The shotgun was not even officially recognized as a distinct building style until 1936 when it received a few paragraphs in an article on Louisiana house types by Fred B. Kniffen, a distinguished professor of architecture and anthropology at Louisiana State University. Subsequently, other scholars posited that the house did not come from Haiti but was indigenous to New Orleans and had originated from a modification of the Creole cottage in the 1840s. For decades, a few scant articles served as the authoritative account on the shotgun.

Kniffen's and other scholars' views were based on a belief, shared by many at the time, that the culture of enslaved Africans had been completely severed after they were transported to the New World. However, by the 1960s scholars started to publish evidence that enslaved people had not only preserved their cultural traditions, but also that these traditions had been most strongly expressed in architecture. This was particularly the case in New Orleans, where many of the enslaved people brought from Haiti had been born in Africa and carried a full memory of their traditions. The shotgun's roots in the African diaspora were eventually substantiated in a groundbreaking doctoral thesis published in 1975 by John Michael Vlach and have been further bolstered by research by the painter John Biggers, the professor Jay D. Edwards, and other scholars.

Yet the origins of the shotgun are still disputed by many preservationists. This is also partly the result of the fact that a comprehensive study of the structure has never taken place. While nearly every wrought iron balcony in the French Quarter and bracket in the Garden District has been documented, the shotgun remains one of the most understudied buildings in the city, despite it constituting nearly 60 percent of the city's housing stock. As of 2009, out of 147 buildings on the Historic American Building Survey in New Orleans, only eight woefully incomplete entries are for shotguns.[57]

New Orleans, through tourism, catastrophe, and gentrification, is now one the nation's best preserved yet most endangered cities. This has led to many of the oldest and most charming neighborhoods becoming stage sets for tourists. Nearly four thousand of the city's homes have been turned into short-term rentals, allowing their often-out-of-state owners to receive in less than a week the same income they could receive in a month by renting it out to a full-time tenant. Meanwhile it is estimated that the city lacks thirty-three thousand units of affordable housing.[58] The shotgun, like many working-class housing types in desirable cities, has become a shell. The exteriors are carefully restored and painted while the interiors are gutted and the working-class residents who once inhabited them are displaced. The shotgun is a reminder that one of the most important aspect of urban housing is the community these buildings foster and the culture they produce. The challenge for cities is not so much preserving buildings but rather the qualities that make them vital, living presences in their neighborhoods.

CHAPTER 4

Chicago Workers Cottage

The Pine Jungles

In the early 1800s, when New Orleans was an important metropolis, Chicago was a mere trading post. The creation of the Erie Canal in 1825 and the advent of the railroads, however, quickly catapulted the city into prominence as it became the country's preeminent industrial center. Fewer than four decades after its in incorporation in 1837, Chicago would not only surpass New Orleans in population but achieve what the Southern city had always aspired to be—a Western rival to New York. Yet architecturally, the city bore little resemblance to its older counterparts on the East Coast. Those places dated back to the colonial period and had buildings and urban forms that mimicked those of the Old World. Chicago, however, with its towering office buildings, monstrous industrial districts, and sprawling neighborhoods of wood-frame houses, was a new and, to many, frighteningly modern type of city.

Superficially, the tiny gabled-roof workers cottage—one of the first structures to appear in the city and which came to define Chicago's housing—bore a striking resemblance to the New Orleans shotgun. Both were rural structures that had been adapted to the city. However, whereas the shotgun expressed the deeply rooted cultural values of its Caribbean and African origins, the workers cottage was a commodity. It was meant to be built rapidly and cheaply, to help fuel the city's industrial economy, and—just like any industrial component—was designed for planned obsolescence. As Chicago transformed from a rural village into one of the largest cities on Earth, these wood-frame houses were torn down almost as fast as they were erected. Whereas the shotgun is still a celebrated symbol of New Orleans, the workers cottage is an afterthought even in its home city. However, it is the workers cottage that makes Chicago not simply a facsimile of European cities, but rather a distinctly American metropolis. Today, the legacy of the workers cottage is embedded in the urban form of almost every city and town in the nation.

ıllıılıılıılıılıılı

In 1780, Bathsheba Lincoln moved with her husband and sons from their large farm in the Shenandoah Valley of Virginia to the frontier of Central Kentucky. Using rocks and trees to demarcate borders, they carved out a homestead and constructed a log cabin for shelter. Scandinavian colonists had first brought this incredibly basic structure to the American colonies in the 1600s; it quickly became the default dwelling of frontier settlers because it was made from one of the most abundant materials on the continent: timber.[1] The Lincolns chopped down a tree, turned it into hand-hewn logs, and—with the assistance of their neighbors in the surrounding countryside—stacked them up using interconnected corners to keep the structure together. It was in a similar log cabin on Sinking Spring Farm that Bathsheba's grandson, Abraham, was born in 1809. A few years later, the family moved to a new homestead in Indiana. There they built another log cabin, but because it was assembled in the freezing cold of winter, a proper mixture of clay and grass could not be made to seal the logs. This resulted in wind and cold sweeping through the home's interiors and famously allowed a seven-year-old Abraham Lincoln to shoot a wild turkey from between one of the cracks.[2]

In an era before mechanized transportation and well-paved roads, waterways were the main transportation arteries by which products and raw materials were moved from the East Coast to the interior. The Ohio River, near where Lincoln grew up, was one of the superhighways of the early nineteenth century and provided him a portal to the larger world. As a teenager, Lincoln was hired by a store owner named James Gentry to take meat, flour, and other goods to New Orleans by flatboat. It was on this trip that he first saw enslaved people being sold on the city's docks. When his family moved to Illinois in 1830, they settled in the downstate town of Decatur, where Lincoln made his very first political speech, which centered on improving the nearby Sangamon River for transportation.

Decatur, Illinois, was a small outpost consisting of only a handful of log cabins. However, it was a booming metropolis compared to the muddy and monotonous grasslands in the northern part of the state near Lake Michigan. Europeans had yet to settle there in great numbers, but the region had been inhabited for millennia by the Miami–Illinois and Potawatomi people. They lived by the Seven Grandfather Teachings of wisdom, respect, love, honesty, humility, bravery, and truth toward each other and all creation.[3] They relied on the small local waterways in the region for transport and trade and named this area on Lake Michigan Shikaakwa, after a type of wild onion that grew there.[4]

The first non-Native to settle in Shikaakwa was a free Black man named Jean Baptiste Point du Sable who established a very successful trading post in what is now Downtown Chicago, directly north of where present-day Michigan Avenue crosses the Chicago River.[5] Du Sable's trading post—which contained a large log cabin filled with art and fine furniture, a horse-powered mill, and numerous service buildings—became a notable landmark in the area. In 1800 he left the region; three years later, the Louisiana Purchase would make it part of the United States. As part of a government strategy to wrest control from the Native inhabitants, du Sable's property became Fort Dearborn, which housed the US Army. However, although Shikaakwa had a river, it was disconnected from any other major water outlet and so remained isolated and remote. The settlement was so tenuous that Fort Dearborn was briefly abandoned during the War of 1812 before being reestablished four years later.

||||||||||||||||||

In 1825, German and Irish immigrant laborers constructed the Erie Canal, creating a 351-mile waterway via the Hudson River between the Great Lakes and New York City. Previously, in order for a product created in a place like Baltimore to reach a place like Cincinnati, it had to travel down the coast by boat and into the Gulf of Mexico to New Orleans. It would then be transferred to another boat and sent up the Mississippi and Ohio Rivers. The Erie Canal allowed goods to go directly east, instantly creating a 1,700-mile shortcut to the Midwest and, in doing so, reordered the geography of the country. New York rose above Philadelphia, Boston, and Baltimore to become the nation's new economic center of gravity, with the canal channeling the rich natural resources of the interior into the city.

However, one crucial ingredient was missing: an industrial city around the Great Lakes, a Midwestern New Orleans that would take in the surrounding bounty and export it to the rest of the country. After the completion of the Canal, a race ensued to find this place, with every tiny market town and provisional outpost in the Midwest vying to become this gateway, with their advantages trumpeted in hyperbolic newspaper articles and advertisements in order to entice speculators.[6] Out of all the candidates, Fort Dearborn—which was nothing more than an army base surrounded by a haphazard cluster of wooden shacks—was one of the most promising in terms of location. It was as far west as a city could be from the Atlantic Coast while still having access to the Great Lakes, and its location lay roughly parallel to the industrial centers of the East. There was also the tantalizing possibility that another canal would be constructed to link the region to the Mississippi River.

In a fever to capitalize on this potential economic bonanza, a metropolis was willed into being on the site of Fort Dearborn. The state of Illinois hired a surveyor, James Thompson, who hastily laid a 350-by-450-foot grid over the settlement in the hopes that the sale of the lots would finance a canal connecting the Chicago River to the Mississippi.[7] However, Thompson's plan was more detached from local circumstances than even the Commissioners' Plan for New York had been. Instead of basing his plan on the local geography or any sort of aesthetic ideal, Thompson based it on the Public Land Survey System, a massive square-mile grid laid across the continent that had been proposed by Thomas Jefferson to facilitate settlement and turn raw land into real estate. In 1833, a treaty was imposed on the local tribes to banish them to reservations in Oklahoma and farther west. Four years later, Fort Dearborn was incorporated into a city, and Shikaakwa became Chicago.[8]

Unlike the cities of Philadelphia, New York, and New Orleans—each of which had spent decades gestating as a colonial hamlet before exploding into a metropolis—Chicago was an instant city. Lots that had sold for $33 in 1829 went for $100,000 in 1836.[9] Yet the structures that were thrown up were not hearty brick dwellings but wood buildings only slightly more refined than a hand-hewn log cabin. They were based on a gable-roofed wooden structure known as an upright and wing that was common on Midwestern farms at that time. The home had a two-room hall-and-parlor floor plan with the addition of a third larger room, all connected railroad-style. This type of home would normally be found perched atop a hill under a large oak tree, its broad porch opening up onto a cornfield.

However, like the Creole cottage in New Orleans, in Chicago the upright and wing was used as the basis for a new, more urban type of structure standardized to fit the city's 25-foot-wide lots. The front door moved from the long side of the house to the narrow end facing the street.[10] Instead of a long railway layout, the floor plan was divided in half, with the bedrooms on one side and the living room on the other (see the floor plan in image 13). Wealthier people would live in larger versions of the home with two front rooms, a kitchen el in back, and several upstairs bedrooms. However, most people lived in a small 18-by-24-foot version, known as a workers cottage. In these homes, the bedrooms are only seven feet wide and barely accommodate a double bed. However, even these small homes have a more comfortable layout than the tiny two-room homes found on the East Coast or the shotgun found in the South. These simple wood homes were present in the city from its earliest days.

As Chicago grew from fewer than three thousand people to over a million in under fifty years, these cottages popped up like mushrooms after a rainstorm as the grasslands around Lake Michigan became a city. With its gabled roof, tall chimney, and minimally decorated doors and windows, the workers cottage looks like a child's drawing of a house, and the "pine jungles" of simple wood-frame homes gave the working-class areas of Chicago a crude, rustic feel that persisted well into the nineteenth century. Sneering critics looking west toward the upstart city said, "Of architectural display there was none. The houses were built hurriedly to accommodate a considerable trade center here and were devoid of both comforts and conveniences."[11] As late as 1890, when Chicago was one of the largest cities in the world, it was still derided as being a "huge flimsy country town."[12]

IIIIIIIIIIIIIIIIIIIIII

Chicago's wood-frame workers cottages looked especially primitive when compared to New York's finely detailed brick row homes or ornate tenements erected by developers like Wolf Baum. The cottages would be thrown up seemingly overnight, transforming an entire field into a bustling neighborhood. Their humble appearance, as well as the incredibly rapid rate at which they were erected, gave the impression that they were shoddy. However, the workers cottage actually represented an incredible innovation in construction.

The early tenements, row homes, and Creole cottages all were built using a medieval construction method called *timber framing*, which required great skill and craftsmanship. A team of artisans would fell a large tree and carefully carve it into the structural components. Because nails were very expensive, each beam was designed to fit into another using an interlocking joint called a *mortise and tenon*. While housing reformers at the turn of the twentieth century thought the standard 25-foot-wide urban lot had been created by horned figures that emerged out of a fiery portal to hell, the measurement was actually rooted in this ancient construction technique. In the seventeenth century, when many East Coast cities were founded, 25 feet was the longest that a beam could be made by animal and hand machinery.[13] In remote areas where there was a lack of skilled craftspeople, instead of timber frame, families had to resort to simple buildings like log cabins that they could erect themselves out of local materials with only the assistance of a few neighbors.

The area in and around Chicago was at a disadvantage when it came to wood-frame construction because it lacked timber. The flat land around the city was mostly grass prairies, and the few trees that did exist were varietals such as oak, elm, and poplar whose wood would shrink and warp when it dried.[14] Fortunately, over the seventeenth and eighteenth centuries, craftspeople in New England developed labor- and time-saving modifications to traditional timber framing. Their simplified construction technique used many smaller pieces of wood instead of several large beams and then attached them using a simplified mortise and tenon joint. As these builders moved into the Midwest in the early nineteenth century, their method became the preferred one for constructing hall-and-wing farmhouses and many other structures.

Local Chicago builders further honed the New England method by using nails—which mass production had recently made affordable—instead of a mortise-and-tenon joint to connect the smaller pieces of wood. This was much faster and cheaper than the timber frame. Instead of having to rely on trained artisans, relatively unskilled people could erect a structure in a week. This proved to be incredibly advantageous in the lightning city of Chicago, and one of the first structures built with this new method was the city's St. Mary's Catholic Church, erected in 1833.[15]

Despite these remarkable innovations, this new method was dubbed *balloon framing* because the buildings were thought to be so flimsy that even a moderate gust of wind would carry them away. Yet this method was integral to the growth of the workers cottage—and, by extension, Chicago—and is still the primary method for building many homes and apartment buildings to this day. Balloon framing allowed a simple wood-frame workers cottage to be assembled within a week. This construction technique, combined with the vast expanses of flat open land around the city, made the workers cottage incredibly cheap. Through balloon framing, workers and immigrants were not only able to purchase a simple cottage, they could also actually construct it themselves.

IIIIIIIIIIIIIIIIIII

The promised canal that would connect Chicago to the Mississippi was finally completed in 1848. Yet while the canal was being constructed, rail travel was already starting to usurp water transport as the most efficient and reliable way to move goods and people. In 1836, construction began on the region's first railroad, which would run 164 miles west from Chicago to Galena, Illinois, near the Mississippi River. Seventeen years later, the train route from Chicago to New York opened, cutting travel time between the cities from two weeks to two days.

By 1856, fifty-eight passenger trains and thirty-eight freight lines came into Chicago daily.[16] By 1860, thirty thousand miles of track crisscrossed the continent, opening up vast expanses of the West for development and resource extraction.[17] Chicago became the hub of this system, with these lines carrying raw materials from every corner of the West into the city: wheat from Iowa, livestock from the plains, and timber from northern Wisconsin and Michigan. These products would be processed and packaged in massive factories that developed within the city along the branches of the Chicago River. The products were then shipped back out on the same rail lines to the rest of the country.

The immense economic scale on which Chicago operated—processing resources from a vast hinterland constituting tens of thousands of miles—was unparalleled in human history and resulted in a monstrous, strange, and entirely new type of urban form. Instead of a compact, mixed-use walking city where workshops intermingled with houses, Chicago sprawled across the prairies, with specialized districts arising to serve specific commercial and industrial functions. Along the mouth of the Chicago River, near where du Sable's cabin once sat, were seventeen grain elevators handling 11.6 million bushels of wheat. West of the city was a massive stockyard and packing district where livestock were turned into steaks, sausages, and roast beef. Along the southern branch of the Chicago River, 400 million feet of lumber were stacked so high they towered over the small offices of the individual merchants, forming a vast city unto itself.[18] The old site of Fort Dearborn, which had once been described as looking "raw and bare standing in its high prairie above the lake shore," was now a commercial district filled with the symbols of the industrial age: office buildings where a new managerial class oversaw the flows of products in and out of the city, immense department stores where these products were showcased, and hotels for travelers who came to purchase the goods wholesale and bring them back to regional cities and towns.[19]

A closer look past the imposing buildings, grain elevators, and factories revealed the city's rustic and provisional foundation. Next to large masonry buildings in the downtown sat diminutive workers cottages that had been converted into businesses. The sidewalks were paved with wood planks with green and black goo oozing out of the cracks. The freight and passenger rail lines that converged on the city sped through crowded business and residential districts at the same level as the streets. By the time of the World's Fair in 1893, six hundred people were killed in the city each year by passing freight cars, and many more were injured or lost limbs.[20]

Among all of this chaos were rows of wood-frame workers cottages that would appear within days in the spaces between the factories and office buildings. The rapid pace of balloon framing was further accelerated by the city's industrial production. Up to this point, the city's builders often combined the balloon frame with more traditional construction methods, such as hand-hewing wood and some joinery, but by the mid-nineteenth century, the city's sawmill cut wood planks into exact specifications, creating fully interchangeable, readily available components.[21]

By 1865, local fabricators like the Lyman Bridges Company sold prefab balloon frame structures, and homes could be ordered out of the catalogues of local department stores such as Sears and Montgomery Ward.[22] Through this, the workers cottage became a Northern equivalent of the shotgun house, spreading across the industrial centers of the Great Lakes from Buffalo to Milwaukee and throughout the West. Yet the workers cottage lacked the deep cultural roots of the shotgun, and instead of being adorned with gingerbread brackets and columns, it was devoid of superfluous ornament.

IIIIIIIIIIIIIIIIIIIII

The considerable railroad presence in Chicago resulted in both a push and a pull. The many lines converging on the city's core resulted in an enormous concentration of commerce and industry. By 1910, a half square mile of the downtown accounted for 40 percent of the city's total assessed value.[23] However, as the tracks also pulled out into the periphery, the rail lines inversely allowed for the dispersion of the population. Unlike Philadelphia, New York, or Boston, there was not a similar concentration of residential density in the core—no tiny alleys, no towering tenements.

Instead, the open, windswept plains enticed people to spread out, making Chicago an early and ardent adopter of new transit technology. The cable car is most closely associated with the patchouli-scented inclines of San Francisco. However, it was Chicago that built one of the world's most extensive cable car networks in the late nineteenth century.[24] These trolleys were quickly replaced by electric streetcars that, by the turn of the twentieth century, went down every major street and avenue in the city. The network was so vast and dense that the tracks had to be elevated in the city core, forming a ring around the downtown that became known as the Loop—a moniker that today is synonymous with the entire district.

However, streetcars were simply one aspect of the city's main obsession: real estate. Chicago in the nineteenth century was like Florida in the early 2000s. Construction rivaled the stockyards and the department stores as the city's main industry. Small talk was made up not of comments on the weather but on the price of land. Newspapers served more as a vessel for advertising building lots than a means of getting information on public affairs. On every main commercial street was a storefront showcasing huge maps of a new subdivision.

Anyone in Chicago who became successful enough to have a little extra money would become a developer. Contractors and store owners joined doctors and lawyers in pooling their resources together to form a syndicate. They would then hire someone to find a piece of land, usually on the undeveloped periphery of the city, and then lure in the services needed to make it viable, the most important of which was transport.[25] Extending a cable car or electric streetcar line to provide access to the property could make the value go up between 30 and 100 percent.[26] In his 1869 memoir *Over the Alleghanies and Across the Prairies*, John Lewis Peyton describes these syndicates as "mapping out the surrounding territory for ten and fifteen miles in the interior, giving fancy names to the future avenues, streets, squares and parks."[27]

In the 1860s, the real estate frenzy in Chicago attracted a Civil War veteran from western Illinois named Samuel Eberly Gross. By the 1880s, Gross had become one of the largest developers in the nation, pioneering many aspects of subdivision development—most importantly, promotion. In 1902, he sued the French writer Edmond Rostand, author of the world-famous play *Cyrano de Bergerac*, accusing him of stealing the plot of a play he himself had written, which had only been performed once, called *The Merchant Prince of Cornville*. He won the lawsuit in a Chicago court but was only awarded what he requested—a dollar in compensation. The notoriety was more than enough.

Gross parlayed his literary skills into plastering the city with advertisements for his communities. These ads were not just for the elite—they were also published in Polish, Swedish, German, and Czech and were featured in the city's immigrant newspapers (see image 13). He would offer free train trips out to his developments and greet disembarking passengers with a marching band, beer, lemonade, and sausages.[28] His flamboyant and highly successful promotion of his real estate developments inspired others. Some went as far to publish their own racy broadsides with names like the *Lawndale Hustler* and *Shedd's Park Cyclone.*[29] However, in most cases, Gross's and other developers' sites were as impressive as a fallow potato field. While developers relied on outside investments such as streetcars and parks to make their projects salable, their own contributions were often extremely limited. In most cases the sites were merely a collection of dirt roads that acted as an extension of the city's standard grid, with only simple wood plank sidewalks to demarcate them.

However, in booming Chicago, the development sites would not remain in this state for long. Instead of having to rely on a savings and loan, Gross was one of the first developers to use an installment plan, and he advertised his parcels as being cheaper than renting. A lot could be purchased for a quarter down with the balance being paid in two to three years with 6 percent interest. Most buyers would construct their own wood cottages on their lots, either for themselves or speculatively. However, Gross was also one of the first developers in Chicago to additionally sell simple, pre-assembled brick or wood-frame cottages. These 18-by-24-foot structures had a first floor with a parlor, kitchen, and two bedrooms, as well as an 8-foot-high attic and a semi-submerged basement below.

Not everyone was satisfied with Chicago's development model. An association of German immigrants complained about the long commutes that resulted from the city's profligate use of land. Anticipating the rhetoric of modern-day advocates for density, a report by a citizens' committee on workers lodging from 1883 wrote, "Within a radius of 15 minutes from the city's business district, high tenement barracks should be constructed, so that time and transportation costs could be saved."[30]

ııııııııııııııııııı

Gross eventually quit real estate mired in debt and checked himself into John Harvey Kellogg's sanitarium in Battle Creek, Michigan, famous for its enemas and virulent racism.[31] His legacy remains in the subdivisions that now compose some of Chicago's most celebrated neighborhoods, as well as a new type of urban environment he helped pioneer. Unlike Philadelphia or New York, where uses were mixed together, Chicago's massive grid was more carefully ordered. Bustling commercial avenues cut across neighborhoods of single-family homes, a model that would become the standard template for the American city. However, Chicago's chessboard of blocks also accommodated an astounding array of uses, containing everything from lush parks to a hellish stockyard to mansions and tiny cottages. Each use would often be contained in its own district, but the urban fabric within the city's grid was prone to rapid and sometimes violent changes. Crude wooden buildings dating from the city's early days would be torn down or physically moved to a different location, then replaced by larger dwellings of brick or stone. Flood-prone, mud-logged streets would be widened and raised several feet in the air. In a matter of months, a quiet residential neighborhood would turn into a crowded slum or bustling commercial or industrial district as the city expanded. Chicago in the late nineteenth century was like the 1990s neo-noir film *Dark City* where every night buildings rearrange themselves as the residents sleep.

The Great Chicago Fire punctuated Chicago's breakneck growth and volatility. On a dry, windy night in October of 1871, a small fire in a wood cottage grew into a ten-story wall of flame, devouring entire blocks. Wood-frame structures dating back to the frontier days were destroyed, as well as stone civic monuments, hotels, offices, and even the board of trade. The Chicago River became so filled with debris and felled bridges one could walk across it. When the smoke finally cleared, an area stretching four miles along the lake and nearly a quarter of a mile inland was destroyed. Hundreds of people were killed and most of the city's population of three hundred thousand was left homeless. Chicago had prided itself on being the lightning city, willing itself into becoming an industrial titan in just a few decades. The fire was a reckoning. The city had become so central to the national economy that its destruction resulted in a mild nationwide economic depression.

The blame for the fire was quickly pinned on the city's wood-frame cottages and the people who inhabited them. The face of the fire became an Irish immigrant named Catherine O'Leary, who was implausibly accused of milking her cow in the middle of the night and knocking over a lantern. Her neighborhood, in a working-class area on the southern outskirts of the city, was described as being "thickly studded with one story frame dwellings, cow stables, pig sties, corn cribs, sheds innumerable, every wretched building within four feet of its neighbor and everything of wood, not a brick or a stone in the whole area."[32] This semirural nature of Chicago's neighborhoods was seen as unbecoming of a city that aspired to be one of the world's greatest. A critic said that O'Leary's neighborhood looked as if a rural town called Lickskillet Station had been lifted off the plains and dropped on the city's periphery.

In contrast to the pine jungle that defined most of the city, Chicago's rich lived in stately neighborhoods that would not have been out of place in Boston, New York, or Philadelphia. On the South Side along Prairie Avenue, titans of industry—including George Pullman, Marshall Field, and Philip Armour—built mansions out of stone and brick. One of the most elegant addresses in the city was a monumental set of eleven limestone row houses along Michigan Avenue called Terrace Row. For the elite, the city's working-class areas were an unknown realm, described in a book about the fire as "terra incognita to respectable Chicagoans."[33]

||||||||||||||||||||

Though Chicago's buildings were devastated, the Great Chicago Fire had mercifully preserved most of the city's transportation infrastructure and industrial facilities. The city bounced back even more furiously, growing in population from just under 300,000 before the fire to 1.7 million by 1900. Yet even as a ban was put in place on wood-frame buildings, the workers cottage proliferated even more rapidly than before. Just a week after the fire, rows of workers cottages were built outside the fire zone as temporary shelters for Chicagoans who'd lost their homes, although many of these homes would last well into the twentieth century.[34] Developers like Samuel Gross promoted the fact that you could build with wood in his new subdivision, which stood just outside the city limits. However, in most cases these areas would eventually be annexed into the city.

For the city's working class, the workers cottage was much more than the housing of last resort. In any other large industrial city of the time, an immigrant like Catherine O'Leary would probably live in a crowded tenement or a rented room in a converted row house. In Chicago she was able to purchase a simple frame home on the fringe of the city for $500. As the city grew, and poor areas that had once been on the outskirts became part of the core, property values went up. This gave working-class residents the opportunity to leverage their cottages in various ways to provide additional income. The small homes occupied less than a quarter of the city's standard 125-foot-long lots, and their lightweight but strong frame construction allowed them to be lifted onto cedar posts and then rolled to the back of the lot. Through a loan from a building society, the owner would then construct a larger home at the front with as many as three units, which they would then rent out.[35] In other cases, additional structures would be appended onto the original home, which would sometimes be known as the "starter cottage."[36] Another common practice, particularly in the crowded Polish neighborhoods of the city, was to raise the cottage up and dig out a second, semi-submerged unit underneath (see image 11). These subterranean spaces became known as Polish flats and were so common that Gross incorporated them into pre-built cottages in his developments. It was also common for cottage owners to upgrade the spartan wood façades with red brick and long, narrow windows and to further adorn them with window crowns, cornices, and decorative brackets in Italianate or other Victorian styles. However, the sides and back of the home would remain in plain wood.

In one of the city's older industrial neighborhoods today, this adaptation is still visible. On West 19th Place in the Pilsen neighborhood sits a row of homes. However, instead of being neatly aligned, they are all set back at different distances from the street. Some have large moats in front with a metal staircase leading down to an entrance of a Polish flat. The fronts of these homes are like a memorial to the neighborhood's various iterations over time. The bottom stories have a red-brick Italianate façade, while the upper stories have plain vinyl siding. On the corner lots, one can see that the narrow cottages are extended by additions appended onto the back.

The Eastern and Southern European immigrants who came into Chicago after the Civil War were given the dirtiest, hardest, and lowest-paid jobs and forced to cram into the most dilapidated sections of the city. The workers cottage allowed these marginalized groups to be homeowners and to leverage their properties to generate extra income, which they could then use to start a business or move out into the suburbs. Through these modifications, people turned a building that was simply an industrial component into a unique home that spoke to the aspirations of its inhabitants.

|||||||||||||||||||

With many of the city's small cottages now elevated several feet into the air, the addition of brick façades, and the implementation of a fire zone, Chicago's neighborhoods developed a more orderly and permanent appearance. The fact that they were freestanding homes lent them an air of respectability when compared to the tenements of New York. However, the workers cottage often concealed conditions that were as bad as any marginalized neighborhood in the country. As the lots became filled with additional structures, very little open space was left. In dense immigrant enclaves like the Near North Side, workers cottages rose up to four stories high and could house upwards of eight apartments. This combined with the fact that the homes were often separated by only a few feet meant the interiors were shrouded in darkness. The German Citizens Association—who, along with other Northern European immigrants, were considered the "labor aristocracy"—thought the back houses turned the cottages into tenements and complained about the proclivity of the Bohemians, Poles, and Irish to construct "small huts where people huddle together like sheep in a fold."[37]

In addition to the back houses, the interiors of the cottages were often continually divided into additional units, which the owner would rent to other families. A report containing a canvass of the West Side slums in 1880 found that the average house had three or four families, with some having as many as twelve people living in one of the tiny subdivided apartments. The facilities in these homes were also primitive. Only 2.8 percent of households in the slums had bathrooms and most used privy vaults—some of which were literally underneath the sidewalk because the street in front of the home had been raised.[38] The report pointed to a Lithuanian family on the West Side who had rented out all the nicest parts of the home, forcing them to live in a dark attic space that they shared with "a very lively rooster."[39]

Chicago did have one advantage over other large cities: James Thompson's decision to place service alleys through each block in his plan for the city. This provided open space between houses and avoided the problem of buildings sitting back to back, as had happened in New York. However, unlike in Philadelphia or Baltimore, these alleys did not become community spaces where people chatted and congregated. Workers cottages had their backs turned to them, without even a window looking out. Today, the asphalt on these alleys is eroded and beaten down by the city's rugged climate, revealing the old porous bricks used to cover them. At the turn of the twentieth century they would not have been paved at all, and during rainstorms they would flood with horse manure and garbage floating in the muck. The housing reformer Edith Abbott wrote in the 1930s that the biggest improvement to the slums of Chicago did not come from any housing law but from the creation of cars, which removed horses from the city and forced the streets to be paved.[40]

Reformers in cities like New York had seen detached, single-family homes like the workers cottage as the answer to urban ills and a way for immigrants to assimilate to American norms. Chicago's cottage-filled slums became a symbol of the hopelessness of this mission. A broad consensus emerged that it was folly to incentivize poor workers to own their own home. On one side of the political spectrum, Friedrich Engels thought home ownership was a new form of serfdom because it tied people to land, which they would become so focused on retaining that they would not engage in revolution.[41] On the other side, reformers came to believe that the workers cottage was an illustration of how immigrants were too poor and ignorant to manage their own property, saying they purchased a house not for the comforts of a "home and garden" but as a way of generating income.[42]

|||||||||||||||||||||

The Great Chicago Fire erased from the central business district any last vestige of its mud-logged, rural-town origins. Just as the advent of balloon framing had changed residential construction, by the late nineteenth century local builders had transformed commercial buildings with the new technology of the steel frame. Instead of relying on heavy masonry walls, these lightweight steel beams allowed buildings to rise to incredible heights. On sites formerly occupied by wood-frame houses, skyscrapers like the Home Insurance Building and the Marquette Building rose over a hundred feet into the air. These new towers had the effect of concentrating great density on just a few square feet, with the architect Cass Gilbert describing them as "machines to make the land pay." This resulted in Chicago's central core becoming one of the most compact business districts in the world. Whereas in New York and London facilities like the train station, department stores, the financial center, and government buildings were scattered across several miles, in Chicago they all sat in one square mile of the Loop.[43] Just outside the core was an alternative skyline of factory smokestacks and church steeples, each demarcating one of the city's ethnic principalities (see image 12). The French gathered around the great Romanesque revival dome of Notre Dame, the Slovaks around the twin baroque steeples of St. Joseph's, and the Poles around the great 200-foot-long basilica of St. Stanislaus Kostka.[44] Their spires rose out from the jagged roof lines of the tiny workers cottages, creating a scene reminiscent of the backdrop of a German Expressionist film.

In 1892, a short stretch of track was elevated onto steel girders and placed in an alley, allowing trains to glide above the city's traffic and swiftly take passengers to their destination. A few decades later, Chicago had a whole network of elevated, or El, trains branching out in every direction from the Loop. These trains were not only much faster than the streetcars but could also carry many more people. Instead of single-family homes, much more substantial residential buildings were constructed around the stations. For the most part, these structures were not for poor factory workers but rather for the new professional class working in the offices of the Loop. Three- and four-flat apartment buildings were clad in a type of limestone quarried in Indiana known as greystone and sat on the same 25-by-125-foot lots as workers cottages. However, instead of spreading the units across the lot, these buildings stacked them on top of one another, leaving ample room for a backyard and allowing for light and air to enter the apartments. Even larger apartment buildings were also built in a U shape that created a large courtyard in the middle. These spacious and light-filled buildings were bolstered by the city's newly tightened building standards, created in response to the Great Fire. This law required two exits for each dwelling unit, leading to the advent of wood fire escapes, which also doubled as decks. By the 1920s, with the towering skyscrapers, Greystones, and courtyard apartments, Chicago was no longer an overgrown prairie town but had become what Carl Sandburg called, in his 1914 poem, "the City of the Big Shoulders."

IIIIIIIIIIIIIIIIII

Even as the skyscrapers and jam-packed cottages and apartments created astounding density in its core, Chicago continued to expand outward on its periphery. The city's spread-out nature dated back to the 1850s, when commuter train stations would quickly appear along the route, making towns like Waukegan and Wheaton—which were over twenty-five miles from the Loop—satellites of Chicago.[45] By 1873, Chicago was the Los Angeles of its day—famous for its sprawl and described as "more given to suburbs than any other city in the world."[46]

Chicago's far-flung appendages became a testing ground for a new vision of urban life, albeit one heavily influenced by a designer living in a small town on the Hudson River in New York state. Andrew Jackson Downing, one of the nation's first landscape architects, believed that small, detached homes were an antidote to the ills of modern society. These ideas predated those of housing reformers by several decades, making him a highly influential thinker. The homes detailed in his 1842 pattern book *Victorian Cottage Residences* were far from the utilitarian wood structures found in Chicago and other Northern industrial cities. Their compact yet intricate floor plans contained libraries, vestibules, and pantries, and the exteriors ranged in style from Gothic to an Italian villa. The evocative descriptions of Downing's homes even alluded to intricate backstories such as "a cottage for a country clergyman."[47]

Because Downing was a landscape architect, the key to his vision was not just the home itself but the surrounding environment. He recommended that instead of homes being packed together along a mud-logged street outside an abattoir, they be placed on lots at least 100 feet wide and preferably much larger, warning that plots under five acres had the risk of introducing city ways.[48] His pattern book included instructions not just on the houses but also on how to cultivate the landscape around them, such as "the choice of fruit for the kitchen garden and how to train vines up a trellis."[49]

Downing did not simply make pattern books but rooted his designs in a moral appeal that would go on to influence many housing reformers. He saw the detached single-family country home as bringing people closer to nature and ensconcing them in the family unit. If the tenement was thought to corrupt its inhabitants, the country cottage was a path for them to reach their highest potential.[50] This became a sentiment shared by other leading intellectuals of the time, including Ralph Waldo Emerson and Henry David Thoreau.[51] However, it would be decades before Downing's homes became affordable and feasible for most Americans—even the well-paid businesspeople and merchants of the 1840s and 1850s couldn't easily escape to the country. As had been the case for millennia, the need to be close to one's job prevented people from living in an orchard on a country estate—but by the mid-nineteenth century, the railroads were making Downing's vision more realistic.

In the 1860s, the acclaimed landscape architects Calvert Vaux and Frederick Law Olmsted were commissioned to design a housing development named Riverside. The site was a large patch of farmland along the Des Plaines River, directly off the Chicago, Burlington, and Quincy Railroads, which could whisk passengers into the Loop in just forty-five minutes. Vaux and Olmsted had just finished designing New York City's Central Park and saw this new commission as another way to fuse nature and city. In contrast to the rigid geometries of the standard city grid, they built curving streets throughout the subdivision to mimic the contours of the landscape, resulting in a street plan that looks almost organic, like the veins of a leaf. A large area along the river was set aside for an open space, and smaller parks were placed into the small nooks and crannies left between the undulating streets. To assure the preservation of this idyllic setting, covenants were imposed on each lot requiring that homes be set back a minimum distance from the street and prohibiting the construction of front fences to make the properties look like they sat in open fields. By the turn of the century, imitations of Riverside arose in other areas: Westchester County north of New York, along the Main Line outside of Philadelphia, and in Brookline near Boston.

In many respects, communities like Riverside were just the latest in a long line of developments that leveraged transportation infrastructure to support vast subdivisions. But developments like those of Samuel Gross in Chicago, Spring Garden in Philadelphia, or Backatown in New Orleans had been built to match the central city's grid, street widths, and lot sizes, making them extensions of the city. Developments like Riverside, on the other hand, did not repeat the existing urban fabric—they were a reaction against it. Homes sprawled across half-acre lots with lawns as big as a small city park, but instead of housing farmers or aristocrats they belonged to upper-middle-class professionals. In the post–Civil War era, Riverside set a precedent for the new communities growing along rail lines outside of large cities—developments that were neither city nor country but a new type of environment: the suburb.

ıııııııııııııııııııı

By the 1890s, even working-class immigrants were being lured out to commuter suburbs like Hammond, Indiana, twenty-four miles south of the city. It was here that a syndicate created a community aimed at Polish residents called Sobieski Park. Streets were named after Polish kings and saints, and a portion of each sale went toward the construction of a Polish church in the development.[52] The crowded neighborhoods around the city's core became just the first stop for immigrants, who would eventually make their way to larger homes on the periphery.

However, just as immigrants were decamping for leafy suburbs, a new group of migrants started streaming into Chicago. Beginning around 1915, six million African Americans left the rural South for large cities in the North and West. Chicago was one of the primary destinations of what is now known as the Great Migration. The city's Black population, which was around fifteen thousand in 1890, rose to eight hundred sixty thousand by 1960. Even though the old neighborhoods around the core of Chicago were depopulating due to the suburbs and new national restrictions were imposed on immigration, segregationists policies forced Black arrivals to cram into a long, skinny area on the South Side measuring only a few blocks wide. Ironically, this was the same neighborhood along Prairie Avenue that had once been home to the city's gilded class. Those affluent residents had long ago decamped to the North Side and the suburbs, and the large urban homes they left behind were subdivided into tenements.[53] This district became known as the Black Belt and transformed into one of the most crowded and dilapidated neighborhoods in the entire country.

The mobility that had been afforded to white immigrants was not given to African Americans. Landlords would not rent to them, and banks would not loan to them. Even if Black residents managed to leave the Black Belt and seek homes in other parts of the city, they were met with fierce and sometimes deadly resistance, particularly from their working-class white neighbors. In the spring of 1919, a seventeen-year-old African American boy crossed into a white section of a public beach along Lake Michigan. He was quickly surrounded by a white mob, who attacked and drowned him. This incident triggered an eruption of violence reminiscent of New York's Civil War–era Draft Riots: white mobs hunted down African Americans in the streets, pulled them from streetcars, and beat and murdered them. Black homes were ransacked and burned. Twenty-four bombings were directed at homes occupied by Black people, as well as at real estate agents known to sell homes in white neighborhoods to African Americans. Only the state militia was able to quell the unrest after thirteen days.[54]

||||||||||||||||||

In 1889, Jane Addams established the first American settlement house, called Hull House. Addams had grown up in a large Federal-style mansion on a five-acre homestead in northern Illinois. Her dedication to housing reform began when, as a young girl, she visited the nearby town of Freeport and caught a glimpse of poverty, asking her father, "Why do people live in such horrid little houses so close together?"

Hull House was based on British settlement houses, which were meant to literally provide a model home for people living in the slums. Tenement dwellers were invited in to attend classes, participate in activities, and take in the beautiful interior, bathed in light and filled with paintings, flowers, books, and musical instruments. This setting was meant to inspire immigrants to transcend their circumstances and aspire to a better life. Hull House became the standard bearer of the American settlement house movement, which spread to cities across the country by the 1920s. Addams would go on to win a Nobel Peace Prize in 1931, becoming the first American woman to receive this honor.

Hull House, with its broad porch, Italianate detailing, and small domed cupola on the roof, was a model of Victorian refinement. When the building was originally built for a wealthy family in 1856, it sat on the western outskirts of the city and was one of the few structures to survive the Great Fire. By the time Addams purchased it, it had been absorbed into the central city. Only a glimpse of the front door could be viewed from a narrow passage between the large buildings lining Halsted Street. The Near West Side, where the home was located, had become one of the densest immigrant enclaves outside of the Lower East Side.

By the 1920s, the district around Hull House, as well as its clientele, was starting to disappear as more and more immigrants left the core for larger and more modern homes on the periphery. During the first few decades of the twentieth century, the area within four miles of the Loop lost one hundred fifty thousand people.[55] This shift toward the suburbs was a national trend—by the late 1940s, as the country was shrugging off the Depression and World War II, cities across the country found themselves ringed by semi-abandoned neighborhoods. These communities were often over half a century old and the infrastructure was hopelessly antiquated. A land survey from 1939 found that nearly 8 percent of Chicago's housing stock was substandard and unfit for use.[56] Suburban areas like Riverside, with single-family homes on large lots, had gone from being an architectural experiment to the new American standard.

The old, dense, mixed-use neighborhoods were seen as relics of a less evolved era. As a sense of optimism pervaded after World War II, planners in cities across the country created grandiose schemes to revitalize inner cities. In Philadelphia, a charismatic planner and bureaucrat named Edmund Bacon unleashed an orgy of destruction on the central city. A sign went up on the arched doorway of colonial row homes reading "Coming Soon! New Modern Community. TREES, Open Spaces, Parking!" Entire blocks were removed for modern apartment towers, freeways, and open lawns.[57] Altogether over six thousand people—the vast majority African Americans—were displaced from Center City between 1960 and 1980 due to these urban renewal efforts.

However, Bacon's interventions in Philadelphia also included the restoration of many old row homes and buildings and were tame compared to what occurred in other cities. In 1919, Al Smith, a son of immigrants who had grown up in a tenement at the foot of the Brooklyn Bridge, became the governor of New York. Smith appointed a young Yale graduate named Robert Moses as secretary of state. Moses would go on to amass almost imperial power in his quest to remake New York City and the surrounding region. Beginning in 1934, he oversaw the leveling of huge swaths of Manhattan, including nearly the length of the East River from the base of the Brooklyn Bridge to East Harlem. Al Smith's childhood home is now an on-ramp to FDR Drive, and the teeming city of tenements can only be experienced in the dire dispatches of turn-of-the-century reformers.

In Chicago, similar urban renewal programs replaced the packed inner ring of factories and workers cottages outside of the Loop with freeways, on-ramps, industrial parks, shopping centers, and university campuses. Although Hull House survives as a museum, the context of the Near West Side slum that once surrounded it is gone—the house is tucked into a corner of the leafy campus of University of Illinois–Chicago. In the pine jungle where Catherine O'Leary once lived, the smell of smoke still lingers in the air. However, instead of packed-together cottages, a Burlington Coat Factory, Chick-fil-A, and other accoutrement of a suburban shopping center fill the neighborhood, and the smoke is emanating from the training center of the Chicago Fire Department, which occupies the exact site of O'Leary's house.

Altogether, urban renewal efforts across the nation destroyed nearly one thousand communities and displaced one million people, with 75 percent being people of color.[58] Even tiny towns like Fenton, Michigan, with a population of six thousand, ripped down nearly its entire downtown, fifty structures in total.[59] Today, the rare urban neighborhoods that escaped urban renewal—places like Greenwich Village in New York, the French Quarter in New Orleans, or North Beach in San Francisco—are some of the most iconic and treasured neighborhoods in the entire country. This is precisely because the type of nineteenth-century urban form they epitomize is so rare. Prior to the 1950s, similarly dense and walkable communities could be found across the country from the West End of Cincinnati to the Lower Hill District in Pittsburgh to Mill Creek Valley in St. Louis. Today they are the sites of parking lots and freeway interchanges. The buildings destroyed by urban renewal across the United States represented the collective work of thousands of artisans who passed down plans over generations and invented regionally specific architectures. The homes they built constituted character-rich neighborhoods of narrow streets lined with small shops and dotted with parks and squares and sheltered millions of working people who powered the nation's economy.

ıııııııııııııııııı

A 2015 photo series called *Color(ed) Theory* by the artist Amanda Williams is illustrative of one of Chicago's most enduring features: its deep-rooted segregation. The work is located in the South Side neighborhood of Englewood, once home to European immigrants who lived in densely packed workers cottages. As white people left the city after World War II, Englewood was absorbed into the Black Belt. By the twenty-first century, many of its homes were abandoned and eventually ripped down, and the remaining ones sat in open fields. To create *Color(ed) Theory*, Williams painted these abandoned cottages in bright colors that symbolized the nation's systematic disinvestment from inner-city neighborhoods after World War II. Among the colors she chose were the brilliant purple of a Crown Royal whisky bag, to symbolize the inundation of liquor stores, and the nauseating orange of Cheetos, to show the lack of access to fresh food. In Williams's photos, the bright colors of these houses pop out from a pastoral winter landscape like a psychedelic homage to Andrew Jackson Downing.

While certain neighborhoods in Chicago have depopulated, others are experiencing an enormous wave of investment. Between 2010 and 2020, Englewood's population fell 20 percent, and nearly three thousand housing units were demolished.[60] Yet during the same period, the neighborhoods within the Loop and inner core were one of the fastest-growing places in the nation. The area surrounding the spires of St. Stanislaus—once an enclave of Polish immigrants—is now part of the inner band of neighborhoods prized for their walkability and access to jobs and transit. But instead of being renovated, the humble workers cottages that once defined these Chicago neighborhoods are being cast aside.

In Logan Square, a few miles northwest of the Loop, nearly half of all buildings demolished between 2006 and 2020 were workers cottages that were replaced by modern, much larger homes.[61] Within two blocks of preservationist Matt Bergstrom's home, there have been twenty-six demolitions within five years; he has watched his neighbors, who were mostly Puerto Rican and Mexican, move farther out into the periphery. He prized the workers cottage because it was a historic vestige of the city that was also affordable, and he felt that these buildings should be preserved. He decided to go to a meeting of local Logan Square preservationists where he met a fellow lover of the workers cottage, Tom Vlodek. However, people at the meeting were uninterested in their advocacy, focusing instead on preserving the large Victorian homes on Logan Boulevard. So Tom and Matt founded the Chicago Workers Cottage Initiative to raise awareness about the structure and advocate for its preservation.[62]

Getting people to care about these working-class buildings, even ones as integral to the city's development as the workers cottages, has been a challenge. If you were to ask a Chicagoan what the city's most emblematic architectural type is, they would likely mention the skyscraper, two flats, or the brick bungalows that developed in a ring outside the city in the mid-twentieth century. Yet out of all of Chicago's industrial outputs and technological innovations, the workers cottage is one of the most important. This building and its balloon frame construction method allowed housing to expand beyond medieval timber frame methods and adopt new forms. A whole universe of spatial configurations became possible. This, combined with the advent of the railroad, allowed cities to expand horizontally. Through this, Chicago created a new urban template that was not imported from someplace else but is distinctly American: small, detached homes laid out across an endless grid.

CHAPTER 5

Portland Bungalow

The Progressive Era City

O ne of the primary aims of American cities has been to fuse the urban with the rural. William Penn designed Philadelphia to be a garden city with single-family homes set back on large lots, and there was no country on Earth in which the suburban country cottage resonated more than in America. Yet at the same time that Andrew Jackson Downing was popularizing this ideal in the early nineteenth century, it was being thwarted by the Industrial Revolution, which drove people into urban areas. Cities became unavoidable necessities, with jam-packed tenements simply the price to pay for economic progress. But as railways opened up large expanses of land after the Civil War, the garden city ideal finally came within reach. In developments like Riverside west of Chicago, builders ensconced detached homes in gardens. Streetcars and mass transit systems made access to these communities more democratic, allowing even working people to escape the cities for the periphery. With these technological innovations came a need for a new type of house—a structure with modern amenities that could be nestled in greenery but was also broadly accessible: the bungalow.

These wooden homes sitting on wide lots came to be emblematic of a new type of twentieth-century city most epitomized by Portland, Oregon. The city core is a cluster of towers and large commercial buildings;

however, it is surrounded by a vast sea of single-family homes, each on its own manicured lot. Instead of the built environment being subject to the constant change that had previously defined American cities, a suite of zoning laws and building codes protect these residential neighborhoods, preventing the intrusion of large apartment buildings or nonresidential uses. Portland's landscape of sprawling, detached bungalows is locked in.

The rise of Portland and other bungalow-dominated cities is a testament to the success of the nineteenth-century reform movement's efforts to reduce overcrowding and improve the quality of life in urban slums. Yet today, as these cities are once again surging in population and investment, the laws that perpetuate their low-slung nature is resulting in a new urban crisis of affordability. The urban challenge of the twenty-first century is how to add new housing to sprawling neighborhoods defined by single-family homes.

IIIIIIIIIIIIIIIIIIII

In 1804, President Thomas Jefferson dispatched a Corps of Discovery led by two soldiers, Meriwether Lewis and William Clark. Their mission was to explore the territory that had just been added to the Union by the Louisiana Purchase and to claim a distant land known as Oregon Country for the United States. Over the next two years, they traveled up the Missouri River and then set out on horseback through the Dakotas and across Montana.

In Idaho they connected with the Snake River and paddled down it in canoes until it turned into the massive Columbia. As they approached the Cascade Mountain Range, the golden rolling hills of eastern Washington morphed into a mountainous landscape of mist-shrouded Douglas fir trees. Suddenly, the walls of the Columbia River Gorge opened up into a flat basin bisected by the Willamette River. To the west was the dark green mass of the West Hills rising a thousand feet into the air, and to the east was a flat plain indented by gullies and punctuated by volcanic cinder cones. The snow-covered peaks of Mount Hood and Mount St. Helens loomed in the distance.

The land on which Lewis and Clark had arrived, now known as the Lower Columbia Basin, was not only physically spectacular but also a veritable Garden of Eden. Its rivers and creeks brimmed with salmon, and large elk and deer roamed the meadows and forests. The rich volcanic soil was some of the most fertile on Earth and filled with a wild-growing, nutritious, potato-like root known as *wapato*. These attributes made the Lower Columbia Basin the most densely populated place on the West Coast, with Chinook-speaking tribes living in compact settlements throughout the region, some of which had as many as three thousand people.[1] Their homes were wood structures covered in white cedar bark, measuring 100 feet long. These buildings were supported by a frame made of huge timber logs, on top of which sat a gigantic pitched roof with the eaves protecting a façade made of wood planks, each over two feet wide.

Decades before the arrival of Lewis and Clark, the Lower Columbia Basin had been discovered by Russian, British, and American traders. In 1811, John Jacob Astor—who would later invest his spoils from trading in the region into New York tenements—had established a trading post at the mouth of the Columbia, which would later become the town of Astoria, Oregon. By the 1830s, nearly the entire Native population had been decimated by disease brought by foreign explorers, and thirty years later the few who remained were forcibly relocated to reservations. Under the federal Donation Land Claim Act, their land was parceled out to white settlers in 320- to 640-acre parcels.

In 1845, a lawyer named Asa Lovejoy sold half of a small clearing of land on the Willamette River to a merchant named Francis Pettygrove with the idea of plotting a new settlement there. This land had once been home to a temporary Chinook village but now served as a rest stop for travelers going between the more established American communities of Oregon City and Vancouver, Washington. At this site, Pettygrove and Lovejoy laid out a grid composed of 200-by-200-foot blocks. Lovejoy, who was from Maine, and Pettygrove, who was from Boston, both wanted to name their settlement after their hometowns. After the flip of a coin, the site became known as Portland. Unlike Chicago, this new city was not an instant boomtown, and it eked out a tenuous existence as an isolated trading post. Hastily felled tree stumps littered the townsite as if the surrounding forest would soon reclaim it, and scoffing visitors from larger cities nicknamed it Stumptown. In 1849 the village was nearly abandoned after almost the entire population left to partake in the San Francisco gold rush.[2] However, the clearing's location still held promise, as it bordered a deep-water moorage. After a plank road was built over the West Hills and into the rich farmland of the Tualatin and Willamette Valleys, Portland soon became the region's main trade center.

||||||||||||||||||||

To this day, the names of Portland's first settlers—Lovejoy, Pettygrove, Ainsworth, Lownsdale, Skidmore—bedeck the city streets, neighborhoods, and parks; their oil portraits peer down from the walls of public schools. In addition to physical landmarks, these New Englanders also imbued Portland with a certain ethos, which was to create a proper and orderly city. Just a decade after its founding, the skyline boasted a cupola-adorned wooden schoolhouse, and elegant two- and four-story brick buildings lined the waterfront. The city's leaders also championed growth and commerce, and by 1900 Portland became the chief city of the Pacific Northwest, with a population of nearly one hundred thousand. Lovejoy and Pettygrove's clearing was now dominated by large office buildings, hotels, and department stores glistening in cream-colored, glazed terra-cotta tile. Train lines running in every direction converged on the 150-foot-tall red-brick clock tower of Union Station. Bustling wharves lined the Willamette, shipping wheat and produce around the globe and bringing immense wealth into the city. Portland was said to match any place in the nation in architecture and refinement.

However, the neighborhoods that lay just beyond the downtown had a more rugged character. To the north was Slabtown, where working-class Swedish, German, and Slavic immigrants occupied small workers cottages. To the south was the city's answer to the Lower East Side: a mixture of churches, synagogues, small homes, and apartments filled with Italian and Jewish immigrant families. In the heart of the city along the river was the nation's second-largest Chinatown, as well as one of the largest Japanese communities. Over half of the city's population was composed of immigrants or their children, who worked in factories and docks along the river.[3] During the cold and rainy winter months, thousands of seasonal workers from nearby logging camps and farms descended on an area of Portland near Burnside Street known as the North End. This notorious district offered cheap hotels and boarding houses as well as diversions for these idle workers, including opium dens, brothels, theaters, and two hundred saloons. Many of these establishments had trapdoors that descended into a network of caverns leading to the river, which were used to move goods to the docks. In a practice known as shanghaiing, passed-out bar patrons would wake up as involuntary labor on ships headed to the Far East. The issue became so serious around the turn of the twentieth century that the British government threatened to ban all their vessels from entering the city.[4]

ıııııııııııııııııııı

Like its Eastern peers, Portland was a walking city: its patrician elite, immigrants, and rowdy seasonal workers all crammed together onto a small, flat outcropping of land on the West Side of the Willamette River. Yet the city would not remain this way for long. In 1887 the Morrison Bridge was constructed, with its wooden truss and swing span making it an engineering marvel and one of the longest bridges west of the Mississippi River. A year later, tracks for horse-pulled streetcars were added to the bridge, which were converted to electric streetcars another year later. The bridge and the trains that ran on top of it facilitated an exodus of middle-class residents from the cramped West Side to the wide-open East Side. By 1910, the bulk of the city's population resided east of the Willamette River, and a 161-mile grid of streetcar tracks reached south to Sellwood, north to Portsmouth and St. Johns, and ninety-two blocks east to Montavilla, bringing people from the residential districts to the West Side.[5] Homes and businesses clustered along the lines, forming tentacles of development. At important stations and where lines intersected, bustling commercial streets of one- and two-story shops, grocery stores, cleaners, and movie theaters sprang up. These shopping streets came to define the new East Side communities. To this day, longtime Portlanders refer to many neighborhoods by their commercial arteries, such as Hawthorne, Belmont, or Alberta, rather than their official names.

In older Eastern cities, the advent of the streetcar had simply enabled the expansion of the city's existing urban form. West and North Philadelphia extended the alleys and row homes of the old colonial city. Backatown of New Orleans built the same type of double shotguns as those near the Mississippi. However, Portland was well over a century younger than these cities when the streetcar arrived. Instead of the streetcar neighborhoods repeating the established patterns of the West Side, an entirely new type of urban form evolved.

In 1889, a wealthy merchant originally from Vermont named William Ladd bought 126 acres of farmland southeast of the new Morrison Bridge. Instead of following the city's traditional grid, he created a wagon wheel of diagonal streets on his land, interspersed with small rose gardens. He envisioned this area not for workers cottages but for large, elaborate homes on 7,000-square-foot lots and mandated minimum setbacks from the sidewalk. Ladd's Addition would soon be complemented by several other exclusive East Side subdivisions, which were in stark contrast to the density and heterogeneity of the West Side. With their large lots and racially restrictive covenants, they had much more in common with Riverside than with traditional urban neighborhoods. However, whereas Riverside was a distant commuter suburb of Chicago, these communities were built within five miles, sometimes much less, of Portland's central business district.

These elite subdivisions helped set the tone for the rest of the city. The city's original 200-by-200-foot grid was only sporadically carried over to the new East Side neighborhoods. This gave developers on the East Side much more liberty to lay out streets and determine lot sizes. This, combined with the mobility allowed by the streetcar, resulted in developers creating lots much larger than the 25-by-100-foot lots that had previously been the standard for working-class housing. Lots measuring 50-by-100 feet became the new standard size in Portland, as well as in other growing twentieth-century cities, particularly in the Midwest and West. In most American cities, 5,000 square feet is now the minimum lot size for single-family residential zones. In many cases, even this large dimension was just a baseline to expand on. In 1909, a development called the Suburban Home Club Tract opened in outer Southeast Portland, with "junior acres" of 100-by-400-foot lots.[6] William Penn's eighteenth-century vision of the garden city had finally become a reality on the East Side of Portland and in other new streetcar neighborhoods across the country.

IIIIIIIIIIIIIIIIIIII

At the same time that railways were opening up the countryside in the late nineteenth century, a broad shift was happening in housing design. In wealthy suburban enclaves around the nation, the conventional rectangular, grid-like, Georgian floor plan was losing popularity to homes that took on almost organic shapes, reflecting complex interior layouts. Upon entering, one would be met with multiple parlors and dining areas, all ornately furnished and decorated. The more private spaces of the home would contain individual rooms for reading, alcoves carved out of bay windows intended for quiet contemplation, and even separate areas for folding laundry.[7] The exteriors were layered in limestone, cedar shingles, and tiles, all in different colors, which adorned multiple porches, balconies, and overhangs made possible by balloon framing.[8] The exuberant layouts and ornamentation of these upper-class homes were meant to ensconce the nuclear family in unique buildings that expressed their individualism.

Today, these elaborate houses built in the latter half of the nineteenth century, commonly known as Victorians, are seen as representing a time of lost beauty and craftsmanship—they are turned into historic landmarks and inspire everything from dollhouses to horror movies. Yet in their time they were the equivalent of McMansions today, with their ostentatious appearances and lavish interior decoration being considered chintzy, garish, and representative of consumer culture run amok. One of the most ardent critics of Victorian housing was the English writer John Ruskin, who regarded these large homes as a symbol of degradation. Born in a Georgian terrace house in London in 1819, he saw nearly all architecture that succeeded the medieval period as robbing the dignity of man. In numerous volumes and articles, he strenuously advocated for buildings and art to mimic natural forms such as those of plants and trees, which he felt were an expression of the divine. However, this was something that could only be achieved through things made by hand, not by the machines pumping out the ornamentation that was liberally layered onto the façades of Victorian homes, as well as onto the furniture and art stuffed inside them. Ruskin was an immensely eccentric man. He lived on a remote lake in northern England where he grew out a Rasputin-sized beard and surrounded himself with older women who would sing songs to him before he went to sleep.[9] However, by the time of his death in 1900, his ideas would go on to indelibly influence art, architecture, and housing. This was particularly true with respect to his advocacy around simple, well-designed dwellings for working people.

The architectural vessel that encapsulated Ruskin's ideas and legacy would not come from England but from the native houses of Bengal, India. Like early Caribbean dwellings, these were vernacular structures made of a bamboo frame covered with mud walls. They sat on raised platforms, with an outdoor gallery to maximize airflow, and were topped by bulging, crescent-moon-shaped roofs made from thatch (see image 15). Beginning in the fifteenth century, colonial expeditions used these huts in temporary camps. Eventually the homes were adapted into more permanent structures to house British officials and became known as bungalows. Instead of being made from mud and bamboo, they were built from sun-dried brick, and the space surrounding the house was made into a covered outdoor room.[10] Several bungalows would be scattered across ten-acre compounds known as *cantonments*, which were often several times the physical size of the Indian cities they sat outside of, even though they contained a tiny fraction of their population. The bungalows and cantonments were meant to create and enforce a physical and social distinction between the one thousand high-level British officials who lived in these landscaped estates and their 250 million Indian subjects who lived in villages and dense cities.[11]

As global trade and communication increased, by the late nineteenth century the bungalow was transported back to England in the form of an upper-class leisure dwelling. As opposed to stuffy Victorian homes, the bungalow was smaller and easier to maintain and could house a single family without the assistance of servants. Their verandahs and large windows made them ideal for elite coastal resorts or country cabins. Like Airstream trailers today, the building became associated with a rustic, earthy bohemianism. In 1899, a London-based artistic and literary magazine even named itself *The Bungalow*. Though it did not deal with architecture, an early essay by the editor describes how the building represented certain egalitarian and free-spirited ideals it was trying to promote:

> In the cities of Northern Europe, where men from all parts find themselves thrown together, a limit is at once placed on everything. The houses have to arrange themselves in order and instead of spreading themselves out they must mount higher up, and then comes the fight for the best position! The wealthy first, then the poor—nearer heaven! Everyone is on a level in the Bungalow—you are either above or below in the towering city dwelling.[12]

‖‖‖‖‖‖‖‖‖‖‖‖‖‖

By the turn of the twentieth century, a textile designer from the north of England named William Morris coalesced Ruskin's ideas into a design philosophy called Arts and Crafts. This movement was the antithesis of Baroque Victorian styles and espoused simple materials, usually unvarnished wood, used in an affordable and utilitarian manner. The Arts and Crafts Movement grew so popular in England that even celebrities became adherents. The author Oscar Wilde went on a US lecture circuit where he discussed domestic architecture, freely lifting quotes from Ruskin and Morris verbatim and without attribution.[13]

The Arts and Crafts Movement's critique of Victorian houses resonated with a diverse coalition of progressive reformers focusing on a wide range of issues. However, the reformers' interest was not based on esoteric ideas about natural beauty but on more practical issues. Suffragists, for instance, saw large Victorian homes as forcing women into isolation in faraway suburbs, where they became enslaved to the house's constant cleaning and upkeep. To public health proponents, Victorians' complex layouts and various nooks and crannies were the perfect environment for germs.[14] In an era when children were dying of disease in dank tenements, housing reformers saw these decadent Victorian homes as being grossly out of step with the housing needs of regular people.

However, in the US, as in England, the Arts and Crafts Movement began as an elite phenomenon. During the nineteenth century, fewer than a dozen bungalows were built in the entire country, and almost all were in the Northeast.[15] One of the first to be constructed on the West Coast was built in 1909 as a vacation home for the scions of the Procter & Gamble Company in the resort town of Pasadena, eight miles north of Los Angeles. To design the house, the Gambles hired a pair of local architects, brothers Charles and Henry Greene. The Greenes' practice had initially consisted of middling Victorian homes that were a pastiche of styles. During Charles's honeymoon in England, he was exposed to the designs and ideas of Ruskin and Morris. The bungalows he saw in the dreary, ale-soaked towns of the British coast seemed to him to be uniquely suited to the casual, indoor-outdoor lifestyle and temperate climate of Southern California. So instead of another Victorian monstrosity, the Greenes built the Gambles an enlarged Arts and Crafts bungalow (see image 15). The exterior was covered in unpainted wood shingles. The rooms radiated off a central hall, each connected to its own large outdoor patio space. Nearly everything in the home was handmade by local contractors, with a unique cloud lift pattern being echoed in hanging lanterns, mortise and tenon joinery, and even picture frames. The Gamble House's furniture cost nearly three times that of a very nice home at the time.

Like the Slate Roof House in Philadelphia, the Gamble House became one of the seminal homes of its time. A carpenter from Upstate New York named Gustav Stickley began to publish designs for a smaller version of the bungalow in his magazine *The Craftsman*. A pattern book called *Radford's Artistic Bungalows* advertised two hundred individual designs, the plans for which could be purchased for as little as five dollars.[16] These designs shrank the bungalow down to a 50-by-100-foot lot, making it accessible to an emerging middle class. Instead of being handmade, its components were mass-produced and could be purchased out of a Sears or Montgomery Ward catalogue and then constructed by a contractor.[17] Through this, the bungalow went from being a frivolous dwelling for effete bohemians that H. G. Wells described as a place of "careless sensuality" to a home that was accessible to a vast cross section of the population. Its modern features and light-filled interiors also made it a symbol of the Progressive movement.

‖‖‖‖‖‖‖‖‖‖‖‖‖

In 1925, a University of Chicago sociologist named Ernest Burgess made a map of Chicago composed of concentric rings. At the center were the towers of the Loop, with the jam-packed workers cottages of the Near West Side, Chinatown, and Little Italy immigrant enclaves just outside. At the farthest edge was a recent twentieth-century addition to the city, labeled the bungalow belt. By the 1920s, Chicago developers had fully transitioned from workers cottages to bungalows. The dwellings still conformed to 25-foot-wide lots but were clad in brick instead of wood and had modern floor plans with kitchens, bathrooms, and large windows.

This dramatic shift from older working-class housing types to modern bungalows occurred not just in Chicago, but also across the country. In late nineteenth-century Oakland, California, working-class neighborhoods near the docks were developed with workers cottages on 25-foot-wide lots. As in Chicago, their owners would gradually add additional structures and rooms over time. Yet by the first decades of the twentieth century,

developers in the Bay Area and other West Coast metropolises quickly
shifted to bungalows sitting on 45-by-100-foot lots with a standard 15-foot
outbaok from the sidewalk.[18] In New Orleans, shotguns were replaced
by tile-roofed homes that looked like they could be in California.[19] The
farthest reaches of Philadelphia; Washington, DC; Baltimore; and New
York were built out with day lighters that merged the features of the bungalow with the shared party wall of a row house, as well as fully detached
bungalow-style homes.

In Portland, the rise of the bungalow corresponded almost precisely
with one of the city's largest periods of growth. In 1905, Portland followed
Philadelphia and Chicago in hosting a World's Fair, the nation's third,
called the Lewis and Clark Centennial Exposition. The centerpiece was a
200-foot-long house covered with pine cones, which became known as the
world's largest log cabin. Despite the fair's underwhelming attractions, it
resulted in massive growth for the city. Banking transactions increased by
150 percent, employment growth outpaced population growth, and the
number of building permits filed went up 400 percent.

Almost all of this growth occurred in the city's East Side streetcar
neighborhoods in the form of bungalows. They sat back on 50-foot lots
buffered with small lawns or gardens and were built in every shape and
size, from boxy two-story "four-squares" with four rooms on each floor in
Ladd's Addition to small 800-square-foot-bungalows for rail yard workers
in Southeast Portland. Due to the abundance of lumber from the massive
Douglas fir trees that surrounded the city, the exteriors were made entirely
from wood. The low-pitched roofs sheltered a small porch held up by
bracketed columns. The bungalow was not just a stylistic change—it represented a huge technological leap in housing. Until 1900, most American
homes, with their hall-and-parlor floor plans, were essentially arranged no
differently from those from the medieval era. Their interiors were like the
depiction of the home in the film *Charlie and the Chocolate Factory*, where
the family's four grandparents occupy a single bed that sits directly next
to a stove and a giant cauldron of laundry. The typical nineteenth-century
house had three to four rooms that functioned interchangeably, being used
for sleep, work, meal preparation, eating, and storage alike. The kitchen
was distinguished from any other room only by the presence of a small
sink and stove, and the bathroom was usually located outside in a privy or

outhouse. Like the large Victorian homes, the bungalow gave each room its own distinct purpose. A front porch opened up onto a living room connected to a dining room. Large picture windows brought in light. In the Arts and Crafts tradition, the shelving, cabinets, and seating were built into the walls. In the dining and living rooms, wood beams ran along the ceiling—however, unlike in the Gamble House, they were not usually structural but simply tacked on.[20]

The crowning achievements of the bungalow were the bathroom and kitchen, which were based off the latest advances in germ theory: Each surface was designed to be easily cleaned, the walls were covered in brilliant white tile, and the floor was made of linoleum. Instead of a rusty spigot and hole cut out of a wood plank, the bathroom contained the new holy trinity of the porcelain sink, bathtub, and toilet. The kitchen became a show place for new time-saving appliances, including washers, refrigerators, and vacuum cleaners.[21] These rooms, which previously had been so wretched and vomit-inducing that they'd been cast off into separate buildings, became the new focal point of the home. Architectural historians Thomas Hubka and Judith T. Kenny call these five-to-six-room layouts the Progressive Era Plan.[22]

With the rising living standards of the twentieth century, these 800-to-1,200-square-foot bungalows with modern amenities became affordable to a broad cross section of society. In Portland, advertisements were plastered across the city for the Union Savings and Loan Association saying, "Don't wait until you have saved enough money to build your home. What you pay in rent will build it for you."[23]

|||||||||||||||||

Portland's new spacious, open bungalow neighborhoods represented a tremendous triumph of the Progressive movement. The American dream of a working family having their own free-standing home had finally been realized. Yet if history proved to be any guide, maintaining these communities as low-density enclaves would be challenging. Many urban districts, from Prairie Avenue in Chicago to the (now lost) neighborhood of Cherry Hill on New York's Lower East Side, had started out as idyllic enclaves for the upper classes only to decline into slums a few years later.

Up until the twentieth century, an urban Darwinism consisting of rapid neighborhood change had prevailed. As cottages were absorbed into the urban core, they would be replaced by towering offices and factories. A home built for the rich would be down-cycled until it housed the most destitute. Housing had been built with this type of change in mind. The geometric floor plans of row homes could easily be subdivided from a single-family home into apartments, and the light wood-frame construction of shotguns and workers cottages allowed them to be physically moved or lifted to add additional units.

Whereas older workers' housing was a cheap commodity, the new technology incorporated into the bungalow made it a complex asset. The very structure made the mutability that had previously defined city housing more difficult. Rooms individualized for different purposes made it hard to subdivide these dwellings into apartments.* Complex wiring and plumbing, as well as more solid modern foundations, prevented them from being raised in order to add an additional floor or relocated to make room for another structure. Moreover, the skills needed to create the plumbing and electricity systems far surpassed those of the average nineteenth-century builder, and increased sanitary requirements for the bathrooms and kitchens alone doubled the price of a house between 1890 and 1905.[24] By the 1910s, the cheapest bungalow on the market was $800, multiple times what a basic workers cottage or row house would have cost a generation before. The rapid change that had characterized neighborhoods of the past would no longer be accepted. New government policies were needed to protect bungalows and their surrounding neighborhoods.

The Progressive movement barely paused to revel in the triumph of the bungalow. Instead, by the early twentieth century they broadened their focus from housing to the design of the city as a whole. The Economic Club of Boston issued a report declaring "the present haphazard system of intermingling dwellings, factories, stores, offices and other buildings in hopeless confusion must give way to a system of town planning in scientific lines. These include the defining of zones in which buildings of specified character and height can alone be erected."[25]

In Portland, the need for such policies was highlighted by the city's experience during World War I. During this brief period, the number of

---

* It was common for some bungalows to have a room in the front of the home which could be used to house boarders.

manufacturing workers doubled, with thirty-three thousand people being employed in large shipyards along the Willamette. Housing production did not keep pace with demand. Chicago-style back houses were erected behind workers cottages on the West Side, apartments were subdivided with windowless rooms, and owners of single-family homes took on boarders. In the wake of this onslaught, Portland's leaders decided that policies were needed to protect the city's character. A new city planning commission was established in 1919 with its first task being the establishment of a zoning code to create a minimum standard for private housing.[26]

Zoning was seen as a progressive tool to give all citizens benefits that previously had been only for the rich. Historically, developers of wealthy areas across the country would place restrictive covenants into the deeds of their houses to control what could be built and who could live there. In Chelsea, on the West Side of Manhattan, covenants had been used as far back as the 1830s to ban stables and to ensure that all homes were built from brick instead of wood.[27] In Riverside, Illinois, they were used to protect the integrity of the development's design, creating minimum setback requirements and even banning fences from being built. However, covenants were most prominently used to restrict access to white residents only. In the Laurelhurst neighborhood of Portland, an exclusive subdivision of undulating streets and a large park, a restriction was placed on deeds in the early twentieth century stating that homes could not be "occupied by Chinese, Japanese or negroes, except that persons of said races may be employed as servants by residents."[28]

The creator of Portland's zoning code, a planning consultant named Charles H. Cheney, wrote that "the poor man with a family is as much entitled to an opportunity to live in a home neighborhood restricted from flats, apartments, business and other undesirable buildings as is the wealthy man, who builds his home in an appropriately restricted tract."[29] In 1924, Cheney divided the city into four zones: one to protect single-family homes, particularly in exclusive areas like Laurelhurst and Eastmoreland; another for multifamily housing; and two others for commercial and industrial areas. The original covenants took precedence over zoning if the former were more restrictive.[30]

||||||||||||||||||||

Just a thirty-minute walk from downtown Portland sits SE 16th Avenue in the East Side neighborhood of Buckman. In an older city, a neighborhood this close to the core would be composed of dense row homes or tenements, but here, the broad porches of bungalows are pushed back from the sidewalk by rhododendron-filled gardens, and the sky is blotted out by massive trees sprouting from overgrown parkways. A leafy calm prevails. The air is scented with the smell of wet earth, and the only sound is that of the wind blowing through chimes or a distant train whistle or lawn mower. Pedestrian traffic is limited to an occasional mail carrier and people walking their dogs. This is a far cry from mixed-use neighborhoods in older cities, where it would not be uncommon for a tavern or corner store to be tucked into the middle of the block and for the streets to be bustling with people going about their day.

Where the Progressive Era Plan marked a new standard for housing, neighborhoods like Buckman made Portland emblematic of a new twentieth-century Progressive Era city. Instead of stores, homes, and businesses being mixed together, zoning segregated each into their own part of the city. A concentrated downtown core of commercial and industrial uses was ringed by broad swaths composed of only single-family homes. Interspersed were business districts that developed along streetcar lines (see image 17). By 1935, Portland had been joined by 1,322 other American cities adopting zoning codes. The dense, mixed-use urban centers of the nineteenth century now became the exception rather than the rule.

For most of the country's history, the suburb had been a transitory state as neighborhoods were developed from rural to urban. Areas like West Philadelphia, Five Points in New York, or Catherine O'Leary's Chicago neighborhood had begun as quasi-rural areas that were later absorbed into the urban core. However, the new zoning systems locked in the character of a neighborhood. These laws were used to preclude the erection of denser forms of housing or commercial uses in a particular neighborhood, so that even centrally located areas like the inner East Side of Portland look much the same in 2023 as they did in 1923.

|||||||||||||||||||||

Since the colonial era, American housing could be divided into two classes. A small minority of people representing less than a third of the population lived in large well-appointed homes, often staffed by servants and ranging from country estates to brownstones. The rest lived in cramped cottages and tenements.[31] In the early twentieth century, as wages increased, a new middle class emerged, which came to be defined by its access to modern, spacious homes. On October 29, 1929, however, the decades-long economic expansion that had made this possible suddenly and dramatically ended with the stock market crash known as Black Tuesday.

The Great Depression, with its snaking bread lines, is often viewed as an employment crisis. However, it was also a housing crisis. Savings and loans still dominated the lending industry. Many of them, like the Union Savings and Loan in Portland, provided loans of less than 60 percent of a home's value and required a down payment of at least 30 percent. As jobs and savings vanished, people became unable to meet these terms, and many customers defaulted on their payments. Between 1930 and 1932, six hundred thousand homes were foreclosed on, and new construction fell by 95 percent.[32] Hoovervilles—shantytowns named after President Herbert Hoover full of plywood shacks with metal roofs and scavenged furniture—sprang up everywhere: from New York's Central Park to an old shipyard along the Willamette River in Portland.

In response, the federal government passed the Home Owners Loan Act of 1933, which provided mortgage assistance and refinancing to at-risk homeowners. This was part of a suite of government interventions into the housing market between the 1930s and '50s. While these programs were adopted as an immediate response to the Depression, they fundamentally remade housing in America. In 1900, less than half of the population owned their home, but by 1960 this number had risen to over 60 percent.[33] This was made possible through agencies like the Federal Housing Administration (FHA), which insured 93 percent of a home's value and required a down payment of no more than 10 percent. FHA loans were also fully amortized, greatly reducing monthly payments. In many US cities it became cheaper to own than rent.[34]

These new federal programs did not only change how housing was financed but also how it looked. In order to qualify for an FHA loan, housing had to adhere to new national standards. Strict insulation and fire protection standards meant that façades had to be built with plywood sheathing and vinyl siding instead of the clapboard of a workers cottage.

New minimum room sizes did not allow for the tight quarters of a trinity.[35] Requirements for lot sizes and setbacks rendered even the standard pre-twentieth-century 25-foot lots no longer viable.

A home's suitability for a loan was further evaluated using an appraisal system that color-coded neighborhoods by risk. Homogenous areas of single-family homes were shaded blue and given the highest grade. Older neighborhoods composed of a patchwork of dense housing, as well as retail and commercial buildings, were given the lowest grades and shaded yellow for "definitely declining" or red for "hazardous." However, what this system—which became known as *redlining*—weighed most heavily was not a neighborhood's physical quality but rather who lived there. Neighborhoods with Southern or Eastern European immigrants, Latin Americans, or Asians were often given a yellow grade due to the "infiltration of subversive races." The presence of just one Black person on a block was enough to redline an entire area.[36] In Portland, only the choicest neighborhoods in the West Hills and elite subdivisions were given the best grade, while the majority of the city was marked yellow and red. Redlining resulted in older urban neighborhoods, particularly communities of color, being systematically starved of resources. In many cities today, neighborhoods redlined nearly a century ago still suffer from high poverty and worse environmental and health outcomes.[37]

In 1947, William J. Levitt, a descendant of Russian Jews from Brooklyn, bought a potato field on Long Island, thirty-six miles east of Manhattan. Drawing on his experience building army barracks during World War II, his company Levitt and Sons constructed two thousand homes, combining balloon frame construction with other labor-saving techniques, including organizing teams of subcontractors on an assembly line. Levittown, as it became known, was joined by similar developments in New Jersey and outside of Philadelphia, totaling 17,447 homes built between 1947 and 1951. These communities were the ultimate expression of the new federal housing regime. The era of small builders constructing one or two homes a year, often in a regional style, was over. Instead, on the periphery of cities, developers threw up thousands of homes with low-pitched roofs and flat façades covered in vinyl. The only ornamentation would be a rain gutter and perhaps a faux brick panel at the base. These new suburbs rejected the urban grid. But instead of mimicking and accentuating natural features like Riverside, Illinois, or Laurelhurst in Portland, the curving streets were rote and mechanical, with the land ruthlessly divided into 60-by-100-square-foot lots (see image 16). Adhering strictly to the new federal lending standards, residential buildings in these developments were strictly segregated from buildings for any other use. Highway-side strip malls replaced the traditional Main Street. As these postwar suburban communities quickly filled with white ethnic families leaving the city, people of color were barred from them. As late as 1960, not a single Black resident lived in the original Levittown.[38]

In Riverside outside of Chicago, a new suburban form had been created: detached single-family homes on large lots in insular communities composed of curvilinear streets. With the mid-century federal housing policies, this form became codified. Developments like Levittown not only physically expressed the new suburban form but also represented a new legal definition of the suburbs. Before, it had been common for developments to be built just outside the city limits and then lobby to be incorporated within the city, as was the case with many of Samuel Gross's communities in Chicago. But by the mid-twentieth century, new developments like New York's and Pennsylvania's Levittowns incorporated as their own homogenous suburbs with their own governments, services, and, most importantly, school districts. These fast-growing suburbs were like New World cantonments: white enclaves sitting outside of denser, poorer, and increasingly Black and brown urban cores.

By 1982, eleven million people had used the new federal programs to buy a home, almost exclusively in suburban communities like Levittown. Over time, homes and lot sizes ballooned until McMansions sat on acre lots fifty miles outside of the central city.[39] Farms, forests, and natural habitats outside of cities and towns were eaten up by low-density subdivisions, strip malls, and industrial parks. Today, the northeast seaboard is a blob of contiguous development stretching 550 miles from Fredericksburg, Virginia, to Kittery, Maine. These communities are almost entirely car dependent, forcing people to drive to reach even the most basic amenities and severely isolating anyone who is unable to purchase or operate a vehicle.

|||||||||||||||||||

While the United States came out of World War II as the planet's dominant superpower, Portland emerged weary and shell-shocked. The city had again experienced unbridled growth during the war. The population of the metropolitan area had grown by a third, stretching housing, mass transit, and services to the limit. Massive shipyards ran twenty-four hours a day, and one of the nation's largest public housing complexes was hastily thrown up on a flood plain along the Columbia River. The workers the war had brought into the city had made it much more diverse, with the African American population growing from two thousand to fifteen thousand.[40] For a still-insular and conservative city, the speed and pace of this change was almost too much to bear. A local hotelier said it was impossible to ride the streetcar "without getting grease spots."[41]

Postwar, Portland largely retreated from the national stage and grew only half as much as its northern rival, Seattle. By the 1960s, the number of people coming into the downtown had dropped by a third, and the population of the suburbs surpassed that of the city.[42] In inner neighborhoods like SE 16th Avenue, old bungalows—their paint now peeling, their roofs covered in moss—became cheap boarding houses. Along the once-thriving streetcar commercial districts, markets and clothing stores were boarded up or converted to smoky dive bars and greasy spoon diners. Neighborhood movie theaters went from showing Saturday morning cartoons to crowds of screaming children to screening X-rated films to hirsute men in trench coats. It was the ragged, rain-soaked city depicted in the early films of the director Gus Van Sant.

An area of Northeast Portland was turned into a redlined ghetto, where 60 percent of the city's Black population was confined. Old streetcar strips like Mississippi Avenue, with their vacant lots and half-demolished buildings, became open-air drug markets.[43] In his 2013 memoir *The Residue Years*, Mitchell S. Jackson describes certain parts of his Northeast Portland neighborhood as "crack central, a mise-en-scene . . . with dopeheads darting in and out of shadows or grumbling up in cars with their windows dropped low."[44]

During the chaos of World War II, the owner of the city's shipyards, Edgar Kaiser, had hired New York's master planner Robert Moses to come to Portland and create a plan for its renewal. In 1943, two dozen planners swooped into the city and holed up in the ballroom of the Multnomah Hotel, with the maestro himself flying in during the final days to unveil the final document, *Portland Improvement*.[45] In the introduction, Moses excoriated the city's conservative leaders who only accepted growth out of a sense of "patriotic sacrifice" and "wished that Portland shall keep as long as possible the flavor of a transplanted New England."[46]

As in New York, Moses largely called for the city to destroy itself in order to be saved. Cast iron buildings along the waterfront, which rivaled New York in number, were leveled, and over the next decade a freeway corseted the downtown and the riverfront. The old Jewish and Italian enclave of South Portland was leveled for modernist office buildings and residential towers surrounded by plazas and parking. African Americans were forced to move several times, once when the old Albina district was cleared for the Memorial Coliseum and freeways and again for a hospital. In order to triage the declining East Side bungalow belt, it was to be made as suburban as possible. Planning documents called for freeways to divide it in order to turn "residential sections into secluded units protected from the encroachment of conflicting urban uses."[47]

IIIIIIIIIIIIIIIIII

In 1964, as the bulldozers were initiating their work on Moses's plan, a young woman from Brooklyn by way of Moscow and Dusseldorf named Vera Katz transplanted her young family to Portland. For someone with such a cosmopolitan background, an isolated river city was an odd place to move. However, Katz and her painter husband longed to escape the pressure cooker of New York, and Portland seemed as far as one could get both culturally and physically.[48]

The Katzes were not an anomaly. As in Philadelphia, New Orleans, and other cities across the country, downtrodden neighborhoods in inner Portland were being revitalized by young families during the 1960s and '70s as part of the back-to-the-city movement. Directly south of downtown Portland, overlooking the Willamette, was one such neighborhood, Lair Hill—one of the few remnants of the city's old West Side. Here, Jews, Italians, and African Americans mixed with other immigrants in subdivided Victorians and workers cottages scattered amidst small brick industrial buildings and shops. By the early '60s some of the homes started to sport psychedelic paint jobs, and longhaired young people could be found lounging in Lair Hill Park. For the most part, the neighborhood's bohemian newcomers integrated well with the longtime residents. Some were even recruited to bolster the minyan at the local synagogue.[49] However, to the small cabal of business and government elite who controlled City Hall, these old inner neighborhoods were still slums. On the East Side, a new traffic artery, the Mount Hood Freeway, was planned to cut through Southeast Portland, barely missing the southern edge of Ladd's Addition. Lair Hill was described as the most deteriorated neighborhood on the West Side, and planners called for its 143 buildings to be demolished.[50]

Yet Portland was changing. During the 1960s, the number of residents between ages fifteen and thirty-four increased from 22 to 30 percent of the population, and many lived in the areas that city officials wanted to destroy.[51] Across the city, young families mobilized against these plans. Vera Katz shifted from working as a volunteer on the Robert Kennedy presidential campaign to organizing her Northwest Portland neighborhood. At the same moment, a forty-five-year-old journalist in New York named Jane Jacobs was girding the back-to-the-city movement with an ideological underpinning. Like others of her generation, Jacobs had cast off suburbia for Greenwich Village, a neighborhood viewed by most planners and elected officials as a tenement-filled slum. Her seminal 1961 book, *The Death and Life of Great American Cities*, directly challenged decades of urban planning orthodoxy. Jacobs described how the dense urban patchwork of her Lower Manhattan neighborhood had, far from robbing its inhabitants of dignity as urban renewal proponents claimed, instead produced a deeply interwoven community. Small shop owners minded the streets, and mothers yelled out of apartment windows for their children. *The Death and Life of Great American Cities* was a paradigm shift in how people viewed cities. It provided a forceful defense of traditional urban neighborhoods as well as a damming indictment of the type of modernist planning being perpetuated by people like Robert Moses.

In 1973, the political coalition that had led Portland for decades was overturned when a thirty-two-year-old named Neil Goldschmidt was elected mayor. Goldschmidt, who had served on the City Council for just sixteen months, was an admirer of Jacobs and wasted no time in translating her work into policy. Instead of tearing down old neighborhoods, the city started to reinvest in them. The Mount Hood Freeway was cancelled, and funding was diverted to a new light rail line designed to reaffirm downtown as the core of the metropolis. A multilane highway along the Willamette was removed for a new waterfront park. A parking garage in the center of the city was turned into a brick-paved public space emblazoned with the names of local residents and called Pioneer Courthouse Square—now known as Portland's Living Room—and Lair Hill, instead of being demolished, became the city's first historic preservation district.[52]

ıııııııııııııııııı

Yet no matter how hard local activists tried to stave off the degradation of their neighborhoods, it was clear that their attempts would be futile if suburban sprawl continued to drain people and businesses from the core. In far East Portland, well beyond where the streetcar once ended, companies like the Cooley-Wolsborn Construction Co. created soggy, moss covered mini-Levittowns of 1,120-square-foot ranch homes.[53] By 1970, the city and suburbs occupied nearly three hundred square miles, sprawling twenty miles in every direction.[54]

To many Oregonians, the state's natural beauty was sacred, and the fear that forests and hillsides would be covered in subdivisions propelled an environmental journalist named Tom McCall into the governor's office in 1967. McCall hailed from a prominent Massachusetts family but lived for part of his childhood on a ranch in the high desert of Eastern Oregon. His journalism career up to that point had been defined by calls for natural conservation, including a 1962 TV documentary called *Pollution in Paradise*. When he ran for office, halting sprawl became a chief pillar of his campaign platform. Soon after he was elected, he railed in an early speech to the legislature about "sagebrush subdivisions, coastal condo mania, and the ravenous rampage of suburbia in the Willamette Valley."[55]

McCall found allies in his quest to conserve Oregon's landscape. One of these was State Senator Hector Macpherson, who feared his dairy farm in the rolling hills of Linn County would soon be devoured by sprawl. With the support of the governor, legislation that Macpherson drafted, called Senate Bill 100, was passed in 1973. This law required each city and metro area in Oregon to create land use plans that would draw a line around developed areas, outside of which development would stop and only agriculture and open space would be allowed. In Portland, the role of creating the urban growth boundary was given to a new metropolitan planning organization called Metro.

The results of this can be seen today in suburban Washington County on the western fringe of Portland. It is a booming area, home to Nike's global headquarters and to massive semiconductor fabrication plants. However, despite almost insatiable demand for development, the sprawl of Washington County abruptly stops. The backs of tract houses make visible the invisible line of the urban growth boundary, sharply delineating the suburbs from the farmland and forests beyond.

While the growth boundary has protected Oregon's natural environment, it also had the inverse effect of directing new growth inward, inside already developed areas. In 1992, Vera Katz went on to become the mayor of Portland after having served as the state's first female speaker of the house. As mayor, Katz led with a distinctly urban vision. Under her leadership, in the 1990s the original 200-by-200 square-foot grid platted by Lovejoy and Pettygrove was extended over an old rail yard to create a new dense urban neighborhood called the Pearl District. In the early 2000s, the dusty vacant lots of an abandoned shipyard where a Hooverville once sprouted were turned into the glassy towers of the South Waterfront. Both these areas were linked together by the nation's first modern streetcar, providing a model of urban revitalization that has been replicated across the world. Today, a gondola suspended by wires floats over Lair Hill like a soap bubble, connecting the South Waterfront to a large medical complex in the West Hills. In a city that had been founded by male WASPs to be a Western version of New England, perhaps the most enduring impact on the city's physical form was by a female Jewish immigrant.

⁙⁙⁙⁙⁙⁙⁙⁙⁙⁙

Carl Abbott, one of the foremost chroniclers of Portland history and development, said in his 2001 book, "One reason the city is so widely admired today is that it looks and works much like a city of the 1950's."[56] Downtown Portland has remained vibrant and human-scaled, with people from outlying areas still traveling there to shop, eat, or see a show. Residential neighborhoods have retained a remarkable level of community cohesion, with formal associations and informal block parties, and are anchored by the old streetcar business districts filled with local mom-and-pop businesses. For the urban jet set that was rehabbing areas like Lower Manhattan and Los Angeles's Venice neighborhood in the '70s and '80s, a 1950s-style small town would not have been a sexy or appealing image. However, by the early 2000s, Portland started to attract the acoustic version of that Iggy Pop crowd that had settled in neighborhoods like the Lower East Side. They rejected larger, more economically dynamic cities to focus on their quality of life. Instead of living in cramped apartments and climbing the corporate ladder, they rented rooms in bungalows and focused on art, music, and their hobbies. Along Division Street—an East Side commercial strip once slated for demolition by the Mount Hood Freeway—these newcomers began opening businesses in dilapidated storefronts. These were not hardware stores or dry cleaners: one specialized in coffee that the owner sourced by scouring farms across the globe, paying nearly three times the normal price and selling the brew as a boutique item. Farther down the street, a former house painter from Vermont painstakingly attempted to recreate a style of grilled chicken typically found along the roadsides of northern Thailand. These businesses exceeded all expectations: by the 2010s the chicken shack, Pok Pok, had turned into a full-fledged restaurant, with locations in Los Angeles and New York. Meanwhile, Stumptown Coffee Roasters was bought by a German conglomerate.

The rise of these companies mirrored the rise of Portland itself as it became a national icon synonymous with a slower paced lifestyle focused on the local rather than the corporate, on biking instead of cars, and on regionally sourced food instead of factory farmed. Portland's success drew such great interest in the city's planning policies that Portland State University opened a special office just to lead tours to visiting delegations. Portland became known as a place not built on any particular industry, but on a lifestyle, and it was satirized by the popular television show *Portlandia* as being a place where "young people go to retire."

Today, downtown Portland stands as a glittering testament to the city's farsighted urban policy. The early-twentieth-century buildings erected after the Lewis and Clark exposition sit harmoniously next to a plethora of new lofts and condos. The street grid is interrupted at regular intervals by well-designed public spaces, from the red bricks of Pioneer Courthouse

Square to the colorful totems of Jamison Square. So many streetcar and light rail tracks bisect the area that a visiting national food critic said it was reminiscent of a switching yard.

However, while downtown Portland has grown spectacularly over the last thirty years, the bulk of the city still retains the low-density landscape of the 1920s. The vast expanse of single-family homes, frozen by the zoning code, has contributed to the state of Oregon having the second-lowest amount of housing per capita in the nation.[57] In the 2010s, the average home price in Portland increased by 75 percent, posing a serious threat to the city's character.[58] As home prices and rents have become unaffordable, the middle- and working-class population that once defined the East Side of the city is being pushed out of the former streetcar neighborhoods and farther into the suburbs. Northeast Portland, with its churches, barbershops, and community organizations, was once the heart of not just Portland's African American community but also that of the entire Northwest. Today the neighborhood's Black population has been cut in half—from twenty-four thousand in 1990 to twelve thousand in 2020, even while the total population of the area has risen by twenty thousand.[59]

Across the country, cities dominated by bungalows and single-family homes are facing a staggering housing crisis, largely due to an inability to add new housing. Academic studies have found that zoning restrictions have raised housing prices by 32 to 46 percent across the country.[60] The challenge of altering low-density residential neighborhoods to allow for more housing has become an existential crisis. This is particularly the case in Portland and other booming Progressive Era cities like Austin, Nashville, and Seattle, which each see single-family homes as an intrinsic part of their identity. If a city's charming bungalows are replaced by modern apartments, does this erode its quality of life? Does the offbeat vibe represented by these quiet residential streets get obliterated by a money-obsessed rat race of glassy condo towers? In the late nineteenth century, the primary question for urban reformers was how to reduce density on 25-foot lots filled with dank tenements. However, at the beginning of the twenty-first century, the paramount challenge facing American cities is how to add density to the 50-foot-wide lots of single-family homes nestled in greenery.

For many planners, the solution to this issue lies behind a double-gabled bungalow on the East Side of Portland. Southeast 60th Avenue is the prototypical Portland street, lined by small one-story houses, with plants bursting from front yards into the sidewalk. However, if you look past the young Douglas firs and Japanese maples, you can see that behind the house in the front of one of the lots there is a smaller structure. This 491-square-foot cottage contains only two rooms but—due to its tall ceilings, clerestory windows, and French doors—it feels much larger. By using small appliances and barn doors, it is able to pack in its own kitchen, bathroom, and bedroom. The cottage even has its own private outdoor patio space.

This cottage, designed by Propel Studio Architecture, is known as the Wedge and it represent a popular strategy in Portland and other cities to add density to single-family neighborhoods: ADUs, or accessory dwelling units. These small cottages tap into a long tradition of urban housing, from mews homes in London to tenements and workers cottages—all forms that add density by developing excess space in the back of a lot. Portland passed a law to allow the construction of backyard homes in 1997, partially due to pressure from Metro. California strengthened its statewide backyard home policy in 2017, and laws enacting similar policies have also been established in places from Arkansas to North Carolina.

Part of the reason backyard cottages are so popular is that they allow density while preserving the physical characteristics of bungalow neighborhoods. A person can drive down a quiet residential street on the East Side of Portland and never know that an extra unit may lurk behind one of the homes. These structures also allow homeowners to gain additional income from their property, or add space for a relative. This has reinvigorated small-scale entrepreneurialism, with a plethora of companies now offering off-the-shelf backyard home models that utilize prefabrication.

The Wedge has won awards and is often featured in the press. Part of the reason its design is so successful is because it sits on an abnormally large 60-by-100-foot lot. This allows the Wedge to have its own access path and patio space without encroaching on the main house. However, most bungalow lots are 50 by 100 feet, and many lots on the same street as the Wedge are only 40 feet wide. On these smaller lots, it is difficult to add a backyard home without repeating the mistakes of the workers cottage—robbing air, light, and open space from both units. To avoid exactly this problem, many municipalities have imposed severe regulations on backyard cottages, requiring on-site parking and mandating a minimum buffer between the property line and main house. All of these regulations serve to further conceal the physical impact of backyard cottages, however, it also disempowers homeowners from configuring new units on their properties in a way that would suit their needs.

The contradiction of creating cities that are dense, sustainable, and affordable while still preserving low-density single-family neighborhoods is forcing a reckoning in many places. The bungalow, though burdened with a colonial and often racist history, represents the birth of modern middle-class housing. However, today it is considered the main barrier to increasing affordability and sustainability. Yet as housing prices continue to rise, elected officials and policymakers are increasingly exploring strategies that move far beyond the single-family home and backyard cottage. Cities like Portland must now attempt the arduous task of moving away from a place modeled on the 1950s and create a city for a new age.

CHAPTER 6

Boston Triple-Decker

The Zone of Emergence

With the spread of the bungalow between 1900 and 1920, families went from living in small, dark homes that often lacked indoor plumbing to living in spacious dwellings with modern amenities. However, with these Progressive Era floor plans also came a new Progressive Era city. Low-slung bungalows sprawled outside of urban cores on 5,000-square-foot lots. Instead of a stoop spilling out onto the street, there was a porch buffered by a front yard, paired with an even larger yard in the back. Instead of apartments or row homes, housing in the US ultimately came to be deeply associated with this model of low-density, detached, single-family houses. However, the new spacious and amenity-filled homes were not just limited to the bungalow.

In the nineteenth century, Boston was one of the most congested and overcrowded cities on earth, and its old colonial core rivaled Lower Manhattan in population density. Yet by the 1920s, a very different type of neighborhood had emerged in the streetcar suburbs outside the confines of the old city. Instead of brick tenements, these areas were filled with wood structures buffered by landscaping. These buildings were not single-family homes but three separate apartments stacked on top of each other on a narrow lot. Typically clad in wood siding, with protruding porches and bay windows, Boston's ubiquitous triple-deckers incorporated elements associated with the bungalow into a multiunit structure. They were not only a dramatic step up from the living conditions in tenements and other working-class urban housing of the time; they also provided hundreds of thousands of immigrants with access to homeownership and therefore a leg up into the middle class.

The triple-decker was just one of many multifamily housing types to flourish in the early twentieth century, all with modern floor plans and ample air and light. Yet rather than seeing these buildings as a tremendous innovation in urban housing, much of the public instead viewed their stealth density as a threat to both the physical and social character of their neighborhoods. Almost as soon as these new forms of urban multifamily housing emerged, the vitriol that had greeted the tenement was directed toward them. This puritanical distrust of urban housing, combined with a new wave of anti-immigrant bias, resulted in policies that effectively banned triple-deckers and many other urban housing types across the nation.

ııııııııııııııııııı

For its first two centuries of existence, Boston essentially functioned as a medieval English village transported to North America. In 1630, a group of English Calvinists known as the Puritans founded the city on the Shawmut Peninsula. This hilly spit of land sticking out into what is now Boston Harbor was so tenuous that high tides submerged the narrow neck connecting it to the mainland, turning it into an island. However, the city's layout did not reflect these geographic constraints—or any overriding urban principles at all—but rather religious ones. Homes were arranged in concentric circles around a central meetinghouse used for public assemblies, schools, and religious services, with no resident being permitted to live more than one and a half mile away to ensure regular attendance.[1] As Boston grew over time, these idiosyncratic origins resulted in a street pattern resembling a tangled web, leading to a popular urban legend that they are based on old cow paths.[2]

Perhaps due to these conservative religious roots, Boston stubbornly clung to a village aesthetic in the eighteenth century while other US cities demonstrated a reflexive ambition to become a great metropolis. Whereas brick dominated in the large Northeast cities south of the Connecticut River, wood remained a popular building material in New England.[3] This meant that instead of adopting the more modern neoclassical architecture coming out of Europe, Boston relied on vernacular rural housing types well into the eighteenth century. The Paul Revere House, in the city's North End, with its leaded-glass windows, steep pitched roof, and second floor suspended over the sidewalk, is the last remnant of this era still standing in central Boston.

As Philadelphia and New York filled with Federalist row houses along gridded streets, Boston was defined by wooden houses set back into gardens. An account of the city from the end of the eighteenth century described it as having an "advantage above most of the large towns on the continent with respect to garden spots. Few houses are without them, in which vegetables and flowers are raised, in some fruit trees are planted; and what is still more intrinsically good and valuable, the inhabitant is supplied with pure wholesome water from a well in his own yard."[4]

In 1793, Charles Bulfinch—one of the most distinguished architects in the country and builder of many Boston landmarks, including the Massachusetts State House and Faneuil Hall—attempted to bring denser and more urbane forms of housing to the city. Like the grand terrace houses of England, his ambitious project, named Tontine Crescent, consisted of sixteen row houses curved around one side of a park. The exteriors of the rows were integrated into a unified scheme with larger homes flanking the row on each side, bedecked with columns. Tontine Crescent was not only more monumental than anything proposed by Robert Mills, who Bulfinch mentored, it also predated Mills's row house developments in Philadelphia by nearly two decades.

One would think that Tontine Crescent would have set the fashion in Boston for years to come. However, the row houses failed to sell, and so the second phase of the development on the opposite side of the park was changed to large, partially detached homes, which were much more popular.[5] The spectacular failure of Tontine Crescent's row homes bankrupted Bulfinch and became a cautionary tale to other developers. Soon after, Mount Vernon Street in Boston's prestigious Beacon Hill neighborhood was subdivided into lots as wide as 200 feet, intended for freestanding mansions.

IIIIIIIIIIIIIIIIIII

By the mid-nineteenth century, what had been a colonial hamlet of wooden buildings, packs of wild boars, and filthy people in tricorn hats trudging through mud-clogged streets was utterly transformed by industrialization and an explosion in population. Between 1830 and 1870, Boston's population quadrupled as immigrants from Europe streamed into the city to work at the shipping yards, in boat building, and in textile factories arising as part of the Industrial Revolution. Old colonial homes, mansions such as the Paul Revere House, and warehouses were subdivided into apartments. Along Broad Street, which today is on the edge of the Financial District, up to thirty-seven people crammed into small two- and three-story houses.[6] Central Boston's twisted and tortuous streets contributed to the area becoming one of the most congested places on Earth by the late nineteenth century. The old urban fabric of colonial Boston was bursting at the seams, and its profligate use of land on a waterlogged peninsula became untenable.

With open lots becoming increasingly scarce, even the city's elite succumbed to more urban types of housing. The gardens and open spaces between the stately, detached houses on Beacon Hill were filled in with additional structures, a change lamented by most of the Boston establishment. An aged Charles Bulfinch, perhaps still feeling bitter about Tontine Crescent, decried that the noble mansions, "trees and all, are swept away" for cramped housing.[7] The writer Ralph Waldo Emerson recalled his childhood playing in large gardens in what is today downtown Boston and taking his mother's cow to pasture along Beacon Street. As he watched the idyllic Boston of his youth get paved over, he moved to rural Concord in 1834 and became famous for his screeds against cities.[8]

Faced with this crowded and dirty environment, many wealthy Boston families—some of whom traced their lineage back to the original Puritan settlers—decided to flee their traditional enclaves in the West End and atop Beacon Hill in favor of rural retreats west of the city. This was made possible by the opening of the Boston and Worcester Railroad in 1834, which ran to the nearby town of Newton in just thirty-nine minutes.[9] These families had coalesced into a ruling elite dubbed the Boston Brahmin, and their departure forced city leaders to pursue a more orderly approach for expanding the city.

Between 1804 and 1900, the land reclamation Boston undertook more than doubled the size of the city, from 783 acres to nearly 2,000. This greatly expanded the neck connecting the Shawmut Peninsula to the mainland and dramatically changed the city's shape, reducing the vast harbor around it to the width of a narrow river.[10] On top of the swamps that had formerly delineated the narrow neck, two showpiece neighborhoods were created to entice the Brahmin to stay in the city. The first, the South End, was filled with three- and four-story brick row homes starting in 1849. These structures are spartanly ornamented and are marked by their distinctive, bow-fronted bay windows. While these structures are relatively plain, they retreat in many places to create lush public spaces. Brick row homes swoop around the curving perimeter of Chester Square like an American version of the Royal Crescent in Bath. In smaller and more intimate spaces like Harriet Tubman Square and Childe Hassam Park, people relax on benches amidst the lush landscaping. Many of the South End parks are so well cared for that they feel more like the backyard of a fastidious master gardener than a public space.

Yet the South End was just a warm-up act for the neighborhood that would be built directly north of the neck in 1859: Back Bay. Unlike the radial streets of the South End, Back Bay is laid out in a regular grid with the main thoroughfare, Commonwealth Avenue, running through the middle. Nearly half of the land was set aside for parks and open space, and the state-appointed commissioners enacted restrictions on the height and design of buildings.[11] Whereas the South End was developed with speculative row houses, the lots of Back Bay were sold directly to end buyers at auction; many were developed individually as large mansions clad in brownstone, brick, and granite to house the city's wealthiest residents.[12]

Both the South End and Back Bay were created with a level of detail and planning that had yet to be seen in any other American city—these neighborhoods achieve a cohesion between buildings, parks, and streets that is still unmatched by any other neighborhood in the country. Commonwealth Avenue—lined by grand row houses and divided by a tree-lined central median studded with monuments—has an imperial grandeur reminiscent of a European capital. One would imagine that the beauty and elegance of these two neighborhoods would have become a template for the future growth of Boston.

However, this would not be the case. The city's residents had given up their gardens and wood houses reluctantly. Their burning desire for these traditional forms was never truly extinguished, but merely lay dormant for several generations. The technological advances of the turn of the twentieth century would finally allow them to regain this ideal. The neighborhoods that would develop along streetcar lines in the latter half of the nineteenth century would be a distinctly new type of urban environment.

|||||||||||||||||||||

By the late nineteenth century, the Shawmut Peninsula had morphed from a rural village into a congested city center that four hundred thousand people commuted into every workday. Along the jam-packed streets, pedestrians and carriages competed with eight thousand trolleys. These privately owned, horse-drawn omnibuses were hailed like a cab, and each had entirely different routes, fares structures, and operating hours. In 1887, the twenty different streetcar operators serving Boston were consolidated into the West End Street Railway, which became the largest unified streetcar system in the world. They adopted innovations now essential to modern mass transit systems, such as standardized fares and color-coded routes. The company was also one of the first to power their streetcars with electricity from overhead wires instead of horses, creating a much faster and smoother ride. The West End Street Railway even played a major role in creating the first subway in the US in 1897, allowing trolleys to bypass the congested streets above via a mile-and-a-half-long tunnel under Boston Common.[13]

Suddenly the twisted, tortured streets of the central city were seamlessly and efficiently connected to the surrounding region. After leaving the central business district, the streetcars fanned out on Washington Street, Dudley Street, Blue Hill Avenue, and other main roads leading to the then-rural hamlets of Dorchester, Roxbury, and Brookline. As riders left the smoke and congestion of Boston and entered the parks, amusement parks, and other attractions strategically placed at the end of the lines, they would notice signs advertising new homes poking out of empty fields. A country estate was now not just for the leisure class. The streetcar allowed a clerk or skilled craftsperson to live in a bucolic environment while still being within commuting distance of their workplace.

Since the 1830s, streetcars had existed in many American cities in the form of horse-pulled omnibuses. These slow, plodding services merely extended the existing pattern of the city they served. In Philadelphia, as Penn's grid was expanded, developers replicated the patterns of the old walking city in the new areas developing on the fringe. The blocks were divided into the same narrow lots, with large row houses on the main streets and narrower ones on alleys and side streets. In New York, the rigid grid created by the Commissioners' Plan was first developed with row houses, later replaced by tenements and towering apartment buildings. However, the much faster and smoother electric streetcars introduced in the 1890s—combined with other new transit services like interurban railways, elevated trains, and subways—greatly expanded how far a person could comfortably travel in an American city. This, along with the advent of the bungalow and the Progressive Era floor plan, resulted in a renaissance in urban housing. In early twentieth century New York, modern apartments were built along subway lines in Brooklyn, Queens, and the Bronx. In Chicago, three- and four-flats and large courtyard apartments replaced flimsy wood workers cottages. On the outskirts of Philadelphia and Baltimore, large day lighter row houses with porches and front lawns filled the countryside.

However, in no American city is the difference between pre- and post-electric streetcar neighborhoods so distinct as in Boston. The city did not simply create new housing types but developed entirely new neighborhoods as well. Part of this was due to the city not mandating a unified grid or exercising power over the layout of new streets early in its history as was done in New York and Philadelphia. Even Boston's two paradigms of urban design, Back Bay and the South End, have vastly different street arrangements that are largely disconnected from one another and awkwardly collide around Boylston Street. The lack of a single grid meant that new neighborhoods would not be prescribed to pre-plotted blocks and lots.[14]

In a process described by Sam Bass Warner Jr. in his seminal book *Streetcar Suburbs*, rail lines and utilities were built through fields and forests along existing country roads. Developers would purchase long, narrow tracts of land stemming off streetcar routes, ranging in size from eight to forty acres. They would then subdivide them with their own street network. The result is that in the outer neighborhoods of Boston, streets weave in and out of each other for no apparent reason and are sporadically connected by short bits of road, some of which terminate in a dead end (see image 19). A popular internet meme contrasts a map of the rigid grid of New York with the confused mess of streets in the former streetcar suburb and current Boston neighborhood of Roxbury. Written on the New York map is, "Because we want you to know where you are and where you are going." The map of Boston says, "Because fuck you."

After the Civil War, horse-drawn streetcar service was still skeletal, slow, and expensive, and the initial wave of suburbanization was largely reserved for the wealthy. The long commutes to and from the central city were only practical for business owners and other well-off families who had control over their daily schedules. For these families, builders essentially recreated the lost houses of the Shawmut Peninsula in the new suburbs: large wood-sided, gable-roofed homes with porches wrapping around the exterior. Yet this country mansion aesthetic was a deliberate illusion. These suburban houses were not single-family homes but duplexes composed of two apartments stacked on top of each other. Great pains were taken to conceal this fact. Each unit had a separate entrance and entirely different circulation systems of staircases (see image 20). Inside, each was appointed with all the amenities necessary for an upper-class Boston family of the time. Instead of the grid-like layout of row homes, they had sprawling Victorian floor plans. Radiating off a central reception hall were multiple rooms for entertaining, including a parlor and a dining room, all adorned with carefully crafted fixtures carved from wood and marble.[15]

The biggest advantage of these suburban structures—which became known as townhomes, connoting their large size but urban characteristics—was the light. Whereas row houses, due to their long and narrow lots, were 25 feet at their widest—and as small as 13 feet for tiny alley trinities—the townhomes were on lots 40 to 50 feet wide. This meant they did not have party walls like row houses, and windows could be placed on all four sides, bathing each unit in light.

The spacious, light-filled homes of the streetcar suburbs led to the row house falling out of fashion in Boston. In Back Bay, large apartment buildings whose units, like those in the streetcar suburbs, offered more dynamic layouts with light on all four sides became preferred over single-family row homes. By 1884, the city had over two thousand elevators in a variety of buildings.[16] This "flat fever" corresponded with a rapid decline of the South End and its narrow brick row homes. The abrupt change in the neighborhood is encapsulated by the story of a wealthy merchant who, after seeing a man in shirtsleeves lounging on a neighboring stoop, exclaimed,

"Thunderation!" and hired movers the very next day.[17] The South End was soon a teeming immigrant slum, with its once-stately row houses divided into tenements.

IIIIIIIIIIIIIIIIIIIII

Due to the robust expansion of Boston's transit system, by the turn of the twentieth century the streetcar went from serving the affluent to all classes of the city. Track mileage increased from 260 miles in 1891 to 408 in 1901, and ridership increased by more than one hundred million passengers a year. This enhanced mobility allowed even working-class residents to leave the slums of the central city and move to the suburbs, with the average length of a commute increasing from 7.5 miles in 1891 to 11.23 miles twenty years later.[18] Crosstown lines in particular allowed lower-class laborers to get to various worksites across the region, as opposed to having to go into the central city and then transfer.[19]

Developers who had bought parcels after the Civil War had originally divided their lots to be as wide as 90 feet, anticipating wealthy residents seeking large single-family houses.[20] Sensing an opportunity to cater to a new demographic, these developers now subdivided the large lots into narrower plots ranging from 40 feet to 27 feet wide on which to build smaller and less expensive housing (see image 19). To make these smaller lots economically viable, the townhouse form was compressed to fit the long, narrow lots, and an extra floor was added to accommodate a third unit, turning the building from a duplex into a triplex. Instead of each unit having entirely separate entrances and staircases, one was built to serve all three units (see image 20).

While this building type was much denser and more modest than a townhome, its structure retained some of the building's architectural features. Set back from the street with landscaped yards along the front, side, and back, it rose three stories from a rough stone foundation made from granite quarried in nearby Quincy. Due to their distance from the inner core of the city, instead of being clad in the brick mandated by the central city's fire zone, they were clad in a tongue-and-groove wood sheathing. Like the townhomes and large Victorian houses, the exterior featured a bay window and large 12-foot-wide porch with the supports turned into a decorative feature, such as neoclassical columns.

The overall visual effect of these new buildings was slightly disconcerting. While the townhouses gave the impression of an elegant single-family house, the bizarre dimensions of these tall, narrow structures made them a conspicuous new presence. On some blocks they were packed cheek by jowl, with only a few feet separating each. They were dubbed *three-deckers* or *triple-deckers*, after an enormous multitiered British warship that itself was nicknamed "the sovereign of the seas."[21] In a 1961 article, the MIT professor Lloyd Rodwin said that few other urban housing types "flaunted their sheer ugliness more brazenly."[22]

However, the triple-decker retained the townhouse's most important feature: providing light on all four sides, with each unit occupying an entire floor. This made the structure one of the first types of mass-built, multiunit housing for the working classes that demonstrated the Progressive Era floor plan. The interior units are typically 1,500 square feet, with an elegant sitting area in the bay window, a dining room, and up to three bedrooms (see image 20). As if to confirm their superiority over the row house, the main room in many triple-deckers was larger than first floor of some narrow South End row houses. Many units also had better light, air circulation, and green space than the upper-class houses of Back Bay.

The large front decks, one for each apartment, were sometimes referred to as piazzas and acted as formal outdoor rooms where the residents could sit on warm summer nights in their Sunday best and observe the goings-on in the neighborhood. A back porch served a more workaday function for doing the wash and drying clothes and was usually made from plain unvarnished wood. There was also a back entrance leading to a common hallway that then branched off into entrances into each unit's kitchen.

The spacious, light-filled units made the triple-decker some of the highest quality working-class housing in late-nineteenth-century America—especially when compared with the center city of Boston, which was becoming denser by the day. Once-grand row houses in the South End and Beacon Hill were turned into boarding houses, and New York–style tenements started to replace old colonial buildings. As late as 1929, only half of all dwellings in the North End had a toilet. This area, which had sprouted around the colonial remnant of the Paul Revere House, had a population density of 799 people per acre, rivaling the densest parts of Manhattan at the time.[23]

Between 1870 and 1920, sixteen thousand triple-deckers were constructed in Boston and across New England. As in Philadelphia and New York, this work was not done by large entities but by nearly nine thousand small builders who would construct one to two houses at a time. Each builder specialized in a specific design and floor plan that they would replicate again and again. These designs were passed down and shared among builders and were heavily influenced by existing buildings, such as the townhouses of rural New England, from where many of the builders hailed.[24]

The lack of a rigid city grid, as well as the broader lots, resulted in triple-deckers demonstrating a diversity that rivaled the row house—which can still be seen in Boston to this day. The Jones Hill section of Dorchester consists of handsome triple-deckers with neoclassical details and sweeping views of Boston Harbor. South Boston has many early versions of the buildings that lack ornamentation or porches and are often so close together that they appear to be row houses. Along commercial streets are mixed-use versions of the building with the bottom story of the bay windows having been converted into street-level retail spaces.

The triple-decker spread across New England, with unique variations found in mill towns and large cities like Worcester, Massachusetts; Woonsocket, Rhode Island; and Lewiston, Maine. Over 1,200 were built in the port town of New Bedford, Massachusetts. In Hartford, Connecticut, there is a unique type that combines two triple-deckers into one building, clad in brick. This creates a much more imposing version of the building, which is known locally as a Perfect Six.

The unique development pattern of the streetcar suburbs has given many of these residential neighborhoods a far different character than other large Northeastern cities. The winding tree-filled lanes in the city of Cambridge or in Boston's Jamaica Plain neighborhood could not be more different from the tightly packed brick-and-concrete blocks in Brooklyn or Philadelphia. Yet just as the suburban Boston townhouses have the external appearance of single-family houses but are actually duplexes, the suburban look of these triple-decker neighborhoods is also deceptive. The streetcar suburbs of Boston are some of the most walkable, densely populated, and transit accessible areas in the US. This is because these neighborhoods, even as they boasted more greenery and space than the urban core, still needed to be within walking distance of streetcar lines, businesses, and services. In order to maximize space for development, the townhouses and triple-deckers often take up the entirety of their lots, leaving only a setback of a few feet on each side. The greenery surrounding the structures is more of a buffer than a usable yard. Many neighborhoods where townhouses and triple-deckers dominate have a population density comparable to the row houses of Back Bay and the South End.

ııııııııııııııııııı

While much of Boston may have had a greener and more open atmosphere than New York, the two shared one key similarity: both were cities of renters. Even though the triple-deckers and townhouses looked like single family homes, they were still apartments, and the abundance of multiunit buildings meant that savings and loans never gained a foothold as they did in Philadelphia or Baltimore. In Massachusetts, such institutions were called cooperative banks and were promoted by legislation passed by Josiah Quincy in 1877. Quincy wanted the middle-class of Boston to be "a house owning people instead of a house renting people." Yet after a small surge in cooperative banks following this legislation, by 1890 only 2 percent of all families in Boston had used one.[25]

For most working- and lower-class Bostonians, the price of a single-family house was too high, even with the assistance of a lending society. Developers found that the demand was for two- and three-unit buildings. With stand-alone houses out of reach, many working-class Bostonians would scrape together a down payment for a triple-decker. The owner would then usually move into the second-story unit, considered the most pleasant because it did not get as hot as the first floor, which was next to the basement broiler, or as cold as the top floor, where heat escaped into the uninsulated attic. The other two units would be rented out to relatives, which would help subsidize the owner's mortgage payments. The new, expensive utilities of the Progressive Era plan were also made more affordable by splitting the cost among the units.[26]

Through this, the three-decker itself became what the savings and loan was in other cities: an engine of mobility that allowed immigrants to leave the crowded slums of central Boston and ascend to the middle class. A study of the city's streetcar suburbs done shortly before World War I estimated that up to 50 percent of the small dwellings and three-unit buildings in those areas were owned by immigrants. Sociologists at the time called the streetcar suburbs "zones of emergence" because they allowed immigrants to assimilate into American society. Through homeownership, residents became more engaged in the broader affairs of their communities, gaining an interest in "government, neighborhood, and the greater community situation."[27]

The structure of the triple-decker also ingrained itself into the life of the community. The front deck of each unit took on almost ceremonial quality and was used when esteemed guests arrived for dinner and for communions, holidays, weddings, and funerals. Young people would have dates there with older relatives sitting nearby in the front parlor, keeping a watchful eye. As the professor Kingston Heath described, the porch symbolized "private ownership, civility and taste"; it was a mark that the building was not a tenement but a socially acceptable structure.[28] This social aspect of the triple-decker also fostered tightly knit communities where neighbors knew and cared for one another. During the 1912 Bread and Roses Strike in Lawrence, Massachusetts, mill workers organized using existing networks of neighbors within the city's triple-decker apartment buildings.

Through this, the triple-decker has gained a kind of mystique as the incubator of New England's immigrant culture. Structures that once housed Irish, Jews, and Italians are now home to Vietnamese in Dorchester, Cape Verdeans in Roxbury, Puerto Ricans and Dominicans in Lawrence, and Somalis in Lewiston. It has also become synonymous with Boston's blue-collar identity and is often highlighted in the many films shot in the region. In *Good Will Hunting* (1997), Matt Damon, playing the titular genius janitor employed at the Massachusetts Institute of Technology, is shown poring over books in his nearly empty three-decker apartment, a bare light bulb illuminating the alcove of a bay window. His best friend, played by Ben Affleck, visits him via the back porch. In countless other films from *Mystic River* (2003) to *Spenser Confidential* (2020), the building serves as a visual shorthand for working-class authenticity.

||||||||||||||||||||

As Boston grew into an industrial metropolis in the nineteenth century, the Brahmin elite consolidated their position on Mount Vernon Street in Beacon Hill. The city below had changed dramatically around them.

The gardens of stately homes had been replaced by row houses, and the old colonial districts of the North and West Ends had been filled with towering five- and six-story brick tenements and boarding houses. These slum apartments were climbing up the northern slope of Beacon Hill like intruders scaling a castle wall.

The tenements and boarding houses signified a broader demographic change. By 1910, Boston was no longer a Puritan village but a melting pot, with 74 percent of the population composed of either immigrants or their children. Before 1882, 85 percent of immigrants coming into the US had been from Northern Europe. However, by the turn of the twentieth century, worsening poverty and anti-Semitic pogroms in Europe, along with increased ship travel, led a much more diverse array of people to seek refuge in America. The total number of immigrants also increased dramatically: Between 1900 and 1910, 7.6 million immigrants entered the country, compared to fewer than 4 million in the previous decade.

Since the mid-1800s, Boston had taken in large numbers of Irish who, by the turn of the twentieth century, had reshaped the city and ascended politically. While the Brahmins did not particularly care for them, they shared a history going back to the British Isles, as well as a language. In contrast, the Brahmins found the new wave of immigrants hailing from Southern and Eastern Europe utterly incomprehensible. In 1907, Henry Adams, the descendant of two presidents and Brahmin royalty, published his acclaimed autobiography. In it, he described a Jewish immigrant he had encountered on the streets of central Boston as "still reeking of the ghetto, snarling a weird Yiddish."[29]

As the writer Daniel Okrent describes in his book *The Guarded Gate*, by the turn of the twentieth century, the red-brick row houses of Mount Vernon Street had become the center of the nation's anti-immigrant movement. Joe Lee, one of Boston's most prominent citizens, founded an organization called the Immigration Restriction League. Meanwhile, Massachusetts senator and Brahmin Henry Cabot Lodge worked in Washington to establish regulations like required literacy tests aimed at barring immigrants from Southern and Eastern Europe.

The elite of America, many of whom had descended from the original colonists, saw the new immigrants from Southern and Eastern Europe as genetically inferior and a threat to the country's future. As Senator Lodge repeatedly said in the 1890s, "We must guard our civilization against an infusion which seems to threaten deterioration."[30] The fervor against immigrants was also undeniably linked to the conditions of the slums in which they lived, as well as to the proximity of the elite to these slums, especially in the large cities of the Northeast. Francis Amasa Walker, the first president of MIT, wrote an article in the *Yale Review* advocating for a large entry fee to be placed on immigrants, citing the photographs of Jacob Riis to say that they "lived like swine." The Immigration Restriction League argued over whether it would be wise to relocate immigrants to farms, with many countering that this would just create more room in the slums that would in turn attract more immigrants. Madison Grant, one of the founders of the Bronx Zoo, said that the swamps of Jewish Poland were being drained into the Lower East Side, which was also "a dumping ground of Italians."[31]

The type of dense housing found in the urban neighborhoods of large US cities—already considered anathema to the American way of life—became a proxy for immigrants. A 1917 article about the "three decker menace" in *Providence Magazine* said that "the recent immigrants from Southeastern Europe have not the home-owning instinct of the earlier races, although sometimes very keen to exploit the benefits of jerry building. Assuming, therefore, that vertical housing is with us for a longtime to come."[32] The Brahmins and other anti-immigration elites found surprising allies in Progressive reformers, who often came from the same Protestant background and shared similar prejudices. Reformer Lawrence Veiller, champion of New York State's 1901 Tenement House Act and secretary of the Tenement House Committee there, spent his later years advocating for the sterilization of disabled people.[33] Jacob Riis, when not describing slum conditions in his 1890 book *How the Other Half Lives*, shared his thoughts on the inhabitants of these buildings, describing the Jews as worshiping money, the Italians as childlike criminals, and the Chinese as godless.[34]

The triple-decker—set back from the street and often nestled in greenery with spacious, modern floor plans—was far from being a tenement. The widespread adoption of the building was even partially due to housing reform laws. A law passed in 1897 by the City of Boston, which required that all tenements be fully fireproof, was amended in 1900 to allow an exception for buildings of fewer than four stories in height, with two or fewer apartments above the second floor.[35] This provision essentially sanctioned the triple-decker, prompting developers to pivot to constructing the building type en masse in the streetcar suburbs: whereas in 1899, buildings with three units comprised only 12 percent of all new buildings built in the city, by 1915 almost half of all new buildings built in Boston were triple-deckers.[36]

This tenement law also shifted the demographics of many streetcar suburbs. By the early twentieth century, immigrants and African American migrants began to bypass crowded central districts like the North, West, and South Ends and moved directly to outer neighborhoods like Roxbury and Dorchester. As Jews, Italians, and African Americans moved into these formerly low-density areas—now made high-density by the triple-decker—these neighborhoods came to be regarded as extensions of central Boston slums. The new immigrants were poorer than the former residents of these neighborhoods, and many of the buildings in which they lived were owned or managed by absentee landlords who allowed them to fall into disrepair. In some cases units within the buildings were subdivided and the landscaping was paved over with concrete, where litter collected over time. However, for the most part, the triple-deckers remained a middle-class structure; whereas the rent for a unit in a central city tenement was between twelve to fourteen dollars a month in the 1920s, a unit in a triple-decker was between fourteen and thirty-five dollars a month.[37] In 1900, the average death rate in the triple-decker-filled streetcar suburb of Dorchester was one in seventy-two, compared to one in forty-eight for the entire city and one in thirty-nine in the North End.[38]

Yet to "native Americans," as longtime New Englanders referred to themselves, the triple-deckers and their foreign inhabitants were regarded as being little better than a tenement, and the structure was referred to as a "cracker box" and "Boston weed."[39] The Great Chelsea Fire of 1908 gave additional justification for banning the wooden building type: 350 acres burned in a dense city full of triple-deckers just north of Boston, leaving tens of thousands of people homeless. This tragedy, combined with a similar fire several years later in Salem, Massachusetts, caused the triple-decker to be regarded not only as an eyesore but also as physically dangerous. However, such beliefs overlooked the fact that the Chelsea fire was not started by a triple-decker resident overcooking their lasagna, but rather by a rag dump in a nearby industrial area. A contemporary report of the fire said the heat was so hot that "buildings made of solid granite crumbled."[40] If the triple-decker was a safety threat, then so too were the city hall, library, multiple churches, synagogues, and other structures that had also succumbed to the blaze.[41]

The Great Chelsea Fire unleashed a rash of increasingly draconian local laws aimed at curbing the triple-decker. Whereas the laws regulating the tenement in New York at the time were based in actual issues relating to health and safety, the laws aimed at triple-deckers were primarily an attempt to ban immigrants from living in certain neighborhoods. By 1912, urban reformers had succeeded in advancing the Tenement House Act for Towns through the Massachusetts State House. This law enabled municipalities to ban new wooden apartment buildings that allowed cooking above the second floor.[42] In the wealthy suburb of Brookline, where many Brahmins had summer homes, triple-deckers were banned on the grounds that they caused "juvenile delinquency," which at the time was a dog whistle for immigrants and people of color.[43]

Five years after the passage of the Tenement House Act for Towns, William C. Ewing, a Brahmin member of the Boston Planning Board as well as a member of the board of directors on the Boston Chamber of Commerce, wrote a letter to the nearby small city of Taunton, which was considering a similar measure. After describing the benefits of triple-deckers over brick apartments, attributable to their spacious light-filled units, Ewing declared that the structure was nevertheless deleterious because it was inhabited by renters. In a sentence that ties the knot between Brahmin eugenicists and housing reformers, he concluded by saying that "the ideal dwelling for the normal family is the detached single-family home."[44]

In 1927, the construction of new triple-deckers was effectively prohibited in Boston with the adoption of a new city zoning code.[45] New buildings were now required to have ample setbacks and to use expensive construction techniques. The accumulation of these regulations made the triple-decker impossible to build.[46] The Boston code was joined by similar laws passed around the country banning a range of urban housing, from the row house to other types of small apartment buildings.

By this point such bans were a mere formality. Three years prior to the passage of the new Boston building code, the anti-immigration measures of the federal Johnson-Reed Act had effectively cut off much of the new demand for such buildings. This act capped total immigration into the country at 155,000 per year and drastically limited immigration from all places other than Northern Europe. Italians were limited to 2,662 people per year, and the countries of what would later become the Soviet Bloc, including Russia and Poland, were limited to 7,346. Areas that had very little representation in the US in 1890, including Greece and all of Asia, were capped at 100 per year. Without the wave of immigrants to live in triple-deckers, there was no reason for developers to build them.[47]

IIIIIIIIIIIIIIIIIIII

A trip down Blue Hill Avenue through the southern Boston neighborhoods of Dorchester and Roxbury reveals an astounding variety of housing types. Triple-deckers, bow-fronted brick row houses, large apartment buildings with stores at the bottom, small pitched-roof houses that look like they could be from a New England fishing village, and townhouse duplexes all sit side by side. The mixture of housing found along Blue Hill Avenue and throughout Boston reflects the liberty that was granted to the city's early builders. Because they could arrange tracts how they saw fit, they were able to adapt their buildings to meet demographic trends and market conditions. Freed from the long skinny lots that had bedeviled developers in New York and Philadelphia, they used the extra space to create new configurations for urban housing that allowed for more greenery and open, light-filled apartments.

Today this sort of innovation in urban housing is rare. The xenophobic laws that banned buildings like the triple-decker in the 1920s have since been tightened with additional restrictions. Many areas where triple-deckers predominate, both in Boston and in outlying cities like Somerville, have been downzoned to only allow two units of housing. In most Boston neighborhoods, each apartment is required to provide at least one parking space, which is nearly impossible on a small urban lot.

However, the qualities that made the triple-decker livable and desirable one hundred years ago have endured to this day: their light-filled and spacious units, broad porches, and locations in quiet residential neighborhoods that are close to transit and amenities. The buildings along Blue Hill Avenue represent a type of housing that has become increasingly prized in planning and policy circles, dubbed *missing middle housing*. This term, coined by Berkeley architect Daniel Parolek in 2010, describes buildings that have the qualities of a single-family home in terms of scale and materials but that contain three to six housing units. Like the townhouses first built in Boston's streetcar suburbs, missing middle housing is designed to be unobtrusive and sometimes indistinguishable from a single-family house when seen from the street.

Today a new movement is underway to once again create missing middle housing types like the triple-decker. Planners and designers see this as a solution to the nation's housing crisis because these structures gently add density to single-family neighborhoods without disrupting their overall physical character. Since missing middle housing provides multiple units on the same size lot as a single-family home would, it is also inherently more affordable, and because they are often composed of rental units, they allow people who would not otherwise be able to purchase a home in a certain neighborhood to still live there.

A bird's-eye view of Boston shows the skyscrapers and huddled-together red-brick structures of the Shawmut Peninsula and surrounding districts. Yet a few miles away, this cluster dissipates into small wood buildings nestled in a sea of trees. Structures like the triple-decker are examples of how the streetcar of the late 1800s freed urban housing from tiny lots, dark and narrow row houses, and claustrophobic tenements. From the Cleveland Double and colonnade apartment buildings of Kansas City to the bungalow courts of the West Coast, countless options became available in terms of how to organize space. These structures blurred the lines between suburb and city, house and apartment, and owner and renter. Yet as the triple-decker shows, even these innovative multifamily buildings became tinged with anti-poor and anti-immigrant biases that no amount of space, amenities, or sunlight could surmount.

CHAPTER 7

Los Angeles Dingbat

The Dumb Box

In many ways, the 275 days of sunshine that beam down on Los Angeles each year are the city's equivalent of the cotton, steel, and other resources that propelled many other American cities into becoming juggernauts. From across the nation, millions flocked to the city precisely for its mild Mediterranean climate. Los Angeles became where people could escape their old lives and reinvent themselves. Architecture was a vital tool in this, with residential blocks showcasing a range of styles, each expressing the individuality of its inhabitants. Yet there was one constant running through almost all of the region's homes: an openness and an integration of air and light. Instead of imposing themselves, buildings sat low on the landscape and, as much as possible, emphasized outdoor space rather than take up their entire lots. Compared to the hulking cities of brick and steel in the East, Los Angeles was an anti-city, and this ideal increasingly came to be codified in local law. In 1904, a height limit of 150 feet was imposed on buildings to let light hit the sidewalks, and setbacks were placed on housing in order to nestle them in greenery.

Over the years these regulations grew more and more restrictive, and instead of buildings being expressions of their inhabitants, they became products of bureaucracy. Due to an enormous population spike in the 1950s and '60s, entire neighborhoods were converted from small bungalows to wood-frame apartment buildings slathered in a rough stucco finish that was bedazzled with cheap ornaments then suspended over parking spaces. Instead of open-plan homes with light-splashed patios, the city's building regulations resulted in popcorn-ceilinged, dormitory-like apartments whose views looked into an identical concrete box across the alley. The magic that had once defined the city's housing was gone, and what was left were simply dumb boxes, or dingbats.

The dingbat was evidence that Los Angeles, once a resort town for Midwestern transplants, had become one of the largest urban conglomerations on earth. Yet instead of embracing this reality, the city's policymakers in the 1970s and '80s doubled down on discouraging dense housing. Today, the city is one of the most expensive in the country, with its high housing costs forcing tens of thousands of people to live on the street. As this crisis forces the tide to turn back to allow denser housing, Los Angeles's innovative architectural culture is once again being unleashed. Designers across the city are reinventing the dingbat to embrace the city's sunny climate and foster community.

IIIIIIIIIIIIIIIIIIII

During the turn of the twentieth century, trains pulled boxcars across the frozen plains of the Midwest. However, the cars did not carry coal or grain but a portal to another world. Life on farms and in small towns was marked by drudgery and scarcity: water was pumped from cisterns and was so scant that people only bathed once a week, except during the hot sticky summers. After a pig was slaughtered, the odd parts of the animal were turned into sausage, and the feet were pickled to ensure there would be enough food.[1] But by stepping into one of these magical train cars, a weary Midwesterner entered a life-size depiction of the sunny West Coast: land of snowcapped mountains, foamy surf, and fertile soil. There, instead of growing withered rutabagas, one could have entire orchards of oranges, a delicacy so rare they were served at ostentatious feasts of robber barons and tucked into Christmas stockings. The exhibits inside these trains, as well as another called California on Wheels, were just one aspect of a national promotional campaign by the Los Angeles Chamber of Commerce that made the city the most publicized in the country.[2] It resulted in Los Angeles and the surrounding county growing from just over thirty thousand people in 1880 to over two million five decades later, eclipsing even the lightning city of Chicago.

By 1920, Los Angeles had become the nation's tenth largest city, yet it had just half the foreign-born population of New York or even San Francisco.[3] The city's growth was not powered by foreign immigrants like its peers back East, but by Midwesterners, with the Iowa Society being one of the city's most powerful social and political organizations during that era. Its annual picnics were attended by over one hundred thousand people, and to this day local place names like Los Feliz and San Pedro are pronounced by locals in a flat Midwestern accent.[4] In Los Angeles and across Southern California, neighborhoods and towns first developed as warm-weather versions of those in the Midwest. Syndicates purchased large tracts of land that would then be platted into grids, each block divided into 50-by-100-to-150-foot lots. A streetcar or railway station would anchor each community and would often be surrounded by a small commercial business district.

While an individual block or neighborhood may have resembled much of the rest of America, the sheer scale of the city and region was something entirely new. Ernest Burgess's famous 1925 land-use model, showing patterns of development outside Chicago, when applied to Los Angeles would not resemble concentric rings but a massive overlapping Venn diagram. Los Angeles would be the largest circle, but clustered around it would be the cities of Long Beach in the south and Pasadena in the north—each their own self-contained community with a downtown, industrial district, and residential areas—interspersed with many other dots of varying sizes scattered over a huge area.

These communities were all linked together by the world's largest rail network. Traditional streetcars radiated out from downtown Los Angeles, running down the middle of streets. These were complemented by a vastly larger network of interurban trains called the Pacific Electric. Known as the Red Cars, these trains mostly ran on their own right of way through towns and open fields, allowing the population to sprawl from Santa Monica on the Pacific to Redlands on the edge of the desert. Via the Red Cars, Los Angeles's municipal size ballooned from ninety-nine square miles in 1910 to 450 by 1930, making it the largest city in the world by area.[5] Yet conspicuously missing was the ring of dense tenements that circled older

American cities. At 2,800 people per square mile, Los Angeles was just one-tenth as dense as New York and one-sixth as dense as Chicago, Boston, or Philadelphia, with 94 percent of the population living in detached single-family homes in 1930.[6] Its neighborhoods were composed not of crowded apartments or row homes but of block upon block of bungalows where even a working man could have his own plot of land.

IIIIIIIIIIIIIIIIIIIII

But many of the transplants that were attracted to Los Angeles did not necessarily want to live in Dubuque with palm trees. They had come west to reinvent themselves and leave their old lives behind in their conservative hometowns. In the 1920s and '30s the city was filled with spiritual leaders like Aimee Semple McPherson espousing new religious ideas. Utopian settlements were established in places like the mountain community of Tujunga and the high desert of the Antelope Valley, and New Age health regimens were espoused, including veganism and sun baths. As described by the scholar Merry Ovnick in her book *Los Angeles: The End of the Rainbow*, architecture became a way for people to express their new identities and ideologies.[7] It was out of this milieu that the ideas of British intellectuals like John Ruskin and American housing reformers were distilled into a radical reinvention of the house in the form of the bungalow. Instead of two to three multipurpose rooms, the bungalow pioneered a new type of freestanding house with modern bathrooms and kitchens that sat on its own open lot. Yet the city's appetite for novelty meant that by the '20s even the once avant-garde Arts and Crafts style commonly used on many bungalows and first popularized in the Gamble House in nearby Pasadena had become passé. Los Angeles's residential side streets showcased a dizzying array of designs from different eras and cultures. Along Rowena Avenue in the Los Feliz neighborhood, a French country house sits next to a fairy-tale cottage complete with a fake thatched roof, both of which occupy the same block as half-timbered English homes and traditional craftsmen-style houses.

These fantastical homes were not made from traditional vernacular practices but were illusions created by stucco, a simple mixture of sand, cement, and water that dates back to the Romans. It was the same material used to create movie sets on the backlots of the large film studios that began to sprout across the city in the 1910s. When applied to a lattice, stucco could be manipulated to resemble anything from a wood beam to a decorative stone frame around an arched window. Stucco was particularly useful for mimicking the old adobe houses that had marked the region during its colonial period under Spanish and Mexican rule, from 1771 to 1847. Entire factories were established in the region, pumping out red roof tiles, ornamental iron window grilles, and gates, as well as Moorish and Andalusian floor tiles that would adorn stucco buildings painted in various shades of beige.

Yet to many visitors, the city's stucco homes were not pieces of charming self-expression but ersatz illusions that concealed a darker truth. The colonial-style homes were a deliberate whitewashing of the region's history, where Native people had been forcibly converted to Christianity in missions established by the Spanish colonists for this purpose. To the author Nathanael West, Los Angeles was seen not so much as a fantasy land but as a place where rubes were bamboozled by hucksters and mystics—or, as he described in his 1939 novel *The Day of the Locust*, a "dream dump."[8] One visiting critic remarked that the city's fantasy homes were merely "hen coops" that had "no proper insulation or interlining, lack foundation or basement and are just shelters for the night."[9]

||||||||||||||||||

By the 1920s, Los Angeles had transformed itself from a resort town to the main industrial center of the West Coast.[10] In the 1923 silent film *Safety Last!*, a bespectacled Harold Lloyd, in a suit and straw hat, dangles from the hands of clock. Surrounding him are the urban canyons of a large unidentified city, with teeming streets below. Many viewers might assume that the movie's location was the scenic backdrop of New York or Chicago. However, what is behind Lloyd is in fact footage of downtown Los Angeles, which stood starkly apart from the garden city that surrounded it. The compact area—filled with Art Deco department stores, office towers, and lavish theaters—accounted for 90 percent of the region's retail trade. Over a million people commuted there each day, and in 1924, the intersection of 7th and Broadway was said to be the busiest in the world.[11] Angelenos regarded the city's downtown as being every bit the equal of Manhattan or the Loop.[12]

Downtown Los Angeles's supremacy was premised on the same factors that had concentrated commerce into Chicago's Loop or Boston's downtown: mass transit. The Pacific Electric fed people into the area from across Southern California through several massive stations. However, most of the trains ran through the area directly on the streets, competing for space with cars, people, and other streetcars. Traffic was so bad that trains took as long to get through a handful of blocks downtown as to then reach their final destination in Santa Monica or North Hollywood. The Red Cars' sluggish pace and confusing web of lines made them a source of ire in the city. The *Los Angeles Times* summarized the Red Car experience in 1920 with a cartoon showing a train covered in signs for various destinations, including one that says, "We don't know where we're going but we're on our way," while a man trying to decipher it shakes his fist and yells, "Go to hell."[13]

The frustration with the city's mass transit made Angelenos very susceptible to the new automobiles hitting the market. By the 1920s, the car had gone from being a toy for rich tinkerers to being affordably produced in large factories. The sprawling Progressive-style cities of the West were almost perfectly adapted to these vehicles. Cars could be easily tucked in a shed behind a bungalow before being rolled out onto the newly paved streets. By the 1930s there were one hundred thousand cars in Portland, which had one of the highest car ownership rates in the country, and eight hundred thousand in Los Angeles County.[14]

Whereas the Red Car had centralized commuters into tight nucleuses around train stations, the car dispersed them. People no longer had to crowd into plodding trains but could go wherever they wanted whenever they wanted. Instead of clustering downtown, commerce oozed down the city's freshly paved boulevards. Retail strips had always been an important facet of Southern California neighborhoods. Syndicates would include a strip of one- and two-story brick and terra-cotta commercial buildings at the edge of a development to symbolize that it was an established community. As the car decentralized the region's development, these strips along busy streets went from simply containing neighborhood amenities such as markets and hardware stores to being regionally prominent destinations. Property values along corridors such as Western Avenue in South LA went up as much as 3,600 percent between 1917 and 1927.[15] In 1929, just six years after *Safety Last!* premiered, a new department store, Bullocks Wilshire, was built a daring three miles east of the downtown shopping district. This cathedral of commerce was an imposing mix of terra-cotta and green-tarnished copper, topped by a 241-foot spire that could be seen for blocks along Wilshire Boulevard. However, the true marvel of Bullocks Wilshire was behind the building: a three-hundred-space parking lot and porte cochere giving convenient access to cars.

The movement of department stores, large office buildings, and theaters out of the downtown and along major corridors resulted in the formation of new commercial centers. Today, the wide boulevards that bisect Southern California are the region's key organizing force. Boulevards like Sunset, Hollywood, Crenshaw, and Whittier have become synonymous with nationally significant cultural and political movements, from cruising and lowriders to the explosion of the counterculture in the 1960s. To a large extent it is the sixteen-mile, high-rise–lined corridor of Wilshire Boulevard, rather than downtown Los Angeles, that is the true center of the region, home to the Federal Building, the Los Angeles County Museum of Art, and the city's most elite shopping district. By the 1940s the region's boulevards, some of which stretch for as many as forty miles, defined Los Angeles as a new type of horizontal city.

|||||||||||||||||||

The Pacific Electric network had roughly sketched out what would become the Los Angeles metropolis, with Red Cars running deep into Orange County and far east to San Bernardino and Riverside. As the car liberated people from the trains, the city sprawled like never before. Open spaces between stations were filled, and houses even began to appear on the hillsides that were too steep for trains but were reachable by car. Yet even as the city sprawled, it also intensified. As commercial boulevards became some of the city's most valuable real estate, it no longer made sense to give the adjacent land over to just single-family homes. As early as 1928, multifamily apartment buildings, which had previously only constituted 8 percent of all new construction, now accounted for over half.[16] The city exploded with apartment complexes that demonstrated the same architectural diversity and creativity of its single-family homes. French chateaus built to house the newest studio starlets were set back against the Hollywood Hills. On side streets, apartment buildings resembling Egyptian temples and Danish villages were constructed.

As with its single-family homes, the Southern Californian apartments did not reproduce existing structures as much as they invented entirely new kinds of buildings. In 1909, on a rectangular lot off of Colorado Boulevard in Pasadena, an architect named Sylvanus Marston grouped eleven small bungalows around a central court.[17] They were built in an Arts and Crafts style and were separated from the street by a rustic stone wall. Their small size made them similar to the Victorian beach resorts in England; however, instead of being placed along a seaside cliff, Marston's development transferred this concept to a tight urban lot.

Apartments within Marston's bungalow court let in light on multiple sides and also offered open space in the form of a shared courtyard. Their low profile allowed them to easily be integrated into single-family neighborhoods. By developing a type of dense multifamily housing that still conformed to Los Angeles's identity as a low-slung city of open space and sunshine, Marston had unlocked a key strategy for the region's growth: blending in with the city's existing fabric became one of the primary goals of many multifamily buildings in Los Angeles. One of the most popular types of structure was the fourplex, which stacked two apartments on each of the building's two floors, fitting four units on a 5,000-square-foot lot originally meant for a single-family home. A large second-story verandah often shaded a small first-floor patio. Many of these buildings provided separate entrances for each unit and, from the outside, were visually indistinguishable from single-family homes.

Designs for these small buildings were reproduced in pattern books such as *Weston's Single and Double Bungalows*, which offered four-family flat plans for fifty dollars that included an "[i]n-a-door-bed in [the] dining room and a breakfast nook in the kitchen."[18] Although the designs of the four flats and bungalow courts were distinct from other multifamily buildings, they were developed in a very similar manner. A person who had accumulated some modest savings could receive a loan to build a multiunit structure; they would then live in one apartment and use the income from the others to pay off the loan.

|||||||||||||||||||||

One of the tens of thousands of people drawn to Southern California during the turn of the twentieth century was a young architect named Irving Gill. A Quaker who had grown up in Upstate New York, Gill had climbed to the upper echelons of his field working in Chicago for one of the great early skyscraper designers, Louis Sullivan. However, like so many Americans of the time, he chose to cast aside his life in the East and start a new one in the West. Gill, like his mentor Sullivan, aspired to push architecture past the gingerbread artifices and historicism of the Victorian era and instead create buildings that spoke to his own time. In one of his few pieces of writing from 1916, he said that in order to do great and lasting work, architects must "dare to be simple; must have the courage to fling aside every device that distracts the eye from structural beauty, must break through convention and get down to fundamental truths."[19] Although he was first drawn to Southern California because the climate promised to improve his ill health, he chose to stay in the region because its openness created the perfect laboratory to test out his ideas.

In 1919, Gill accepted a commission to build a bungalow court in Santa Monica that would provide cheap lodging for seasonal vacationers. This type of common, speculative housing was considered beneath someone with Gill's pedigree. Charles Greene of the firm Greene and Greene, who had designed the progenitor of the California bungalow, the Gamble House, had derided the courts proliferating across the region as having the "monotony and dreariness of a factory district."[20] However, while in Chicago, Gill had been exposed to Hull House and the work of Jane Addams and had come to see low-cost housing as a perfect medium to demonstrate his ideas and also elevate the working class. For his commission in Santa Monica, called Horatio West Court, he created a series of simple dwellings contained in white cubes, separated by small patios and archways made not from stucco but from concrete painted white (see image 22). The interiors were a public health official's dream, with flush doorframes and concrete floors rounded up at the walls so that dust would not collect.[21]

With its clean lines and geometric composition, Horatio West Court placed Gill on the vanguard of modernist architecture, a movement inspired by the new ways of building created by the Industrial Revolution. The center of modernism at the time was Vienna, where architects like Adolph Loos were erecting unadorned geometric boxes like the Steiner

House. Los Angeles, tucked half a world away, was an unlikely place for modernism to flourish—the city was regarded, even in its own country, as a garish place filled with poorly made and eccentric buildings. Yet the openness and appetite for unconventional structures that had brought Gill to Los Angeles also attracted other innovative designers.

By the 1920s, Frank Lloyd Wright had built several important homes in the city, made from precast concrete blocks and resembling Mayan temples. However, Wright's biggest legacy in the city was the bridge he provided between Vienna and Los Angeles. One of his apprentices was a young man named Rudolph Schindler who had studied under Loos. Schindler summoned his fellow Austrian Richard Neutra to Los Angeles and the two became the godfathers of modernism in the city. Neutra and Schindler are best known for their single-family homes, including Schindler's own house in West Hollywood, which combined concrete walls and glass and wood sliding doors that melted the separation between indoor and outdoor. However, these architects also advanced the city's tradition of innovative multifamily buildings. Works like the Bubeshko and the Sachs Apartments scaled up the city's hillsides like an Umbrian village, and each unit included a private entrance and outdoor space. By the 1930s, modern architecture had claimed its spot next to the Tudor, Norman, and colonial revival buildings that lined the residential streets of Los Angeles.

||||||||||||||||||||

Just off Sunset Boulevard, past the café tables of a Cuban coffee shop, sits Parkman Avenue. Along this tree-lined street, the startling diversity of early twentieth century Los Angeles housing is on full display. At 933 is a bungalow court capped by minarets and onion domes, all in brilliant white stucco, as if it had been airlifted from the coast of North Africa. Less flamboyant tile-roofed duplexes and small houses with chairs and kiddy pools in the front yards are interspersed with larger fourplexes and apartment buildings. Parkman Avenue demonstrates how the Progressive Era house—with its large windows, multiroom floor plans, and modern amenities—was not just limited to the bungalow but was also transferred to apartments. From the triple-deckers in Boston to the four-flats in Chicago to the bungalow courts in Los Angeles, these buildings were modern while still being rooted in regional architectural traditions. In Los Angeles, these types of structures can be found across the city but particularly in the older neighborhoods that were developed before World War II, like Silver Lake, where Parkman Avenue is located. When flying into LAX or seeing an aerial photo of the city, people often assume the low-slung buildings sprawled across the landscape are single-family homes, when in actuality many are small apartment buildings. These apartments have contributed to Los Angeles's transformation from one of the lowest-density major US cities in the early twentieth century to one of the most densely populated today.[22]

The nationwide wave of innovation in multifamily housing was partially influenced by the new building and planning regulations of the 1910s and '20s. This ranged from building codes banning darkened tenements in cities like New York and Chicago to zoning codes preventing tanneries from opening on the ground floor of an apartment building. Yet while there was broad agreement that the most egregious housing practices of the nineteenth century should be outlawed, property rights were still considered sacred. Early zoning codes in cities like Los Angeles and Portland still gave property owners broad liberty over what they could build on their land. In Los Angeles's 1926 zoning code, commercial uses and multifamily houses were allowed in the vast majority of the city, with only 10 percent of land zoned exclusively for single-family homes.[23]

However, to many Progressive reformers who had battled disease-ridden and dilapidated slum housing, and to people trying to control where low-income families and people of color could live, multifamily housing was still as noxious as a rendering plant. They felt that the unfettered ability to build apartments could turn even the nicest neighborhood into a teeming slum. Because of this view, the single-family home was lifted up as the only decent dwelling, and laws to protect them from encroachment were fiercely advocated. But to the general public at the time, these views were considered to be government overreach into the private lives of citizens. In Portland, the planning consultant Charles Cheney, who was hired to create the city's first zoning code, was condemned in the local paper as "a dapper and dandified little gentleman" who was robbing the middle class by preventing them from turning their land into apartments or stores.[24]

The open, light-filled Progressive Era apartment buildings that were being constructed across the country also obviated the need for these regulations in many places. In Los Angeles, the bungalow courts and small apartments were considered a source of pride. In 1915, city officials declared that "four-family flats, as constructed in Los Angeles, are especially desirable" and "there should be no restriction upon the continuance of such construction."[25]

Yet over time, the zoning code was gradually strengthened. In 1936, Los Angeles's original code, which had previously only had five broad categories, was further broken down into various residential zones such as low (allowing only single-family homes), medium (allowing small apartment buildings), and high (allowing larger apartment buildings). New requirements were also put in place mandating setbacks between the building and its property line to create yard space, and—in response to the rising rate of car ownership—at least one parking spot now had to be included in multifamily buildings. The cumulative effect of these regulations and similar ones across the country was that by the mid-twentieth century, the construction of new bungalow courts, fourplexes, and other types of small multifamily housing was effectively banned. In Worcester, Massachusetts, after World War II, the zoning code was revised to mandate that residential lots be at least 5,000 square feet. This rendered unusable the 3,500- and 4,000-square-foot lots that had been meant for the region's traditional three-decker apartment buildings, and for decades the city was plagued by vacant blighted lots where nothing could be built.[26] In 1962, Philadelphia introduced parking and other requirements that made trinities and other types of row houses "non-conforming" and therefore outlawed.[27] By the 1950s, the explosion of innovative multifamily housing across the country that had begun in the 1910s had been extinguished not in one fell swoop, but through many tiny cuts.

IIIIIIIIIIIIIIIIIIII

In 1923, the Swiss architect Le Corbusier wrote what would become a bible of modernism, *Towards a New Architecture*. The book laid out five points for how housing should be built, including elevating it on supports, or *pilotis*, to free the space underneath for other uses such as parking; covering it with a flat roof that could support outdoor space such as a garden; and incorporating horizontal ribbon windows. Le Corbusier's book illustrated a huge divergence from how housing had traditionally been built and also marked a shift in how architects viewed common workers' housing—it went from being derided as the realm of the untrained builder to a serious concern. Modernism became seen as a way to streamline housing production by making simple, affordable dwellings for the masses.

By the '60s, buildings very similar to what Le Corbusier described started to proliferate across Los Angeles. In areas like West LA and Hollywood, entire tracts of dilapidated bungalows were replaced by flat-roofed, stucco-slathered rectangles containing as many as twelve units, all suspended over several parking spots on impossibly narrow stilts. This apartment boom was incentivized by tax regulation that regarded rental housing as a business and permitted deductions for depreciation. The boom was further fueled by a broader generational change occurring in the 1960s: young people were delaying starting a family or purchasing a house and were instead choosing to rent close to their jobs. Near airplane plants, office buildings, and film studios, entire neighborhoods filled with small apartment buildings. To appeal to these young singles, the façades of these structures were adorned with starbursts, lamps, and other mid-century ornaments and were plastered with plywood signs displaying evocative names like Taj Mahal, The Tropics, Hi-Life, or simply The Pad.

The designers of these buildings were not disciples of Gill or Neutra but architects whose methods guaranteed a solid return to the doctors, lawyers, and small merchants who were investing in these projects. Their designs were not due to an adherence to modernism but to an increasingly stringent zoning code. The buildable area on a typical 50-by-150-foot lot had been further reduced by a mandatory 15-foot buffer from the sidewalk and a 5-foot side yard setback.[28] Within this diminished envelope, builders also had to accommodate at least one parking spot for every 1.25 units.[29] Constructing a bungalow court that looked like an Italian piazza or Moorish castle was no longer possible. Design became simply a geometry problem. In order to solve this equation, investors turned to people like the architect Jack Chernoff, who specialized in reverse engineering building regulations to create profitable apartment buildings. He told the *Los Angeles Times* in 1972, "We'll push the law to its ultimate. Sometimes the apartments aren't the keenest looking buildings, but they're the best money-makers." From his studio, filled with apprentices straight out of high school, Packin' Jack (as he was known) pumped out plans for over 1,300 apartment buildings between the mid-1950s and the early '70s.[30]

Architects like Gill, Schindler, and Neutra had taken great care to achieve the simplicity of their designs, and the interiors of their buildings were generous, light-filled, well-appointed living spaces. By contrast, the type of mid-century apartment taking over Los Angeles due to increased building regulations was simply an anonymous dormitory, or as Le Corbusier put it, "a machine for living." They had low ceilings, wall-to-wall carpet, and rough plastered walls reminiscent of the stucco on their exteriors. The living and dining rooms typical of a bungalow were combined into a single space, and the closet and bathroom were oriented so as to buffer one unit from the next.[31]

The outdoor space, which had always been a focal point of Los Angeles housing going back to the grass-and-willow-pole wickiups of the region's Native people, was reduced to an asphalt driveway and an elevated walkway that gave access to each unit. Fire codes prevented chairs or even small plants from being placed on the walkway, and because it passed directly by the living room windows of each unit, residents often kept their venetian blinds perpetually drawn, casting the interiors into darkness. A recent transplant to the city in the early 1970s said, "When I first got out here, I couldn't get over the kind of architecture and the type of apartments. There's just nothing homey or nice about them."[32] Befitting their status as a dumb box, these buildings became known as *dingbats*, a word meaning a stupid or eccentric person that was used by builders in the region to describe cheaply constructed housing. At a 1954 presentation on a new subdivision in Eastern Los Angeles County, a builder told the city council, "The term dingbat is not derogatory. . . . It merely means something thrown up quick and shoddily built."[33]

||||||||||||||||||||

Los Angeles in the early decades of the twentieth century had been sprawling and relatively low-density; however, because of its robust transit network, it was also pedestrian oriented. The city was laid out on a grid, with sidewalks and a network of pedestrian staircases linking the steep hillside areas. The quiet blocks of small apartments and single-family homes were contrasted by bustling main streets lined with two- and three-story commercial buildings chock-full of small restaurants, bookstores, movie theaters, and pharmacies, which could be found in almost every neighborhood in the region.

By the mid-twentieth century, the dingbat had fundamentally transformed many Los Angeles neighborhoods, as streets once lined with bungalows became enclaves of apartments. Yet perversely, even as the city became much denser, it also grew more automobile-oriented. Instead of small spaces in front of each building where neighbors could congregate and children could play, the dingbat had a driveway often double-parked with cars. Areas like Palms or West Los Angeles became auto-scapes, with cars in driveways, parked along the street, and tucked under buildings.

The cars rapidly started to infect the commercial boulevards. In the 1920s and '30s, parking had been considered unsightly.[34] The on-site parking lot at the Bullocks Wilshire department store had been a huge innovation in retail design, but the lot had been discreetly tucked behind the building, which was built right up to the sidewalk and greeted pedestrians with enormous display windows and a decorative frieze above the massive entrance. However, as the car took over the city in the 1960s and '70s, parking moved to the front, facing the street, as a new type of retail building called a strip mall devoured the city. The once-solid wall of one- and two-story retail buildings along the city's main boulevards became gap-toothed as strip malls replaced old commercial buildings. A visitor to LA in 1935 had complained that the streets were so crowded with pedestrians you could "hardly walk and it takes hours to get anywhere."[35] However, by the 1970s many of the city's main streets had become devoid of people, and the sidewalks served primarily as a skid-marked path for cars to drive over on their way to the parking lot.

Los Angeles had always been considered a La La Land of eccentric people and buildings. However, the dingbats and strip malls had shifted the city's built environment so far out of the American mainstream that it became a subject of curiosity for contemporary artists. Beginning in the 1960s, Ed Ruscha made a series of photo books cataloguing different aspects of the city's architecture, from apartments to parking lots, from swimming pools to entire streets like Sunset and Hollywood Boulevards. In the '80s and '90s, photographers such as Judy Fiskin and Catherine Opie made eerie black-and-white portraits of dingbats and strip malls.

These images depict the buildings as isolated objects removed from any context. They revel in their strangeness, are devoid of people, and have the static quality of insurance documentation. Someone from a previous century viewing these photos might have difficulty determining what these structures even are. Standard elements such as a front door or even windows are nonexistent, replaced by garages, a parking space, or blank walls covered in signage. In this artwork, Los Angeles is not so much a city but a lifeless stage set.

llllllllllllllllllll

By the 1970s, any ounce of glamour the dingbat once had was gone. Upwardly mobile workers had moved on from their dim, cramped spaces to newer, larger buildings with courtyards and swimming pools. The dingbat became a refuge for a more downtrodden inhabitant, providing cheap lodging for alcoholic writers and anti-social drifters. These tenants epitomized what had been the turn-of-the-century housing reformers' worst fears about transient apartment dwellers. As one dingbat resident told the *Los Angeles Times* in 1972 about these buildings,

> In other parts of the city if you don't have a 9 to 5 straight job, people start wondering about you "what's that cat doing? Why's he always hanging around during the daytime, don't he work?" Here you can do what you want. As long as you got the money for the rent, man, nobody cares who you are or what you do. I can dig it.[36]

However, these derelicts were increasingly outnumbered by a new group of people coming into the city. In 1965, President Lyndon Johnson signed the Immigration and Nationality Act, which repealed the eugenicist quotas on non–Northern European immigrants that had been put in place forty years earlier. Suddenly, entire continents became eligible to come to the United States, and the country experienced a wave of immigration not seen since the turn of the twentieth century. However, these arrivals did not flood into the old tenement districts of the East Coast but rather into the dingbats of Los Angeles. What in the 1950s had been the nation's whitest, most native-born, and Protestant large city became one of the most diverse the world had ever known.

In a 2019 piece for the *New Yorker*, the writer Héctor Tobar described his childhood in 1970s East Hollywood. This neighborhood, once filled with bungalows, had by his youth become subsumed by dingbats and small apartment buildings. Tobar, whose parents had come from Guatemala, played in the streets with the children of fellow immigrants from Czechoslovakia, the Philippines, Mexico, and Lebanon.[37] By the early '90's, Los Angeles had become the nation's new melting pot, accommodating 25 percent of all arrivals to the country, twice as many as New York City.[38]

As this transition occurred, the lifeless, flat buildings depicted in Ruscha's images became animated. The lollipop strip-mall signs hanging over the city's commercial boulevards became the weather vanes for a neighborhood's demographic change, with new restaurants selling pupusas, kabobs, and sisig opening next to the established tanning salons and donut shops. The catwalks of the dingbats became places where people leaned on the railings to chat with their neighbors, and during neighborhood potlucks driveways were temporarily blocked off and filled with tables and large, inflatable bounce houses.

। । । । । । । । । । । । । । । । ।

The profound change happening in Los Angeles left some longtime residents shell-shocked. The 1982 film *Blade Runner* opens with a panning shot of an orange-skied city of flame-belching towers. A title card introduces this hellscape as "Los Angeles November 2019." Familiar early-twentieth-century Los Angeles landmarks such as Union Station and Frank Lloyd Wright's Ennis House were subsumed into a dystopian nightmare. *Blade Runner* was a projection of many longtime Angelenos' fears: overdevelopment turning the suburban anti-city into a concrete jungle, a place so utterly inundated by foreigners that English was displaced by a pidgin of Japanese and Spanish.

By the time *Blade Runner* was released, Los Angeles had become one of the world's largest cities through a collusion of bankers, the real estate industry, and politicians that the author William Fulton calls the "growth machine."[39] A dispersed movement, largely made up of middle-class, white homeowners living in neighborhoods that were becoming denser and more racially mixed, assembled to challenge the power of this machine. Yet unlike in Portland, in Los Angeles residents did not coalesce around investing in mass transit and historic neighborhoods as an alternative to sprawl and urban renewal. Instead, they rallied around a draconian crackdown on any kind of development.

In 1986, voters approved a ballot measure cutting density along commercial boulevards in half and downzoning huge swaths of the city to only allow single-family homes. A year later, a slow growth activist from the bohemian coastal neighborhood of Venice, Ruth Galanter, was elected to the Los Angeles City Council, defeating the council's powerful president, Pat Russell. Even historic areas like Parkman Avenue, with its diversity of small apartment buildings, had the number of units allowed on a lot reduced by half or sometimes even fourfold.[40]

IIIIIIIIIIIIIIIIIII

The liberal zoning of 1970s Los Angeles had allowed apartments and dingbats to be built in large stretches of the city, creating the potential to house a population of ten million. Yet by limiting density, by 2010 the city had reduced housing capacity to just four million—close to the city's actual population at the time—and in over 70 percent of the city, only single-family homes could be built. Throughout the 1980s, LA's planning department had felt that the downzoning was reasonable and could still accommodate the nearly four hundred thousand residents they estimated would move to the city between 1970 and 2000.[41] However, the actual growth during this period ended up being more than double their estimate.

In the San Fernando Valley neighborhood of Pacoima, twenty miles from the downtown, ranch homes sit on large lots with the wilderness of the San Gabriel Mountains looming in the distance. In this neighborhood, some residents keep horses in their yards, and feed stores sit next to strip malls. Pacoima is seemingly the textbook definition of Southern California postwar suburbia. Enormous arterial streets cut through a sea of single-family homes, with commercial shopping centers confined to major intersections. Yet although this area is superficially suburban, a far different reality lies behind the front lawns and driveways.

Since 1950s and '60s, when the area's tract homes were first laid out, a clandestine group of contractors paid in cash have transformed the neighborhoods' small houses. Garages have been converted into apartments and cottages constructed over backyards. The main houses on these lots have been subdivided into separate apartments, with unit numbers tacked onto the doorways. These dwellings run the gamut from tiled-roofed casitas with gurgling fountains to barely insulated structures with an extension cord running into the main house for electricity. UCLA architecture professor Dana Cuff has found that in Pacoima, nearly 45 percent of lots have one or more houses on them, and this number climbs to as high as 60 percent in other parts of the city.[42] The conversion of these small single-family residences into multifamily housing has contributed to Los Angeles having the most overcrowded housing in the nation.[43]

While Pacoima has become denser and is now largely inhabited by working-class immigrants, the intransigent zoning code has locked in its suburban form. One of the neighborhood's large arterials, Glenoaks Boulevard, is lined not by storefronts but by single-family homes. However, small stands have been set up along the sidewalk where vendors grill tacos and sell chopped fruit with chili powder to people waiting for the bus or biking home from work. Trucks filled with produce and dry goods park along the curb, creating mobile convenience stores. In sum, a street zoned by the city only for houses has been transformed into a mixed-use shopping district by its residents. Such interventions found across Pacoima are indicative of how immigrants have transformed inherited structures with their own values, imbuing them with a unique sense of place. Urban planner James Rojas describes this sort of adaptation as *rasquache*, or DIY urbanism.[44]

However, much of this activity is illegal. Many of the vendors along Glenoaks are criminalized by public officials, and a large portion of the back houses are not up to code. For prior generations, these activities—from the pushcart sellers in Lower Manhattan to families in Chicago building additions onto their cottages—had been legal and gave immigrants a leg up into the middle class. However, with increased regulation, many of these pathways that had been available to earlier generations of Americans have been cut off.

|||||||||||||||||||||

In 1990, an architect named Tim Smith was sitting on a beach in Hawaii, reviewing the latest uniform building code. Buried in the minutia was a small but crucial amendment: wood-frame construction could now go as high as five stories over a concrete podium if the wood was treated for fire and if sprinklers were installed. This was a game changer—instead of using expensive materials such as concrete or steel, multifamily housing could now use much cheaper wood-frame construction. Smith decided to utilize this method on a housing project called Casa Heiwa he was designing in Los Angeles's Little Tokyo neighborhood. He was able to reduce the cost of the project by 40 percent and cram one hundred apartments onto the compact downtown site.[45] A new building type had been invented, one that now constitutes the vast majority of new housing in Los Angeles today and has also migrated across the country. These structures are known by the building code designation type five, or simply as *podium buildings*.

From Seattle to Minneapolis, old one-story streetcar business districts have been transformed by apartment buildings that place five to six stories of wood-frame construction over a concrete podium. Due to their conspicuous presence, they have become the most visible symbol of the movement back into urban cores and, accordingly, are highly controversial. Like their dingbat ancestors, podium buildings are seen as speculative structures meant to wring out as much profitable space as possible, but now on a much larger scale. Unlike their diminutive ancestors, these structures can hold as many as five hundred apartments.

Podium buildings are criticized for having shoddy construction and poor living environments. The wood-frame construction requires the flooring to be laid directly onto joists covered in gypsum board and plaster, which, combined with the sheer density of the buildings, causes sound and vibration to carry through each apartment. Each floor consists of a long hallway with units on either side, known as a double loaded corridor. This configuration results in long, rectangular apartments which, like the poorly ventilated tenements of the nineteenth century, have windows on only one side of the unit. Because of the lack of light, it often only makes sense to build studios or one-bedroom apartments.

Because every inch of the podium building has been engineered to garner as much profit as possible, the role of the architect is often reduced to simply finding ways to "break up the mass" of these large, slab-like structures. Like Victorian homes, the façades are layered with different colors and textures to make what is essentially a large shoe box appear more complex. However, instead of using the type of jigsawed wood and slate as in the late nineteenth century, they are covered in a concrete siding called Hardie board that can be made to look like anything, from wood to brick. The discordant mishmash of metal siding, stucco, glass, and varying types of Hardie board makes some of these buildings appear as though a construction yard threw up. But underneath the garish exteriors, they are simply anonymous rectangles that have no relationship to the culture or architectural tradition of their location. In many cases, podium buildings are simply copied and pasted across the country by large developers.

ıııııııııııııııııı

In 1914, architect Irving Gill started construction on the building that would be considered his masterpiece: the Dodge House, a sprawling sixteen-room home composed of interlocking white concrete cubes, located in a sparsely settled, unincorporated area of Los Angeles County. A few years later, Rudolph Schindler picked a half-acre plot two blocks up Kings Road on which to construct his own home. Today this area, now known as West Hollywood, is a startling example of how much Los Angeles has changed in the last century. The Dodge House was replaced in 1970 by a two-hundred-unit condominium complex. The Schindler House, once surrounded by open fields, is now disguised with tall bamboo and hemmed in by large four- and five-story apartment buildings. What once was a sprawling, semirural area of single-family homes now has a population density nearly twice that of Chicago.

Kings Road is representative of many dense Los Angeles neighborhoods composed of mid-century apartments. Heavily regulated by the zoning code, these buildings are a uniform mass of gray and beige stucco. However, next door to the Schindler House, a striking lime-green building provides relief from the monotony. Known as Habitat 825, this apartment building pulls itself back from the sidewalk to create a small landscaped public space complete with benches. It uses the same construction method typical of podium buildings, with wood frame over concrete, but instead of double-loaded corridors it is composed of two interlocking masses, with the front doors of the units framing an outdoor courtyard. Just as Schindler and Gill had tried to reinvent residential architecture in the early twentieth century, Habitat 825, designed in 2007 by the firm Lorcan O'Herlihy Architects (LOHA), is part of a movement of Los Angeles architects reinventing the podium building. These designers reject gloomy double loaded corridors to infuse outdoor public space in ways that are reminiscent of the bungalow court (see image 24).

One of the firms on the forefront of this movement is Michael Maltzan Architecture, whose work mines the history of Los Angeles housing. Their apartments are usually clad in white stucco, alluding not only to Irving Gill but also to the dingbat, which is furthered by portions of some of their structures being elevated on stilts. However, in Maltzan buildings like the Crest Apartments, built in 2016, the space underneath is used not for parking but rather becomes a green space for residents. Maltzan's most dramatic work is One Santa Fe in the Arts District near downtown Los Angeles. Longer than the Empire State building is tall, this mixed-use structure, when viewed from the east, is like a stucco city wall hemming in downtown Los Angeles. One Santa Fe is composed of several interwoven bars that form public spaces, including a piazza lined by stores. Nearly a quarter of the 438 residential units are covenanted affordable housing. The building is designed to anticipate the continued rapid growth of this formerly industrial area and makes room for a future connection to a new park planned along the Los Angeles River.

The work of Maltzan, LOHA, and other firms such as Brooks + Scarpa and Koning Eizenberg Architecture build on the lineage of housing in Los Angeles to envision a denser and more sustainable city. Many fuse the podium apartment with the bungalow court by lifting the courtyard above the first floor and surrounding it by several stories of apartments. Their buildings, instead of meeting the street with a driveway, embrace the public space of the sidewalk, bringing new life to Los Angeles boulevards. Across the city, strip malls and parking lots have been converted to new mixed-use housing, providing respites of shade, greenery, small cafés, grocery stores, and storefronts on once-desolate streets (see image 23). As Maltzan describes, these buildings are an attempt to "not meet the city at the scale of the city today" but to "project how the city might continue to emerge" as "Los Angeles gets denser."[46]

Yet the intentions of these architects are cold comfort to low-income residents who see their designer buildings as sleek Trojan horses carrying affluent new people to displace them out of their longtime homes. However, the true reality of gentrification in Los Angeles and many other cities is far more insidious. While new podium buildings are highly visible, the main cause of displacement is actually due to older, rent-controlled structures being bought by speculators. A few blocks from Parkman Avenue in Silver Lake, old dingbats have been gutted, their carpet replaced by engineered wood floors, dog runs are crammed into any residual open space, and rents are raised.

Faced with these alternatives, even grassroots activists are increasingly seeing podium buildings as a solution to the housing crisis. In 2016, a coalition of social and environmental justice organizations placed a measure on the ballot in Los Angeles that resulted in a new program called Transit Oriented Communities.[47] TOC, as it is known, subverts the city's regulations by giving developers relaxed parking requirements and allowing for increased density in exchange for providing covenanted affordable housing. Since its inception, this program has produced thirty-seven thousand units of new housing, eight thousand of which are deed-restricted affordable units.[48] Whereas affordable units directly subsidized by the city have an average cost of nearly $600,000, ones produced by TOC come at no cost to taxpayers.[49] Because the TOC units are integrated into market-rate buildings, they also tend to be built in wealthier areas of the city, giving low-income people access to neighborhoods they could not otherwise afford. This program shows how podium buildings, rather than being tools of displacement, can produce housing for all people.

|||||||||||||||||||

Just like the dingbat, the failings of most podium buildings are the result of explicit policy. Building codes in many cities essentially incentivize developers to build the largest, most expensive, and banal structures possible. Because multifamily housing is allowed in so little of the city, the few parcels that do permit it become extremely valuable. Largely antiquated fire requirements calling for two separate points of egress lead to double-loaded corridors and railroad-style apartment layouts. Parking requirements force developers to excavate deep into the ground to create garages, increasing the cost of construction by up to 25 percent.[50] Once built, the traffic in and out of these parking lots also undermines the pedestrian experience. On one busy street in downtown Los Angeles, crossing guards are required to stand near the entrance of a new podium building's garage to prevent pedestrians from being hit.

Because the few places zoned for multifamily housing often only exist on sites already developed with smaller apartment buildings, the zoning code also perversely pits new multifamily buildings against older ones. Even programs like Transit Oriented Communities do not apply to single-family areas—only to commercial and multifamily zones. Because of this, small four-to-ten-unit apartment buildings are being replaced by large twenty-to-fifty-unit apartment buildings, displacing low-income, rent-controlled tenants.

The twentieth century saw the birth of new types of multifamily housing that had all the amenities of a single-family home. However, with each passing decade, new regulations were added until most apartment buildings were reduced to bland, poorly lit, inhospitable stucco boxes adjoining parking spaces. Yet increasingly innovative architecture firms are finding ways to work around these restrictions to create buildings with air, light, and open space and which engage and activate the streets around them. Instead of incentivizing bad design, policies should be recrafted to encourage more livable apartments. This could ignite the experimentation and ingenuity for which American multifamily housing was once known.

CHAPTER 8

Vancouver Point Tower

Cult of the View

Until the late twentieth century, Vancouver, British Columbia, was a prototypical Progressive Era city. However, instead of being sprawled across a dusty plain, its leafy bungalow-filled neighborhoods jut out on a peninsula into the Strait of Georgia and are surrounded by craggy peaks protruding from fir-shrouded mountain ranges. The contrast between its quotidian built environment and its jaw-dropping natural setting has led critics to call it an "spectacular city in a spectacular location."[1]

Yet today, Vancouver's cityscape of slender crystalline towers is almost as impressive as the scenery that surrounds it. Clad almost entirely in glass, these residential structures, known as *point towers*, rise to a height of twenty-eight to thirty stories. Instead of creating the dark, hardscaped environment often associated with tall buildings, at street level they are surrounded by two- and three-story townhomes that allow air and light to penetrate the sidewalk, preserving views of the water and mountains. The harmonious relationship between these buildings and Vancouver's spectacular natural environment has made the city a model of how to create dense communities that do not diminish, but rather contribute to, the city's quality of life.

The point tower emerged out of large-scale redevelopments of the city's downtown waterfront and represents an approach to urban planning that concentrates density in strategic areas while leaving the bulk of the city's single-family neighborhoods untouched. The futuristic backdrop of the point towers—combined with the low crime rate, beautiful parks, and efficient transportation network—has made Vancouver one of the most desirable places to live on the planet.

Even as the city has created entirely new skylines composed of tall towers, Vancouver has also become one of the most unaffordable places on Earth. Instead of helping relieve the affordability crisis, the point tower has become a symbol of it: the condominiums within these sleek, glassy towers are essentially custom-made for wealthy buyers. The building is an example of the unintended consequences of urban revitalization efforts that focus on improving livability through splashy redevelopment projects while simultaneously still banning smaller, more affordable housing options. What good is there in creating utopia if no one can afford to live in it?

|||||||||||||||||||||

Whereas most cities celebrated for their thoughtful planning—such as Copenhagen, Paris, or even Montreal and Toronto—developed fine-grained neighborhoods of narrow streets, beautifully crafted buildings, and public spaces over hundreds of years, Vancouver is one of the youngest cities in North America. In 1901, it was nothing more than a remote western outpost with barely twenty-six thousand people. In the half century that followed, the city's physical development was that of a typical Progressive Era city, with streetcars crossing from the downtown over False Creek to service commercial main streets and single-family homes on the Burrard Peninsula. The residential stock was developed via the same processes as other West Coast cities, with land divided into large subdivisions and then developed with bungalows. Vancouver's neighborhoods at this time were described as places where "English style hedges surrounded California style bungalows."[2] By the 1950s, Vancouver resembled Sacramento or Omaha if either was placed in a landscape from *Lord of the Rings*.

It was not until the post–World War II era that Vancouver took a sharp turn from its North American peers. In the United States, this period was marked by large-scale urban renewal projects involving the wholesale destruction of entire neighborhoods. Virtually every city on the continent girdled their downtowns in massive freeways that not only blocked access to waterfronts and severed neighborhoods but also cannibalized surrounding land uses. Block upon block turned into wastelands of surface parking lots, drive-through businesses, and gas stations to service the immense amount of traffic being pumped into cities. One of the only exceptions to this North American death-by-freeway experiment is Vancouver.

When driving north on Highway 99, after crossing the Frasier River and entering Vancouver's city limits, the freeway dramatically transitions to an arterial street lined by single-family homes. Meanwhile, the great Trans-Canada Highway, which runs from the Pacific to the Atlantic and links virtually every major population center in the country, gets within four miles of downtown Vancouver before abruptly turning north and crossing the Burrard Inlet as if it had hit the border of a hostile territory. Vancouver is the only major city in North America to have virtually no freeways within its limits.

This unique quirk is related to the city's isolation, as well as residents' popular protests against freeways. But primarily it is due to Canada's urban policies in the years after World War II. While the US federal government forced freeways, sprawl, and urban renewal on its cities through programs like the Housing Act of 1949 and Federal-Aid Highway Act of 1956, in Canada, cities were largely left alone. Communities were not uprooted and displaced, and neighborhoods were not scarred by polluting, noisy, unsightly freeways to the degree that Americans were south of the border. Instead, postwar development was more contained to established urban centers. Whereas transit ridership plummeted in the US during this period as government policies prioritized auto infrastructure, in Canada it remained steady, and many Canadian cities made substantial investments in new rail lines and systems in the 1970s and '80s. The end result was that 40 percent of US central cities lost population in the 1970s while only 8 percent of Canadian ones did.[3] Canadian cities are essentially an alternate reality version of those in the US—one where, instead of being destroyed after World War II, they were allowed to grow naturally. Today Canadian cities like Calgary, with 1.5 million people in its metro region, have skylines and transit systems several times larger than US cities that have four times the population.

Many planning decisions in the US were motivated by anti-Black racism—which cast neighborhoods of color as disposable slums and led white people to flee to the suburbs. Canada's postwar urban policies can partially be attributed to the country's much more homogenous population during this period.[4] The one notable example of urban renewal in Vancouver occurred in the 1960s when fifty-three acres of Chinatown and the adjacent Strathcona neighborhood were demolished for redevelopment. This led to the displacement of 3,300 people—largely immigrant Chinese—as well as the destruction of the city's only Black community, Hogan's Alley.[5]

IIIIIIIIIIIIIIIIIIIII

A profound manifestation of the difference in postwar urban policy between Canada and the US is Vancouver's West End neighborhood. Sandwiched between downtown and the thousand-acre primordial outcropping of Stanley Park, this area was once an upper-class bastion of Victorian mansions. But like so many neighborhoods near central cores, by the 1940s it had become a refuge for elderly and low-income residents, with many of the large old homes converted into boarding houses. A poor and dilapidated neighborhood like the West End would have been first on the list to be obliterated in the postwar United States. An elevated freeway would have been shoved down its narrow tree-lined streets in order to allow commuters from the North Shore suburbs to access downtown. The remaining blocks might have been cleared of their old homes for modernist towers.*

Yet due to its location north of the forty-ninth parallel, the original fabric of the West End remained and the neighborhood was allowed to develop organically. White-collar workers, young bohemians, and LGBTQ residents, prizing its location close to downtown offices, started moving into the neighborhood in the 1950s. The area proved to be so popular that in 1956 it was rezoned from a building cap of six stories to allow for high-rises.[6] In little more than a decade, the population of the West End doubled, and this strip of land between English Bay and Vancouver

---

* A good contrast to the West End that demonstrates the difference between Canadian and American postwar planning is the South Auditorium Urban Renewal District in Portland. This area was located just south of downtown and had similar characteristics to the West End but was completely demolished and replaced with insular super-blocks and concrete towers. Instead of being integrated into the fabric of the city, today it is a sleepy isolated enclave in an otherwise vibrant downtown.

Harbor went vertical as twenty- and thirty-story towers rose up next to old, wood-sided, single-family homes.[7]

However, the high rise boom in the West End did not get off to an auspicious start. On Morton Avenue overlooking English Bay Beach sits a nineteen-story slab whose horizontal windows look like the vents of an air conditioner. Opened in 1959, Ocean Towers was the first new residential high-rise to take advantage of the rezoned West End. While the building is only 27 feet deep, its sixty-eight suites and penthouse apartments are strung along a double loaded corridor that spans the building's nearly block-long width. Instead of viewing the crystal blue waters, anyone who is unfortunate enough to live behind Ocean Towers has to face a massive beige wall. The city's planning director at the time, Gerald Sutton-Brown, called the rezoning that unleashed Ocean Towers "one of the Biggest mistakes in Vancouver History."[8]

In its flagrant disregard for the views of its neighbors, Ocean Towers had committed a mortal sin in Vancouver. While the slate gray skies and constant drizzle may not make it an ideal location for a Sandals Resort, when viewed by a frostbitten resident of Saskatoon or Waterloo the city is positively balmy. With its mild Pacific Northwest climate, Vancouver is the closest thing Canada has to a Miami or San Diego, and people flock there from across the country to indulge in its year-round outdoor lifestyle. A critical aspect of this is having views of the dramatic mountains, bays, and inlets that surround the city. Access to these vistas has become a driving force in the city's residential architecture, which the writer and architect Lance Berelowitz has described as the "cult of the view."[9]

Yet Ocean Towers did not result in a regressive backlash against high-density housing, and policymakers did not codify a quixotic garden city ideal into law. Instead, in 1962, the city passed one of the first in a series of revisions fine-tuning its provisions for high-rise buildings. Over the next decade and a half, over forty buildings that were nineteen stories or higher were built in the West End.[10] The form of these early towers is rooted in mid-century planning principles that sought to couch high-density living in verdant environments, a style inspired by the architect Le Corbusier dubbed "towers in the park." Instead of being pressed against the sidewalk, the buildings are set back and surrounded by landscaping and parking lots. As a result of a 1962 zoning revision, the allowed height of a building became a ratio of how much footprint it took up on the lot, which planners call floor area ratio, or FAR. This, combined with the fact that the buildings had to fit into the city's preexisting narrow 122-foot-deep blocks, resulted in towers in the West End being 20 percent narrower than most other high-rises on the continent. In response to the girth of Ocean Towers, the city created a new type of slender residential high-rise. The slimmer profile of these buildings makes them much less visually intrusive, preserving views and also allowing air and light to hit the street (see image 26). When seen from afar, the West End looks like a piece of a hyper-dense megacity like São Paulo has been picked up and dropped into a Pacific Northwest rainforest. At street level, however, the quiet greenery-filled streets, where residents tend to flower gardens in parkways, make the area feel like a neighborhood of single-family homes. The West End towers are the high-rise equivalent of the bungalow.

IIIIIIIIIIIIIIIIIIII

As opposed to the modern glass-sheathed towers that define Vancouver in the popular imagination, the plain, boxy buildings constructed in the West End in the 1960s and '70s bring to mind old seaside apartment blocks for high-level Soviet bureaucrats. Constructed from precast concrete, the rough exteriors are shades of gray and beige that look like they were purchased at a discount paint warehouse somewhere in the prairie provinces. The one distinguishing feature that adds any sort of visual interest and complexity to the buildings are the tiny balconies that jut out into the British Columbian mist. These platforms, which sometimes measure only a few square feet, are as much a symbol as they are an actual useable space. They act as reassurance that while you may live on the thirteenth floor of a building that looks like it belongs on the outskirts of Volgograd, it's still possible to step outside and, if you cock your head a certain way, watch the sun set over Grouse Mountain or spot an eagle mauling a coho in English Bay. The balconies and the slenderness of these early West End towers are a physical manifestation of the cult of the view, and they set a precedent for the design of high-rise buildings in Vancouver.

Urban housing has always included aspirational qualities, dating back to the decorative doorframes of colonial row homes. Yet these details often came a distant second to utilitarianism. The Boston triple-decker offered

spacious, light-filled apartments, but its design was mandated by the narrow dimensions of the lot and the need to cram as many units as possible
into a confined area. The slick signage of the Los Angeles dingbat was a
desperate way to convince ambitious migrants to Southern California that
these gloomy and shoddily built structures had a touch of Hollywood glamour. However, with Vancouver's West End high-rises, aspiration usurped
economics. With their narrowness, height, and balconies, they were not
just meant to house city residents but also to act as physical branding of
the Vancouver lifestyle. In an innuendo-laced description, the 1966 documentary *West End 66* called these structures a "magical habitat of a new
midcentury hybrid, the swinger. Behind curved and angled perimeters of
twentieth century gingerbread they live modern, with pool, party room,
patio and permissive management."[11]

।।।।।।।।।।।।।।।।।।।।।

In J. G. Ballard's 1975 novel *High-Rise*, the mechanical systems of a tower on
the outskirts of London break down, causing the building's two thousand
inhabitants to retreat into a primal state, with warring tribes and eventually
cannibalism. Ballard's novel depicted life suspended above the rest of the
city as severing any connection its residents had to the outside world—or
to reality itself. As new politicians were elected to office in the 1970s, this
fear of towers was echoed in Vancouver's urban policy. Instead of blunt
rezonings, city leaders desired more refined tools that would dictate not
just what could be built but also how it would look and relate to its surroundings. In 1977, the False Creek South redevelopment constructed in
Fairview, a residential neighborhood just south of downtown, was designed
to have "village like intimacy."[12] Nearly half of the site was left as green
space, and the three-story stucco townhomes are so timid that they recede
back from the narrow lanes that cut through the development.

However, in 1992 the opening of a new Vancouver complex called 888
Beach Avenue led to a new era of high-rises. This full-block development
occupies an oddly shaped site on the Downtown Peninsula between the
Granville Street and Burrard Street Bridges and was created almost by
accident. The site had been zoned for very high density to accommodate
what planners thought would be a hotel. However, the plans were changed
to a residential project, and the Vancouver architect James Cheng was hired

to design it.[13] With 888 Beach Avenue, Cheng took the basic features of the West End towers—the greenery, balconies, and slender width—and accentuated them (see image 25). Two residential high-rises with narrow floor plates were constructed on opposite corners of the block in order to make the complex look like multiple buildings, as opposed to one large mass. Rather than being the bland punch card boxes of the West End, the exteriors of the towers are floor-to-ceiling glass and are contoured like the bow of a ship, recessing as they get higher, with the northern tower taller than the southern one. This not only maximizes the views and privacy for residents but also gives the buildings a more elegant profile when viewed from the water. Cheng's buildings, instead of buffering themselves from the street like the West End towers, embrace the public realm. The base of 888 Beach is composed of townhouses that create a separation between the towers and allow light to enter the units and the surrounding streets. These townhomes also give the ground level of the building a human scale. With their stoops and bay windows looking onto the street, as well as their small landscaped entryways, the townhouses make pedestrians feel that they are in a neighborhood and not at the hard-edged base of a giant tombstone.

With 888 Beach Avenue, the buildings' aspirational qualities became the driving force of the design. Cheng said that his goal for the project was to create a "serene oasis in the city."[14] The lobbies have impressive double-height ceilings, and water and greenery are spread throughout the complex, including a lushly planted elevated open space between the two towers. Nearly the entire structure is designed to maximize the view from the interior. In most North American high-rises, building codes mandate that there be two separate stairwells for fire safety. This results in wide buildings, with the average high-rise in North America having around fourteen units per floor. However, 888 Beach Avenue is dramatically smaller than other North American high-rises, allowing for slender floor plates and creating much more livable interior spaces. The buildings' narrower profiles are achieved through an innovation called the scissor stair, which combines the two stairwells in a double helix formation with a fire wall separating them. As a result, the north tower of 888 Beach has only six units per floor and the south tower only has four. Instead of the narrow shotgun layout of units strung along double loaded corridors found in most large apartment buildings, the apartments inside 888 Beach have windows and even balconies on multiple sides, each angled to have a sweeping view of the surrounding landscape (see image 27).

ıııııııııııııııııı

With its townhome base, glass exterior, and slender floor plate, 888 Beach Avenue created the archetype for the modern point tower. The building was also completed just as the city was about to massively reinvent itself. In the 1970s, Vancouver was not yet a tourist destination or at the top of international livability rankings but rather a working port city, scoffed at by Torontonians as nothing more than a "loggers' long weekend."[15] The waterfront that encircled the Downtown Peninsula had long been composed of barrel works, chain makers, and lumber mills with beehive burners whose black smoke would hover over the polluted waters of False Creek.[16] After World War II, with the port facilities having moved to other parts of the region, much of the land sat fallow and abandoned.

But just as with the World Columbian Exposition in Portland, Vancouver's city leaders decided to host a World's Fair, called Expo 86, which would turn the city from an obscure outpost into an international showcase. This event was staged on the land next to the aging port and industrial facilities along False Creek, and during its summer-long run, twenty-two million people visited the Expo—nearly the population of Canada at the time.[17] However, the intended audience was not the little boy from Regina clutching cotton candy, but investors from across the globe. The geodesic dome, the floating McBarge selling Big Macs, and the fare mascot, Expo Ernie, were all just part of an elaborate real estate open house aimed at international developers.

By the 1990s, two new residential communities—False Creek, south of Downtown, and Coal Harbour, north of the West End—had transformed the Vancouver waterfront with tall glassy point towers. Both are massive, with more than ten thousand units of housing, enough to accommodate nearly 3 percent of the city's total population. The Downtown Peninsula, whose skyline was previously composed of some commercial office buildings and the boxy towers of the West End, was reimagined as a cluster of highrises that in the 1990s seemed to be directly transported from the future.

An intriguing sculpture stands on the Vancouver Harbor waterfront: it is a precariously leaning shack, cast entirely in aluminum, elevated by four plinths. Titled *LightShed*, by Vancouver artist Liz Magor, it is a cryptic memorial to the rough-and-tumble area of ship repair shops and floating shacks that once occupied Coal Harbour. It now stands defiantly amidst million-dollar yachts and a phalanx of glass buildings. Regulations guiding the redevelopment of both False Creek and Coal Harbour codified the 888 Beach Avenue design into law, capping the height of buildings at thirty-two stories and mandating an 80-foot separation between towers.

While Coal Harbour is more serene and contemplative, False Creek's location closer to Downtown makes it more of a bustling urban hub. Along the waterfront, the townhome podium has been elevated one story, with the ground floor of the building composed of shops and restaurants. One of the most unusual sights for visitors accustomed to the American approach to redeveloped urban neighborhoods is the presence of children. Wanting diversity, planners mandated that the redevelopment of False Creek and Coal Harbour designate 20 percent of homes as affordable and 25 percent for families. In Coal Harbour, the Vancouver Parks Department operates a community center with childcare and a gymnasium. A similar community space in False Creek features a nineteenth-century steam engine as well as toy train sets where neighborhood children fend off interloping tourists.

An aerial photo of the Downtown Peninsula during Expo 86 shows a cityscape pocked by surface parking lots not too dissimilar from other urban centers across North America. Since then, more than one hundred new residential high-rises have transformed Downtown Vancouver into a miniature Manhattan. Nearly every parking lot has been replaced by new development, and towers are now cantilevered over heritage buildings and shoehorned into leftover spaces next to sports arenas and bridge on-ramps. Big box stores such as Costco and Home Depot, rather than being surrounded by a sea of surface parking lots, are topped by dense housing. Yaletown, once an industrial district located directly north of False Creek, has since the 1990s been the site of so many new point towers that the few remaining warehouses are isolated to a single street and protected by a historic designation. It is now difficult to discern where False Creek or Coal Harbour ends and the rest of the city begins.

Yet the dominance of the point tower has given portions of central Vancouver a placeless quality. Instead of the idiosyncratic features that older cities develop over time, there is the bland anonymity of glass and concrete. On a typical overcast day, the blue and turquoise windows turn the same slate gray of the sky, and it's hard to distinguish one tower from the next. The townhome bases, protected by a rampart of box trees and foliage, become monotonous. Nearly all the point towers built in central Vancouver since the 1990s are condominiums, and HOA laws prevent someone from altering or even painting the façade, as would happen with a traditional row home. However, the lack of easily recognizable details does give the city one major advantage: Vancouver is the fifth most popular filming location in North America for movies, TV shows, and commercials. Throw up some signage, put some out-of-town newspaper boxes on the sidewalk, and interject a few digital enhancements, and the city is a decent stand-in for other places around the globe. Vancouver portrayed Pyongyang in *The Interview* from 2014, a film that sparked an international incident; San Francisco in the 1996 film *Homeward Bound II: Lost in San Francisco;* and, much less convincingly, the Bronx in the 1995 Jackie Chan vehicle *Rumble in the Bronx*. While Vancouver portrays other cities around the world, it almost never plays itself. However, it is possible that in the decades to come, as the point towers settle in, they will go from being a mere backdrop to a distinctive and cherished feature of the city. Many other examples of common urban housing—like the Boston triple-decker and the Philadelphia row house—were also called bland and monotonous when they were first built, but today they are celebrated and fiercely protected.

ııııııııııııııııııı

As arable land in the Frasier River Valley outside Vancouver began to be gobbled up for new housing development after World War II, policymakers set out to create a better strategy for handling the region's growth. In 1975, the metropolitan planning body, the Greater Vancouver Regional District, passed the Livable Regions Strategic Plan. The process of creating this document was contentious: environmentalists, who wanted to protect open space, squared off against landowners, who wanted to cash in. At the public workshops held to gather input on the plan, undercover cops were stationed to break up fistfights.[18]

However, this plan has been integral in shaping the region through achieving what the former Vancouver city council member and urban planning scholar Gordon Price calls "the grand bargain." This bargain left the vast majority of Vancouver's built fabric—the bungalows surrounded by gardens on gridded streets and the suburban split-level homes on cul-de-sacs—untouched. In exchange, eight regional town centers were designated in the Livable Regions Strategic Plan, which would tuck pockets of skyscraper amidst the sprawl and absorb new population growth.[19]

A critical tool for realizing these town centers was a new regional transit system known as SkyTrain, with the first line debuting during Expo 86. South of the border, rapid transit often has a distinctly second-rate quality. Many American cities have invested in light rail lines that seem to avoid every important destination and instead run through industrial districts every twenty minutes. Older cities grapple with legacy systems where rats carry pizza across the platforms and workers must scour *Antiques Roadshow* for replacement parts. Whereas transit stations in the US often use the design language of public restrooms, SkyTrain stations have the air of Scandinavian spas, with some being constructed from locally sourced fir planks. The trains are entirely separated from traffic, running on elevated structures or in underground tunnels. SkyTrain is also one of the first and longest fully automated transit systems on the continent—there are no drivers, making it possible for the trains to run at two-minute intervals. During weekdays it is possible to board a station escalator while a train is leaving and for another one to arrive as you reach the platform. By creating fast and convenient transit across the region, the SkyTrain allowed the point tower to migrate from the Downtown Peninsula to the suburban fringe. Today the town centers designated in the Livable Regions Strategic Plan form a constellation of skyscrapers across the metropolitan area, seamlessly linked by a network of SkyTrain lines.

In the years after World War II, returning veterans moved their families out of the urban core to suburbs like Burnaby, west of Downtown Vancouver. The town's quiet streets are lined by single-family homes, driveways, and well-groomed lawns. Yet as Burnaby was designated as one of Vancouver's eight regional town centers, one feature that sets it apart from other suburbs across North America is the wall of glass looming in the distance. As you cross Grange Street, you leave the suburban milieu behind for the Metrotown district, which is clustered around several Sky-Train stations. This area still retains a suburban street grid of large blocks and busy arterial streets, giving it a more haphazard quality than on the Downtown Peninsula. The point towers do not define nor dominate the environment, but rather sprout up next to strip malls and gas stations, as if a misguided contractor had accidentally built a thirty-story tower instead of a drive-through Arby's.

Yet the point towers that dot the landscape give this suburban neighborhood a vibrancy—and a skyline that rivals the downtowns of many other large cities in the US. The tallest skyscrapers in metro Vancouver are not in the Downtown Peninsula but clustered around SkyTrain stations in the western suburbs (see image 28). Vancouver's regional centers have become the poster child in urban planning circles for transit-oriented development, or TOD. The point tower has proved to be a powerful tool for shifting people from cars to more sustainable forms of transportation. More than 20 percent of residents in Burnaby use transit for daily commuting.[20] The main Metrotown SkyTrain station is one of the busiest in the entire system, with ridership numbers that rival and sometimes exceed the stations on the Downtown Peninsula.[21]

Vancouver's reputation as a center for sustainable urban development has made it a mecca for aspiring urban visionaries. Many Vancouver planners, architects, and developers have become consultants to cities across the globe, espousing the gospel of Vancouverism. Through this, balcony-bedecked point towers in their familiar blue hues have migrated not just across metropolitan Vancouver but also across the continent and the world. Dubai Marina is a petroleum-wealth-fueled homage to False Creek, where towers rise along a manmade river interwoven with a streetcar.[22] The factories of Brooklyn and Queens, when viewed from the East River, are being blotted out by mega-sized point towers as part of the city's rezoning of the waterfront. In downtown Los Angeles, surface parking has been filled with glass high-rises that overshadow sandy-hued Art Deco office buildings. A large percentage of them were developed by the Vancouver company Onni, which hired the Vancouver firm Chris Dikeakos Architects to design them, and they look indistinguishable from those in Metrotown.[23] Even Portland, Oregon—Vancouver's rival planning utopia—has tried to emulate False Creek and Coal Harbour in its redevelopment of the South Waterfront district.[24] In the future, all cities could look like Vancouver.

IIIIIIIIIIIIIIIIIII

Vancouver's remarkable urban achievement is not just its beautiful neighborhoods but also how it has turned a typical North American Progressive Era city into a more sustainable place. The city, once typified by bungalows and suburban sprawl, is now the most densely populated city in Canada and the fifth densest in North America—even though it ranks only seventy-first in population.[25] Certain portions of the Downtown Peninsula rival New York City in terms of people per square mile. While other cities have grown denser while still staying stubbornly reliant on the automobile, Vancouver has managed to make a meaningful shift to other transportation modes. Since the rise of the point tower in the 1990s, the number of car commuters has decreased by nearly 8 percent, and the SkyTrain system has some of the highest ridership of any mass transit system on the continent.[26] Vancouver also has the second-highest rate of walking and biking commuters of any city in Canada and the US, comprising more than 12 percent of the population.[27] As the world tries to grapple with climate change, automobiles remain a large barrier to achieving emissions reduction targets. Vancouver offers a powerful model for how to decrease reliance on cars while creating sustainable, livable, and beautiful communities. Yet while Vancouver's planning efforts have undoubtedly improved the city's quality of life and environmental health, a growing chorus of critics have responded with the question: "for whom?"

After World War II, Vancouver was at first largely shunned by many Canadian investors due to its struggling economy and reputation for militant trade unionism.[28] One of the few people willing to take a risk on redeveloping False Creek was Li Ka-shing. Born to a Teochew family in 1928, Li fled Guangdong Province in China for Hong Kong during the Sino-Japanese War. He left school as a teenager to support his family by working for a plastic company. By the 1950s he had managed to start his own firm, which would eventually become one of Hong Kong's biggest real estate developers.

Li's investment in False Creek raised awareness of Vancouver in Hong Kong, just as the people there were seeking an exit strategy in anticipation of the 1997 handover of the territory back to China.[29] As of 2020, four hundred thousand residents of Chinese origin live in metropolitan Vancouver.

In once-sleepy suburbs like Richmond, night markets rivaling those found in Taipei or Singapore take place on sprawling parking lots.[30] The vast majority of Vancouver's Chinese immigrant community are middle- and working-class people who live in modest homes on the city's fringe. These immigrants, who earn 40 percent less than their white counterparts, are particularly impacted by Vancouver's astronomical home prices.

Vancouver has also been one of the main destinations for a very different type of immigration. The city is one of the world's epicenters of a phenomenon called *capital flight*, where extremely wealthy people living in volatile or politically repressive countries secure their money in more stable places—the primary vehicle being real estate.[31] Since 2014, it is estimated that $800 billion from around globe has been invested in metro Vancouver.[32] Advertisements for condominiums in point towers greet people exiting the airport, and you can't even check out from the grocery store without a sign on the conveyor belt urging you: "Don't miss your next opportunity to invest in amazing." Development has become one of the main drivers of the economy. As one developer told the *New York Times* in 2022, "when it comes to real estate in Greater Vancouver, it's our Microsoft, our Tesla."[33] Yet this industry has not benefited all of the region's residents. In the past decade, the price of housing in the city has increased more than in the previous three decades combined.[34]

Ocean Towers did more than help spur slender towers—it was also the city's first condominium. Since then, almost all new point towers have not been rentals but condos. With their sleek designs, desirable locations, and sweeping views, they are custom-made to absorb wealth, and the fact that their units are secured on a high floor and often have a doorman allow them to be unoccupied for long periods of time. Over 12 percent of all condos in Vancouver remain vacant for most of the year, and this number is estimated to be much higher in the point tower–rich communities of the Downtown Peninsula.

In Coal Harbour there is a ghost town–like quality, in spite of the neighborhood's physical density. The number of year-round residents is so low that many retail spaces cannot retain tenants due to a lack of business.[35] Oliver Bullough, a journalist who researched foreign wealth in his 2019 book *Moneyland*, calls these types of neighborhoods "bank accounts built from brick and mortar"—or in Vancouver's case, glass and concrete.[36]

Many residents fear that Vancouver has ceased being a city at all and has instead become a luxury resort for the rich. In 2022, a poll found that 61 percent of Vancouver residents were considering leaving the region due to high housing costs.[37] The situation even caused the federal government to intervene in 2023 by issuing a two-year ban on foreign buyers. Prime Minister Justin Trudeau made it a campaign issue, with his website proclaiming, "Homes are for people, not investors."[38]

This foreign buyer phenomenon has made the point tower not just a symbol of progressive planning but also of the perils of globalized real estate. As the building has migrated from the Pacific Northwest to world financial centers like New York, designers have distorted its two defining qualities—slenderness and emphasis on views—to the point of absurdity. Dozens of towers as slim as 57 feet and as tall as 1,000 feet now sprout out of Midtown Manhattan like overextended graphite on a mechanical pencil. The units in the buildings, which occupy a full or half floor, can sell for upwards of $90 million and are often bought by limited liability companies to shield the identities of their wealthy and frequently foreign buyers.[39] New York's skyline is starting to resemble a modern version of the Italian hill town of San Gimignano, where noble families in the twelfth century showed off their wealth by building impossibly tall and skinny towers that were also empty.

|||||||||||||||||||||||

Historically, the main driver of urban housing in North America has been efficiency—building the greatest number of units on the smallest footprint. Yet the point tower, with its complex engineering and costly concrete construction, is perhaps the least cost-effective structure one could build. Due to the massive expense of building high-rises, the value is only recouped through putting as many units as possible around a central core composed of elevators, stairwells, and mechanical systems. However, because of the emphasis on view sheds, the point tower only puts six and sometimes as few as two units around the core. Through this, the point tower sacrifices efficiency for lavish apartments with sweeping views, making an inherently expensive building type even more pricey.

Yet the main failure of Vancouver's planning is not that it built point towers instead of more efficient buildings, but rather that it has not built enough of them. Walk a mile in any direction from the glass towers of the Downtown Peninsula and you will find the same car-centered, single-family-home suburbia that proliferates across North America. While certain areas of the city have been utterly transformed into a Canadian Hong Kong, 80 percent of the city is still zoned exclusively for single-family housing due to the grand bargain of the Livable Regions Strategic Plan. While the average price of a condominium is $700,000, the average price of a single-family home is more than twice as much and increased by 159 percent between 2006 and 2016, versus only 61 percent for condos.[40] It is the city's single-family homes, not the point towers, that have become the true luxury housing in Metro Vancouver.

In the grips of the massive housing crisis, the grand bargain is being renegotiated. In 2018 the city launched the Making Room Program to explore how to open up single-family areas to missing middle housing, from row houses to cottages.[41] Along Cambie Street in the residential neighborhoods south of Downtown Vancouver, fences sit in front of abandoned mid-century homes, which will soon be cleared to make way for new mid- and high-rise buildings that are the result of a rezoning in response to a new SkyTrain line. These strategies could boost housing production in the city by up to a third. If these initiatives are successful, the future of Vancouver could look less like the glass towers and pristine open spaces of Coal Harbour and more like the West End.

Below the skyline of the crusty concrete high-rises from the 1960s and '70s, the West End has a wide array of housing types: the average block contains everything from high-rises to three-story brick apartment buildings to a few surviving single-family Victorians, some of which have been converted into duplexes. It is the historic center of gay life in the city and has accommodated waves of immigrants, from Germans in the 1950s and '60s to recent arrivals from Eastern Europe and Asia. It also is the most affordable neighborhood on the Downtown Peninsula—far cheaper than the point tower neighborhoods of False Creek or Coal Harbour. This mix of building types makes it one of the few truly economically diverse neighborhoods on the Downtown Peninsula. Whereas the point towers in the rest of the city have a generic blandness, the West End towers have a homey, lived-in quality—the balconies brim with plants and patio furniture, and their railings are draped with flags.

Replicating the West End's architectural diversity could be a tactic to increase affordability and would involve rezoning the enormous swath of the city dominated by single-family housing. Creating more flexible planning regulations that encourage various types of missing middle housing—and not just point towers—will allow smaller developers to build incrementally over time, instead of multinational corporations targeting foreign buyers. It could also result in more rental housing instead of condos by spurring small landlords looking to create income-generating properties. This more jumbled, chaotic, and far less sexy approach to development is usually not the path to get on the cover of *Monocle* magazine or lure in foreign investment. A granny flat built behind an old bungalow on the city's working-class East Side would carry little cachet to billionaires, who might have trouble finding room for their life-sized, Swarovski crystal–encrusted Siberian tiger sculpture.

Yet in a globalized real estate market, simply adding more supply is not a panacea to the city's affordability crisis. Vancouver has been on a building binge since the 1960s, and the city is as expensive as ever. It is unlikely that the housing built through the Making Room Program will be enough to accommodate the level of demand from people across the globe who want to live in Vancouver. Renter protections and an increase in covenanted affordable housing and social housing, as well as tighter limitations on foreign investments in real estate, are also essential.[42]

Through careful planning, Vancouver used its geographic assets to build some of the finest urban neighborhoods in the world, all within the lifespan of a millennial. Yet the affordability crisis threatens to turn the Vancouver Achievement into the Vancouver Icarus. The city has choked on its own success and is becoming a place almost no one can afford. It is rapidly going from a model to a cautionary tale on the perils of concentrating density, amenities, and infrastructure investments into a relatively small area while ignoring the rest of the city.

CHAPTER 9

Houston Townhouse

The House and the Town

In a state that is adding nearly one thousand new residents each day, Galveston, Texas, is a bygone relic. Sitting on a narrow barrier island in the Gulf of Mexico, the city is physically separated from the rest of the state. Today it is a sleepy seaside tourist town, where palm trees sway along charming streets lined by old balcony-bedecked buildings. However, in 1900, Galveston was Texas's most important city and one of the country's busiest ports, with goods shipped into the interior over one of the longest causeways in the nation. The skyline was studded with the large domed entryway of Ball High School and the towers of City Hall. Galveston was a compact Victorian-era hub—a Texan San Francisco or New Orleans—and was on course to be one of the leading cities of the South. However, on August 27, 1900, a hurricane inundated the city with swells several stories high, bringing immense devastation and killing nearly ten thousand people.

This calamity marked not just the fall of Galveston but also the rise of a new type of place. Today, the bulk of the nation's population and job growth are not taking place in the antique cities that date back to before the nineteenth century, but in the booming metroplexes of the Sunbelt. These rapidly growing cities, stretching from the deserts of the Southwest to the humid forests of the South, do not follow any type of traditional pattern of urban development but are sprawling conurbations. They are a tangle of massive freeways weaving through subdivisions, with office parks randomly splayed across the landscape. The paradigm of this new type of city lies just fifty miles north of Galveston: Houston.

If Vancouver is considered the apex of smart planning in North America, then Houston is where commerce and development have been allowed to trample over the public good. Flying in, as you descend below the murky haze into George Bush Intercontinental Airport, a massive carpet of buildings unfurls on a pancake-flat plain. The tightly packed towers of the city's downtown protrude into the sky, but other equally tall buildings seem to jut out randomly all around it. In the distance is an entirely separate skyline composed of the distillation columns of the region's petrochemical plants, some of which rise as high as 330 feet into the air. Along the freeway heading into town, woodlands dissipate into a confusing mess of structures: the columns and classical frieze of the Luz del Mundo Temple, bungalows, auto mechanics, warehouses, public storage facilities, and large busts of former presidents and Texans. It is as if the type of rigid zoning code that controls most American cities has fallen on the floor and been scattered like puzzle pieces.

Yet while the polished and planned cities of the Coasts have become increasingly pricey and ever more bland, the frenetic cityscape of Houston has seen astounding growth and seems to pulsate with life. While other urban centers have become playgrounds for the wealthy, Houston is seeing middle- and working-class families move in from across the country in droves—as well as an increasing share of the nation's immigrants. Today, it is arguably the most diverse city in the nation, and a closer look at the buildings along the freeway reveals a mix of businesses and stores representing cultures from across the globe. Houston—as well as other booming Southern metro regions like Dallas, Atlanta, and Austin—have a dynamism that makes the more traditional cities of the Coasts look like overgrown Galvestons.

Yet perhaps Houston's biggest departure from Vancouver is that it is affordable. The average price of a home is half that of one in Portland or New York, and a fraction of one in Los Angeles or San Francisco. Houston has been credited, especially by evangelists of the free market, as the antidote to the nation's housing crisis—a city where lax regulation has allowed it to build enough housing to meet demand. Over the last decade, entire Houston neighborhoods of bungalows and small homes have been replaced by tall, slender single-family houses, separated from one another by only a few feet and known as townhomes. However, the city has done little in terms of broader civic investments to support the added density these structures have brought. The Houston townhouse shows the limitations of housing alone in terms of building sustainable and equitable neighborhoods.

||||||||||||||||||||

In 1833, a pair of land speculator brothers named Augustus Chapman Allen and John Kirby Allen left Upstate New York for Galveston. They came to buy land that would allow them to control the cotton and timber trades. However, finding Galveston already oversubscribed, they went fifty miles inland to a decidedly second-choice location, purchasing six thousand acres of flat clay soil at the intersection of the White Oak and Buffalo Bayous.[1] This swampy, hurricane-prone area had all the advantages of New Orleans—except access to one of the world's great rivers. Yet over the decades, the city that would grow out of this settlement would demonstrate an incredible ability to surmount its challenging circumstances through a combination of luck and unbridled ambition.

Almost immediately after founding their settlement, the Allens started sending out promotional brochures and advertisements. They named the city after the hero of the Texas Revolution, Sam Houston, in a successful bid to become the capital of the Republic of Texas, and the city grew with the establishment of government offices and foreign consulates. Over time, Houston built an industrial base by luring rail lines and widening the bayous to create an outlet to the Gulf. Through these shrewd decisions, when Galveston was destroyed by the hurricane in 1900, Houston immediately replaced it as the region's trade center and propelled itself to becoming the main city of the Gulf. A few months later, ninety miles east of the city at what became known as the Spindletop gusher, oil blasted a hundred feet in the air for nine days, giving birth to a new industry whose center would be Houston.[2]

The relocation of people and businesses due to the Galveston storm and the discovery of oil at Spindletop marked the beginning of an economic boom in the city that has yet to abate. The region's population has roughly doubled every fifteen years. However, the city's urban fabric has never been able to catch up. Even as it became a large city, Houston had the appearance of a Western frontier town, with shotguns and cottages floated into the city from New Orleans standing along unpaved streets.[3] Nothing seemed to be permanent, with buildings being ripped down and new ones constructed, as if the city had to constantly rebuild itself before it was reduced to rubble like Galveston.

During the turn of the twentieth century, while other cities embraced the reforms of the Progressive movement to tame the era's wild and booming cities, Houston stood apart, most notably in its lack of zoning. The *Houston Post* ridiculed this aspect of the city, writing that "public spirited citizens may proceed to erect their glue factories, slaughterhouses, fish markets or other smelly industries where they please. And we suppose the legibility of sites in the vicinity of beautiful churches, residences and schools will not be overlooked."[4] Yet when put to a local referendum in 1948, voters rejected the creation of a zoning ordinance—and did so again in 1962 and 1993. The city remains the largest in the country without a zoning code, and Houston's leaders attribute the city's meteoric rise to its unbridled embrace of growth. As sociologist Stephen L. Klineberg writes, the city's ethos has been that "the only legitimate role for public policy is to facilitate and support private sector development, all in the firm belief that this was the surest way to promote the common good."[5]

Without any overriding policy to guide and control growth, Houston failed to cohere into one city, instead becoming several grafted onto each other. The tiny core retained the original 250-by-250-foot grid laid out by the Allens. However, with the widespread adoption of the car in the 1920s, the grid was largely abandoned in favor of master planned developments like the elite River Oaks, west of the downtown, and Riverside Terrace, to the southeast, both of which featured undulating streets. In 1948, a development called Oak Forest, built to the north, was the largest residential subdivision in the United States until Levittown was constructed several years later.[6] In cities like Chicago, these types of large-scale residential developments were green oases that existed in opposition to the overriding street pattern of the rest of the city. However, in Houston there was nothing to oppose, as nearly the entire city was a collection of insular subdivisions.

In 1965, the Astrodome sports stadium was completed seven miles south of downtown Houston to house the city's new Major League baseball team. The massive structure, which looks like a missile silo bedecked with skylights, was not only the world's first domed stadium but also the first to have air-conditioning. In yet another triumph over the city's geography, fans were able to enjoy a baseball or football game during a Houston summer without passing out from the heat. As air-conditioned office buildings, grocery stores, and homes spread across the landscape, the city's growth was sent into hyperdrive. In 1940, Houston had not even been among the twenty largest cities in the country, but by 1982 it had surpassed Philadelphia to become the fourth most populated in the nation.

In the 1950s and '60s, the city's postwar boom was supercharged by Texas's powerful Congressional delegation in Washington. House Speaker Sam Rayburn, along with Senate Majority Leader and later President Lyndon Johnson, brought tremendous resources into the region, including the Johnson Space Center. However, it was the freeway system that finally brought order to the city. In the late 1950s, planning had begun for Interstate 610, a beltway to enclose a roughly ninety-five-square-mile portion of inner Houston. By the '70s, when the loop was finally completed, it had become more like a spider web, crisscrossed by freeways leading in and out of the city and connecting to even larger beltways farther out. These ribbons of concrete acted like the boulevards of Los Angeles, driving growth and imposing order on the city. As Barrie Scardino Bradley writes in her 2020 book, *Improbable Metropolis*, "Highways became the stalks on which new subdivisions sprouted."[7] Today the freeway network is Houston's most recognizable feature, and the 610 loop carries as much symbolic and geographic import as the rivers buffeting Manhattan.

IIIIIIIIIIIIIIIIII

In Progressive Era cities of the early twentieth century, growth had been linear—development was strung in a line along commercial arterials. However, in a post–World War II freeway city like Houston, growth became more like grapes on a vine, with large developments strung along major freeway off-ramps and intersections. In 1970, for example, The Galleria mall opened just outside of the 610 loop where it intersects with Interstate 69. Six hundred thousand square feet of retail space, a four-hundred-room hotel, and a Neiman Marcus department store were all united under a sweeping glass atrium modeled after the Galleria Vittorio Emanuele II in Milan. However, whereas the Italian arcade had been built in the center of the city, connecting the massive Duomo di Milano cathedral with the famous Teatro alla Scala opera house, The Galleria was set amidst subdivisions and open fields. But in just a few decades, the shopping complex would be flanked by tall office buildings and residential towers. Today the area has more hotel rooms than downtown Houston and is the second-biggest job center in the region.[8]

Just a little over a mile north of The Galleria sits a low-slung single-story brick complex called 5000 Longmont, built in 1961. From the main arterial, Post Oak Lane, the complex's jagged roofline of protruding vents and air conditioning units makes it look like a processing center or perhaps a cold storage facility. However, after turning the corner onto the more residential Longmont Drive, the roofline is revealed to be sixteen attached homes running along a private lane with a swimming pool in the center. Throughout the early 1960s, developments of attached houses like 5000 Longmont began to pop up close to the new office parks that were being built in outer Houston. Like the Los Angeles dingbat, these complexes were a response to rising property values and demographic changes of the postwar era. By 1970, the number of households occupied by a single person nationally had grown from 8 in 1940 to 18 percent, and an even larger percentage of the population was composed of childless couples.[9] Complexes like 5000 Longmont provided smaller units requiring less maintenance and also offered the convenience of shared recreational amenities, like pools and tennis courts. However, instead of being rentals, as was the case with dingbats and other apartment complexes, these homes could be purchased outright.

The 5000 Longmont complex was soon followed by much larger developments, including the 159-unit Lafayette Place in 1965 and the 180-unit Victorian Village in 1967.[10] The buildings in these communities are essentially larger and more light-filled versions of the row homes in Philadelphia or London, with rectangular floor plans and bedrooms stacked over ground-floor living and dining rooms. However, unlike older models, these Houston row homes did not build off a long tradition of such housing in the city. Before World War II, the city recorded the construction of only a single pair of row homes from the 1880s, which, like Tontine Crescent in Boston, were soundly rebuffed by the general population.[11] Therefore, these new Houston townhomes were advertised not as charming throwbacks but rather as thoroughly modern arrivals. Brochures with colored-pencil drawings depicted residents lounging by the pool and barbecuing in mid-century grandeur. Instead of referring to the dwellings inside these developments as row homes—with their connotations of sooty industrial neighborhoods—they were called townhomes. This is a Baroque term originally used to describe the large urban houses built by the elite in the eighteenth and nineteenth centuries. By the mid-1970s nearly five thousand townhomes had been built in Houston, 80 percent of which were located in the prosperous Westside of the city.[12]

While in isolation each home looked like a row house, as a whole these townhouse complexes were just denser versions of a suburban subdivision. Whereas traditional row houses integrated into existing neighborhoods and stood close to the street on compact lots, the townhome complexes of Houston eradicated the street. Like The Galleria, the townhomes were arranged in large, insular subdivisions that often required driving past a guardhouse or opening a gate to gain access (see image 30). The townhome complexes contributed to the explosive postwar growth of Houston, which, rather than making a cohesive city, instead resulted in isolated enclaves half-heartedly stitched together by large roads and the freeway network.

ııııııııııııııııııı

In 1972, in the midst of the city's frenetic growth, the architect Howard Barnstone decided to do what he described as a "professor-ish experiment."[13] Barnstone was a pioneer of Houston townhouses—he had designed 5000 Longmont and several other large developments.[14] However, he wanted to see if it was possible to adapt the Houston townhome to small infill lots within the urban core; a key consideration was how to also integrate the automobile. In suburban townhome complexes, garages were often placed behind the structure facing an alley, but on smaller urban lots this was normally not an option. Barnstone built three prototype 16-foot-wide townhomes in the backyard of a duplex he owned in a leafy neighborhood near Rice University. Each of the homes was almost the exact width of the garage door, which was placed at the ground floor with two floors of living space stacked above. Barnstone's experiment had created a new urban template for the townhome, bringing all the advantages of the large townhouse complexes—such as limited maintenance costs and full ownership—to the center of the city.

As Barnstone was finishing his prototypes, an art dealer named Fredericka Hunter was planning a new home. Hunter had originally wanted a space with large walls to show off her art collection, similar to the lofts found in areas like SoHo in Lower Manhattan.[15] However, she found this sort of raw industrial space hard to come by in Houston and decided to hire a former associate of Barnstone's, Eugene Aubry, to design her one instead. Hunter selected a parcel on Roy Street in an area known as the West End, located a few miles northwest of Downtown Houston. This was a working-class neighborhood crisscrossed by rail lines, composed of modest bungalows and shotguns interspersed with industrial buildings. Using these industrial structures as inspiration, Aubry built a duplex and clad the building in corrugated metal. With its prominent garage and flat roof, the structure looked more like a warehouse than a home. Known as the Tin House, it became the center of Houston's art scene in the 1970s and '80s and hosted parties and openings where famous rodeo cowboys mingled with artists like Andy Warhol and the composer Philip Glass.[16]

Like Barnstone's prototype urban townhome, the Tin House provided a model for adding new dense housing in Houston. With its art-world pedigree and star-studded parties, it gave cachet to both the townhouse and the neighborhoods of inner Houston. As a new oil boom enveloped the city in the 1970s, daring builders hired experimental design firms to build urban townhomes inspired by the Tin House. A swath of the city stretching from the West End south into Montrose became a showplace for this innovative housing.

In the 1980s, the Miami-based firm Arquitectonica built several urban townhome complexes in which the rectangular mass of the structure was punched out with oversized circles and triangles. Extruding fins and bay windows were added, each individually painted in pastel colors (see image 30). On Floyd Street, Taft Architects built the Grove Court Townhouses, which curve around a small green space like the houses fronting Chester Square in the South End of Boston. These urban townhomes, as well as other complexes built in Houston in the '70s and early '80s, differentiated each unit through setbacks and rooflines to create a cohesive composition. However, this belle époque of the urban townhouse was short-lived. With the oil bust of 1986, one out of every eight Houstonians became unemployed, and the cowboy developers willing to build avant-garde townhome developments either went bankrupt or left town. As the city recovered in the 1990s, the few firms that survived eschewed experimentation and built more conservative dwellings. The design of the urban townhouse went from referencing postmodern architecture and industrial spaces to borrowing the aesthetic of the suburbs, with red roof tiles and wrought iron railings, the rusticated brick of a Southern plantation house, and vaguely modernist white cubes with steel accents. These styles were all compressed onto the homes' narrow façades and interspersed with a healthy dose of earth-toned stucco. The designers of urban townhomes of the early 1970s had been happy to leave open space or create a setback in order to fulfill their aesthetic vision. However, the impetus of the post-bust urban townhomes was to max out every square inch of developable space. This has resulted in the average size of an urban townhome built in Houston post-1990 being over 2,100 square feet—nearly twice as large as the typical early-twentieth-century bungalow, and 600 square feet larger than the townhouses built by Arquitectonica.[17]

The average townhouse today typically has a ground floor that is entirely dominated by a double garage facing the street, which at first glance gives the impression that one can only enter the house by clicking on a remote control. However, the door is actually tucked out of sight on the side of the house via a narrow three-foot gap that separates each home from another, and it is so discreet and seldom used that the path leading to it is often paved in gravel or dirt. The ground floor has a foyer that doubles as a laundry room with an adjoining bedroom and bathroom. Stairs next to the laundry machine take you to the main floor of the house—a large open space that serves as the living room, dining room, and kitchen. French doors open up to a small balcony perched over the garage. The top floor contains the primary bedroom suite as well as an additional bedroom, each with its own bathroom.

Like an early-nineteenth-century New York City tenement, the building takes up so much of its lot and is built so close to neighboring structures that it is difficult for light to penetrate the interior. Instead of having an articulated façade with bay windows and other features that could help define the various spaces of the house, each room is simply an enormous rectangle. Compared with homes from the nineteenth and early twentieth centuries, the proportions of many of these post-bust urban townhomes feel like they were designed for a giant. The living room walls rise ten feet high as opposed to the standard eight, making even the biggest flat-screen television feel like it's floating in a vast, beige, spackled ocean. The primary bedroom can seem as though a mattress has been left in a hotel conference room. To ensure privacy, rooms toward the back of the house only have clerestory windows, like a medieval dungeon. In one such home, the dining room table on the main floor sits in front of a large window. However, because the only thing it reveals is the blank wall of a neighboring townhome three feet away, a large painting is suspended over it.

ııııııııııııııııı

Around the corner from the original site of the Tin House sits a block of Blossom Street that still feels like early Houston. Large oak trees arch over a cracked asphalt street whose edges dissipate into the dirt path that serves as the sidewalk. Shrouded in shrubbery, the neoclassical columns and pitched roofs of old turn-of-the-century homes sit behind worn fences made from wood and wire. A sign tacked onto a tree in one yard reads, "Wild Life Habitat, Hunting Fishing, or Trapping is prohibited," harkening back to a time before this area was surrounded by a dense thicket of towering townhomes.

Since 1990, nearly thirty-four thousand townhomes have been built in Houston, which now account for 8 percent of all homes within the 610 loop.[18] The proliferation of urban townhomes has made parts of inner Houston entirely unrecognizable, with a large swath of the city now an unbroken chain of slender houses in a patchwork of architecture styles. Even the original Tin House on Roy Street has been torn down for more densely configured buildings. The semirural stretch of Blossom Street only survives because it was declared a historic district in 2022, with one official calling it the "'last remnant' of the neighborhood's past amidst rapid development."[19]

In most American cities, the type of transformation occurring in inner Houston would be all but impossible. Rigid zoning codes and building restrictions prevent most single-family homes from being ripped down and replaced with denser forms of housing. However, in Houston the lack of zoning and lax subdivision rules makes this relatively easy. The city has historically maintained a minimum lot size of 5,000 square feet for single-family homes, but all that was needed to subdivide it into smaller parcels was a variance, or a request for relief from certain zoning provisions that cause a hardship. The hearings for these variances, instead of being pitched battles between neighborhood residents and developers that are common in most cities, normally take five minutes (it can stretch to thirty if the project is particularly controversial). Under state law, these variance cases must be decided within thirty days or they are automatically approved. In 1999, this process was streamlined even further when the minimum lot size within the 610 loop was reduced to as small as 1,400 square feet.[20] This has resulted in single-family homes being demolished and the lots subdivided for three or more townhomes. Whereas most pre-1999 urban townhomes are attached, this reform has resulted in new structures being detached, separated by tiny three-foot gaps.

Yet similar to the cities of the nineteenth century, wealthy neighborhoods are able to insulate themselves from the onslaught of townhomes and other intrusions by deed restrictions. In the absence of zoning, these covenants control what types of buildings can be built, their size and orientation, and—although now void due to the Fair Housing Act of 1968—what races can live there.* Since they are private agreements, city officials do not enforce these covenants, so vigilant homeowners' associations must collect funds from residents to hire lawyers and challenge projects that fall astray of the restrictions. Originally, nearly all subdivisions in Houston carried some sort of deed restriction on land use, which was a requirement to qualify for loans backed by the Federal Housing Administration (FHA). However, in many neighborhoods, particularly poor and working-class ones, these restrictions have lapsed over time, making these communities susceptible to an array of noxious land uses, from petrochemical plants to garbage dumps.[21]

While Houston's land use policies have been successful in creating tremendous amounts of housing, they have largely failed to create equitable

---

* Because deed restrictions are not just antiquated pieces of paper but vital documents, in Houston there is a movement in the city to get racist language removed from them.

or even desirable neighborhoods. Ironically, while the city famously lacks zoning, it has many other regulations that go beyond even those of liberal coastal cities. Homes with more than three bedrooms are required to have at least two parking spaces and to adhere to setback and height restrictions. All residential buildings with more than two units are considered commercial development and require sprinklers, additional parking, and have much longer approval times. This makes small apartment buildings essentially impossible to construct, with one developer estimating the break-even point to be more than twenty units.[22]

Rather than representing a libertarian free-for-all, the Houston townhouse is instead—like Vancouver's point tower—the result of explicit government policy. However, whereas in Vancouver planners agonized over setbacks, view corridors, the relationship between the building and the street, and creating socially integrated neighborhoods, the Houston regulations have resulted in sections of the city having both the car-dependent design of the suburbs and the congestion and crowding of the city.

From the air, the West End looks like the dense urban patchwork of San Francisco or the Northeast, with tightly packed pitched-roof homes. However, on the ground, one is met with large double garages. The narrow sidewalks traverse open drainage ditches on little gangways and are often blocked by double-parked cars spilling out of the driveways, making the best option to walk in the congested streets. However, in most of the city's neighborhoods, there is no place to walk to. Unlike Vancouver, Los Angeles, or Portland, Houston never developed a robust streetcar system, and the few lines that did exist were mostly focused on downtown and neighborhoods to the southeast. As a result, the city developed few compact neighborhood business districts, and the ones that did exist have been obliterated by freeways or disinvestment.

Yet instead of new development helping to create more walkable areas, due to Houston's planning regulations they often do the opposite. In 2019, the beloved H-E-B grocery chain opened a location at the corner of Washington Avenue and Heights Boulevard in the heart of the West End.[23] The 96,000-square-foot store features a wine bar, a butcher selling twenty-one-day dry aged beef, and a tortilleria, all ensconced in 232 units of housing. This type of large-scale, mixed-use building, with a grocery store at its base, is exactly the type of development that is typically used to make communities walkable, allowing people to grab daily items without using a car. In many places, similar developments have helped anchor and revitalize entire business districts, with shops and restaurants taking advantage of the spillover foot traffic from the grocery store.

However, because buildings in Houston are required to have a minimum 25-foot setback, the West End H-E-B store is not built close to the sidewalk but instead is pushed back by a slender row of parking spaces.[24] In order to enter the store on foot, one must first walk through a gauntlet of cars frantically looking for spots before most of these vehicles give up and park in the large garage directly above the store. New podium apartments built on major corridors in the city often do not even have retail on the ground floor because parking and other restrictions make it difficult to do so. Instead of contributing to a walkable urban area, recent development in Houston has caused neighborhoods to become even more car-oriented. Bill Fulton, the former director of the Kinder Institute for Urban Research at Rice University, says that Houston's land use policies have resulted in it being "the place where developers come to do their worst work."[25]

iiiiiiiiiiiiiiiiii

Houston's townhomes are indicative of two seemingly opposing trends in American housing. Since 1973, the average size of a house in the United States has nearly doubled and is now 2,687 square feet. This is despite the fact that during this period, the mean household size has gone from just over 3 people down to 2.5, resulting in the average American having twice as much room at home as they did fifty years ago.[26] Yet even as people want ever bigger living spaces, there is also a growing desire to live in central, urban areas where space is limited. By providing large, modern, and amenity-filled homes on compact urban lots, the Houston urban townhome is seemingly the answer to this paradox. Because of this, the building type has transcended the urban policy vortex of Houston to spread throughout the country.

Portland, Oregon, incentivized the creation of townhomes in 1995 after permitting smaller lot sizes in certain areas. This led to many ranch homes in East Portland being bulldozed and replaced with several skinny, pitched-roof homes clad in vinyl siding, with the ground floor dominated by a protruding garage. Alluding to a pig's nose, they were dubbed "snout houses," and city officials quickly implemented design regulations to bar them. One city commissioner justified these restrictions by saying that homes should be able to pass the "trick or treat test," meaning that when kids approach, "they actually get a sense that somebody lives in the house, and they can find the door. Imagine that."[27]

In Cleveland, as a result of a 2018 overhaul of the zoning code, nearly two dozen urban townhome developments have been built. In fast-gentrifying areas near the city's core, vacant lots and industrial buildings have been replaced by large rows of townhomes clad in metal and fake brick, with a battery of garages on the ground floor. For a city that has lost nearly two-thirds of its population since 1950, one would think these homes would be a welcome investment. However, they have been dubbed "slot houses," and the Cleveland chapter of the American Institute of Architects issued a forty-four-page letter asking the city to repeal the portion of the code allowing them. A city councilman representing the central city called the buildings "ugly as hell, and not pedestrian-friendly."[28]

The desire for ever larger houses in dense urban areas is also manifesting itself in more insidious ways. On East 75th Street in the gilded climbs of Manhattan's Upper East Side sits a collection of four row homes. Their façades alternate between flat Georgian detailing and ornate pitched-roof brownstone. In the back, however, a glass curtain wall links them together into one massive façade that faces onto a large garden. What appears to be four separate buildings is actually the false front of a single 19,400-square-foot mansion built by the Russian oligarch Roman Abramovich.[29] His home is just the most flamboyant example of how the wealthy are warping urban environments in order to make ever-larger homes. A study by the New York Department of City Planning found that in the Upper East Side, despite adding two thousand residential units since 2010, the total number of housing units actually went down due to people combining multiple apartments into a single unit. One resident said that twenty units in his building alone have been lost in this way.[30]

This trend of mansionization is not just happening in traditionally wealthy enclaves but also in gentrifying neighborhoods. In Brooklyn, along St. Marks Avenue in the neighborhood of Prospect Heights, finely crafted Victorian-era brownstones that were originally built for large families were, throughout the twentieth century, subdivided and turned into apartments and even boarding houses for immigrants from the Caribbean. As this neighborhood has since gentrified, many of these homes are returning to their Gilded Age roots and are being converted back into single-family mansions. The crown molding and inlaid walnut cabinetry are stripped away and painted white in an interior design scheme reminiscent of an Apple Store. Backyard gardens are leveled and turned into Astroturfed play spaces for young children.

In the Logan Square neighborhood of Chicago, Whipple Street was once part of the belt of working-class neighborhoods surrounding the downtown Loop. However, over the last decade, the small workers cottages that lined the street have been ripped down. Rising in their place are brick-fronted homes with low-slung roofs, reminiscent of the prairie style of architecture and each containing five bedrooms, four bathrooms, and over 4,000 square feet of living space. Even the city's two- and four-flat apartment buildings are being bought whole and converted to large single-family homes. A report from DePaul University found that Chicago has lost nearly 12,000 two-, three-, and four-flats since 2013 due to this practice.[31] A similar phenomenon in St. Louis has resulted in four hundred units being lost.[32]

There is an inverse relationship between the size of a home and the vibrancy of a neighborhood. Across the nation, urban streets like St. Marks and Whipple once pulsated with life. On hot summer nights, people escaped their crowded homes, sat on stoops and porches, and watched their children play in the street. The local tavern or diner became an extension of people's homes, where they decompressed or had a meal. However, today there is an eerie quietness, as people no longer feel the need to engage with their neighbors but instead retreat into their palatial homes.

ıııııııııııııııııı

In 1908, the architect Adolf Loos distilled his modernist style into the design of a tiny bar in Vienna. With its coffered ceiling, checkered floor, and mint-green seats, the American Bar became the meeting ground for Europe's leading artists and intellectuals, from Sigmund Freud to Egon Schiele. As fascism descended on Europe, many of these great minds would find themselves exiled to the United States. In 2015, a temporary art installation in what was one of the main landing points for these émigrés,

Los Angeles, meticulously recreated the American Bar. The original Viennese American Bar occupies a tiny storefront off a narrow pedestrian alley in the city's medieval core. In Los Angeles, the bar was placed not on Rodeo Drive or Sunset Boulevard but in a garage space of the Mackey Apartments, a proto-dingbat designed by Rudolph Schindler. The garage door was replaced by an Art Moderne façade with a light-filled awning and floor-length vertical windows. For several nights, instead of housing a dormant Kia Optima, the interior was filled with the sound of glasses clinking and people talking.

This installation, called Los Bar, was a project funded by the MAK Center for Art and Architecture.[33] However, it was also a poignant statement about how even a parking space could be reimagined as fin de siècle Vienna. Several years later, during the Covid-19 pandemic, this type of transformation went from an experiment to a common practice. After several months of being confined to their homes, many people decided to park their cars on the street and fill their garages with desks, easels, and even looms. On warm days, the garages opened, these spaces were exposed to the public, and suburban streets became like old walking cities, where neighbors informally called on each other and casually chatted in the street.

This type of metamorphosis is increasingly occurring on a more permanent basis across the country. In Philadelphia's Fishtown neighborhood, the garage base of a row home built in 2011 has been turned into a small café with a plant-based menu. Instead of a parking spot, the garage door rolls up to reveal a small counter and several tables, and the driveway is an outdoor patio. Due to new laws in California, the ground floor garages of mid-century dingbats and apartment buildings from San Francisco to Los Angeles are being converted into apartments.

Both temporary experiments like Los Bar and more permanent transformations like the Fishtown café show how housing has the potential to change and adapt. This is the promise that the urban townhomes hold for Houston. Today, areas like the West End are the worst of both the suburbs and the city. People are cramped against their neighbors with little open space, yet still have to drive to get even a cup of coffee or some groceries. However, one day these buildings could evolve to support more walkable and vibrant communities. The townhouse is built at a small scale with shoddy wood-frame construction, which vibrates like a small earthquake

when the washing machine is in use. It's not hard to envision these buildings being adapted or replaced. Instead of a mini mansion, the interior
could be divided into two or even three units. The ground floor could go
from housing cars to neighborhood amenities. Urban townhomes could
gradually be replaced altogether by a mix of small apartment buildings,
storefronts, or offices, and instead of rows of identical houses, the city's
neighborhoods would have the diversity of Parkman Avenue in Los Angeles
or the historic urban cores of the East.

ııııııııııııııııı

A few miles east of The Galleria mall is Levy Park. On this small site, a
space-age playground with sky-blue hills made of foam and water-shooting
orange halos sits next to a community center where you can take free sing-
ing lessons from the Houston Opera or check out a bucket of art supplies.
People spill out into the park at café tables in front of several restaurants.
Children from all ethnic backgrounds and social strata climb up a rock
wall and then careen down a massive concrete slide while their parents
strike up casual conversations. Levy Park creates a center of gravity, a social
unifier, amidst a discordant mix of skyscrapers, parking lots, townhomes,
and shopping centers. This park is just one of an array of impressive new
civic spaces that have been built in Houston over the last two decades.
Even the once malaria-ridden bayous have gone from drainage ditches to
ribbons of green, with a network of bike paths and trails allowing cyclists
and pedestrians to safely traverse the city. The bayous may soon rival the
freeway as the symbol of Houston and the city's key organizing force.

These efforts are reminiscent of the visionary leaders who built parks and
infrastructure to relieve the crowded, slum-filled cities of the nineteenth
century. In 1878, Frederick Law Olmsted was hired to clean up the muddy
marshes on the periphery of Boston. The result was the city's famed Emer-
ald Necklace—a chain of parks hemming in tight rows of triple-deckers.
In Philadelphia, row houses butt up against the two thousand acres of
Fairmount Park, which emerged out of efforts in the mid-nineteenth
century to protect the city's water supply along the Schuylkill River. In
turn-of-the-twentieth-century Chicago, clearings were created among
dense blocks of apartments and workers cottages to form neighborhood
parks. Many contain elaborate field houses where the largely immigrant

residents could play sports and take classes under a vaulted plaster of paris ceiling. These parks and public spaces made cities livable, providing a respite from cramped homes. They were democratic, allowing newcomers, immigrants, and longtime residents alike to coalesce into a single group of citizens. These pieces of infrastructure are a reminder that cities are not defined by their housing and private realms, but by the public spaces that tie them together.

Similar to public spaces, the best types of urban housing act as community anchors and enhance the areas around them. The stoop of a row house, the porch of a shotgun, and the balcony of a triple-decker all serve as public thresholds for the home, inviting neighborly interaction and serving as a public gathering space. These features make the street more than just a place to anonymously pass through—they turn neighborhoods into communities.

Instead of enhancing their surroundings, buildings like the Houston townhome are extractive. Their large mass blocks the sun and they flood neighborhoods with cars, giving nothing to the public realm and trying only to maximize private and profitable square footage. This results in cities that are not composed of communities but a series of private domains clustered closely together. Ultimately, the urban townhome and structures like it are the result of a broader failure to invest in infrastructure and public space. Because the cities have failed to provide sufficient options for people to walk or use transit, the building meets the sidewalk with a driveway and parking lot. Because there are few parks, bars, cafés, or other gathering spaces nearby, the interiors of the homes need to be incredibly large to accommodate activities that might otherwise take place elsewhere.

Yet cities are constantly evolving, and perhaps no place is changing as much, or as fast, as Houston. The city has recently made impressive strides to reform its urban policy, undertaking a lauded redesign of its bus network and investing in high-quality transit infrastructure such as new rail and bus lines. Planners are also trying to better orient new buildings around transit, and in 2020 Houston passed an ordinance eliminating parking requirements and loosening setback regulations in central neighborhoods.[34] Throughout history, as infrastructure and the environment changed, so did urban housing. Structures were divided into multiple units, added additional stories, and were even physically moved. By allowing for lots smaller than the 5,000-square-foot Progressive Era standard, Houston took an important step in opening up its neighborhoods to more housing. The urban townhouses that have resulted from this reform should not be looked at as static objects but rather as works in progress, an initial volley in a decades-long metamorphosis. As Houston continues to invest in infrastructure that fosters more walkable and community-oriented neighborhoods, the urban townhouse will evolve along with it.

The Tiny Tower

A s Girard Avenue makes its four-mile run across North Philadelphia, the neighborhoods along its route provide a timeline of US
urban development. Factories and church spires are some of the only tall
structures that stick out among a flat plain of the two- and three-story
row homes that provided affordable housing for the working class in the
nineteenth and early twentieth centuries. By the 1930s, these communities
were considered slums, and a seven-block area of the Poplar neighborhood
was demolished and replaced by public housing in the form of low-rise,
garden-style apartments. Instead of meeting the street with a small stoop,
these dwellings were closed off to their surroundings and oriented around
internal courtyards. Initially, this development provided modern housing
for working families, including Bill Cosby's. However, after years of delayed
maintenance, the mechanical systems—from the electrical wiring to the
sewage disposal—began to break down. As anyone with means refused to
live in the development, empty apartments were taken over by drug dealers.

In 1996, the neighborhood was demolished yet again. Recalling the
wildest fantasies of nineteenth-century reformers, the dense apartments of
the public housing complex were replaced with pitched-roof suburban-style
homes on 6,000-square-foot lots, complete with cul-de-sacs. Even as policymakers were creating a bastion of suburbia in the middle of Philadelphia,
a trickle of upper- and middle-class people were starting to return to the
city. By the 2000s, this trickle became a cascade, and today, just a stone's

throw away from Poplar, the Northern Liberties neighborhood is seeing new podium apartment buildings and high-rises, which are changing the scale and density of this traditionally low-rise area.

Yet amidst the frenetic changes along Girard Avenue, the city's traditional fabric of narrow streets and row homes has remained mostly intact. In Brewerytown, near Fairmount Park and the Schuylkill River, old diminutive brick façades have been refurbished with fresh coats of paint and flower boxes have been placed under windowsills. Old storefronts house cafés and beer parlors serve hazy IPAs. A daycare sits on the ground floor of the John Decker and Son Architectural Sheet Metal Works, and the upper floors have been turned into modern plant-filled lofts. Yet the façades of the buildings still serve as a literal outdoor catalogue, displaying the various kinds of decorative brick, awnings, and cornices that were once manufactured inside.

While the ornamentation on the John Decker building can be found on row homes across the city, a small contemporary house on the narrow, alley-like street directly behind it displays none. The row homes that once surrounded this home have been demolished, and these vacant lots reveal the building's minuscule depth: 20 feet to match its 12-foot width. Instead of maroon-colored brick, it is clad in white corrugated metal and its tall front windows are offset to reveal an interior stairwell (see image 31). Although this structure has been featured in the pages of glossy design magazines, it builds off a centuries-long legacy of residential architecture in Philadelphia.

This home, built in 2018 and nicknamed Tiny Tower, was designed by the local firm ISA, which has gained a national reputation for constructing light-filled and livable spaces on impossibly small and narrow lots. Tiny Tower essentially updates the city's trinity row houses for modern times and shares many of its features, including a single small room on each of the building's three floors and a kitchen in the basement. However, it integrates clever details to make the interior feel modern and larger. A deck has been built on the roof. A gap between the first floor and kitchen allows smells and noises to waft up to the living room, making it feel like one large space. Whereas the rooms inside a modern townhouse drown in excess and are filled with superfluous space, in Tiny Tower, the rooms are ruthlessly efficient but pleasant and intimate.

Just as in the trinity, the most important aspect of Tiny Tower is its stairwell. Standard wood stairs covered in drywall would have taken up too much room, so instead a more slender one was fabricated out of steel. Doing this accounted for $50,000 of the home's overall $250,000 budget, but it was compact enough to allow for decently sized living spaces. In most trinities the stairs are in the back, but in Tiny Tower they are placed at the front of the house, thus becoming an architectural feature. Its perforated steel guard rail acts as a giant window blind, allowing light to come into the home while still ensuring privacy.

ISA is just one of many innovative firms across the country reviving their city's tradition of urban housing. Architect Jonathan Tate was educated under Samuel Mockbee at the acclaimed Rural Studio run by Auburn University, where students are taught through designing and then physically building homes for poor families in rural west Alabama, Tate's home state. After Hurricane Katrina, Tate became one of the many Young Urban Rebuilding Professionals (YURPs) drawn to New Orleans, and he eventually went on to found his own firm there, OJT, in 2011. Their work comes out of a deep love and respect for the city's traditional housing stock as well as from frustration with some of its realities. Many of the firm's clients are people who came to the city specifically wanting historic homes but who, after a decade or longer living in them, yearned for more modern types of housing. As Tate notes, "the room to room to room layout" of the shotgun "is a maddening way to live in one's contemporary life."[1]

One of OJT's projects, 3106 St. Thomas Street, sits on a side street of the Irish Channel neighborhood, next to the Lagasse Brothers medical supply warehouse (see image 32). With its metal façade, at first glance the house could be just another industrial building that populates this area near the docks along the Mississippi River. But while 3106 St. Thomas superficially looks nothing like a traditional New Orleans house, on deeper inspection you can see echoes of the city's traditional architecture: the pitched roof that is reminiscent of a Creole cottage, the floor-to-ceiling windows, and the 10.5-by-45-foot dimensions, which echo the shotgun house. A key element of all of OJT's work is for their structures to contribute to the city's street culture. In a project called Bastion, this is done through a semipublic social space running along the side of the structure that can be used by residents or opened to the broader neighborhood and city. As

Tate says, "I am fundamentally an urbanist and I care way more about how buildings inform urban space than just how they look."

|||||||||||||||||||

Tiny Tower and 3106 St. Thomas show that reviving the lost tradition of affordable urban housing does not entail the wholesale replication of older building types, with gingerbread millwork fabricated out of plexiglass and stucco dyed to look like brownstone. Rather, by being rooted in and building off the existing fabric of the city, it is possible to create new forms of housing that are affordable and accessible but that also respond to contemporary needs and desires. Brian Phillips, the founder and principal of ISA, says that Tiny Tower is indicative of how Penn's grid is "still managing how the city prices itself."[2] On Philadelphia's wider lots, builders are constructing large new row homes that can sell for upwards of $1 million. Tiny Tower shows how well-designed, light-filled, and affordable homes can be built on the smaller legacy lots located on the courts and alleys across Philadelphia. As Phillips says, Tiny Tower "points towards serious affordability or density in a high-pressure market," and it's a model he hopes will be replicated by other builders across the city.

Similarly, 3106 St. Thomas in New Orleans is part of an initiative by OJT called the Starter Home* program, which seeks to create more affordable housing options in the city. This is achieved through developing small, vacant lots in established neighborhoods, where preexisting homes are often very expensive. Developing more efficient homes on these remnant lots creates an opportunity for middle-class residents to move into these areas. Tiny Tower and 3106 St. Thomas—both at $250,000—are below the median price of a home in the quickly gentrifying neighborhoods where they are located.

However, Philadelphia and New Orleans have long traditions of urban housing as well as a legacy of compact urban lots. Whereas in younger cities Tiny Tower would give a reviewer from the building department a coronary, in Philadelphia the structure is able to take advantage of the municipality's more permissive building codes. Tiny Tower was facilitated by Philadelphia's 2010 revision of the zoning code, which did away with parking requirements and allowed for greater density.[3] In New Orleans, OJT found a zoning bylaw that said that any historically platted lot, regardless of its size, was legal to build on without adhering to density or setback requirements.

Of course, most American cities are not composed of shotguns or row houses but detached single-family homes sitting on lots that are 5,000 square feet or larger. In these places it is not so much about filling in vacant legacy parcels or updating historic housing types, but rather about creating entirely new ones. Increasingly, across the nation, cities are clearing the way to do exactly this. In 2018, Minneapolis replaced its old zoning code with a new one called Minneapolis 2040, which allows up to three homes on the 70 percent of the city's lots that previously only allowed one. In 2019, Oregon passed House Bill 2001, which requires all cities in urban areas with more than ten thousand people to allow for a mix of housing, from duplexes and granny flats to bungalow courts and small apartment buildings. Two years later, California passed a law called SB 9, which permits owners of parcels zoned only for detached single-family homes to split them into two separate lots and build up to two homes on each.

Since the Progressive reformers of the mid-nineteenth century, American policymakers have had an almost puritanical obsession with both encouraging and then protecting detached single-family homes. These recent pro-density reforms represent a sea change in urban planning in the United States. Yet the actual amount of housing that has been produced by these laws has so far been anemic. As of 2022, Minneapolis's decision to abolish single-family zoning has produced only ninety-seven units of new housing.[4] In California, although SB 9 reforms are barely getting off the ground, experts predict it will have similarly underwhelming results. A study by the Terner Center at University of California at Berkeley found that SB 9 could produce 127,000 new units of housing in Los Angeles County, which, while significant, is relatively modest compared to the 1.4 million eligible lots.[5] The main failure of these laws is that they still do not give enough flexibility, due to trying to mandate that new development have the qualities of low-rise single-family homes. Even the fact sheet on SB 9, created by the housing advocacy organization California YIMBY, touted the fact that it "respects neighborhood character."[6]

It is the *urban* qualities of historic housing that allow for light-filled and livable interiors. Row homes are tall, narrow, and built right up to the street and neighboring buildings, and through this they provide a relatively large single-family home with its own yard. The triple-decker in Boston and the fourplexes in Los Angeles stack apartments on top of each other, allowing the interiors of each unit to have light on all four sides. Yet laws like 3D 9 do not allow a lot to be divided into 12-foot-wide parcels for row houses, nor for the units to be stacked, but instead force units to be dispersed across a lot so as to result in low-slung buildings that can be concealed from the street. Instead of giving California designers the ability to create a version of Tiny Tower or 3106 St. Thomas that is appropriate for their region, these restrictions make it nearly impossible to build multi-bedroom homes that have ample light and privacy. These policies, though a major accomplishment, need to be further adapted to allow for more flexibility, creativity, and experimentation in order to produce dense, livable, and affordable housing that will be widely adopted by both builders and the public.

｜｜｜｜｜｜｜｜｜｜｜｜｜｜｜｜｜

It is not policies that will get us out of the housing crisis, but rather actual buildings and the people who develop them. In 2019, Donovan Adesoro was fresh out of college, working as an engineer for Occidental Petroleum in Houston. After nearly three years trudging through his day-to-day, he could not imagine doing the job for another forty years and started looking for a side hustle. Through investigating online, he became interested in real estate and learned about a strategy where he could purchase a home and then subsidize the mortgage by renting out the extra rooms to two or three other people. This concept dates back to the boarding houses of the colonial period, and today it has been revived on various online platforms as *house hacking*.

Adesoro purchased a recently built duplex in the south Houston neighborhood of Sunnyside. After renting out the second unit to tenants and the rooms in the main house to several roommates, he was not only able to pay his mortgage, he even had extra money at the end of the month. He started looking for other duplexes, but in a city enraptured by 2,500-square-foot townhomes, he found that very few were being built. Seeing a gap in the market, he decided to pivot to real estate development, but coming from a family without extra money to lend him and being straddled with $30,000 in student debt, he needed to find another way to raise funds. By reaching out to various investors on online forums and Facebook, he was able to raise enough money to purchase a 5,000-square-foot lot in Sunnyside and construct a duplex on it. Today, at twenty-six years old, he has built seven duplexes and owns twenty-five vacant lots, with plans to construct new housing on them. He has become a rare source of missing middle housing in Houston—and, even rarer, a Black developer in an industry that is less than 5 percent Black.

The urban housing built in the eighteenth, nineteenth, and early twentieth centuries is a true American innovation. It was largely built by and for immigrants and working-class people and allowed them to ascend into the middle class. Many of these structures have endured to this day and now form the bedrock of many of our nation's most celebrated urban neighborhoods. Yet, due to its association with immigrants, as well as a broader bias against density, urban housing was largely banned in the twentieth century. As a young person of color, Adesoro and people like him are not only carrying this tradition into the twenty-first century, using social media to raise capital instead of ethnic churches and taverns, but they also are helping make small-scale urban development inclusive to all people regardless of skin color. While most large developers are building luxury housing for the wealthiest, Adesoro is building duplexes occupied by middle- and working-class people, who are in turn using it as an economic stepping stone. Our urban policy should act to support rather than hinder small builders like Adesoro. By creating zoning policies that once again allow for innovative building types, we can take the bespoke housing types produced by firms like OJT and ISA and build millions of homes across the nation. Through this we will not just raise the supply of housing but also will build homes that reflect the diverse needs of our communities.

As of 2022, the United States was nearly four million homes short of what is needed to maintain a stable market.[7] To address this crisis we could, on the one hand, continue to double down on the policies of the twentieth century and replace open land with sprawling, car-oriented suburbs, exacerbating climate change and further atomizing our society. Or we could open our most desirable, economically dynamic, and amenity-rich locations to more housing. Doing this does not have to mean destroying established communities. Rather, this can be achieved through building a diversity of housing at a range of scales that reflect the unique circumstances of individual neighborhoods. Podium apartments like those reshaping Los

Angles can be built on commercial corridors, entire new skylines can rise in downtowns and next to transit stations as in Vancouver and its suburbs, and residential neighborhoods can be filled with missing middle housing that builds off the legacies of our nation's regional building types. These new structures should be complemented by a range of other policies to protect tenants and provide affordable housing for the lowest-income families. While this means that these neighborhoods might physically change, by creating affordable options for both longtime residents and new ones, their intrinsic character will be retained.

ACKNOWLEDGMENTS

This book took many years to come to fruition and was made possible through the assistance of so many people. My professors Peter Dreier, Robert Gottlieb, Jonathan Martin, Clara Irazábal, Alejandro de Castro Mazarro, and Robert Beauregard, who first exposed me to many of the concepts in this book. The librarians and the resources of the Los Angeles Public Library. Marlene Dubas, who provided early feedback. The classes of Jane Friedman. My agent, Sarah Phair, who saw the potential of this book, helped me develop it. The advice and guidance of Julia Kramer as well as David Tamarkin and Michael Szczerban. Tom Vlodek, Matt Bergstrom, Ian Dickenson, William Fulton, Donovan Adesoro, Brian Phillips, and Jonathan Tate, and especially Gordon Price, who gave me a tour of the Vancouver SkyTrain network. My friends Madeline Wander, Tom Carroll, and John Guevara for their feedback and assistance. Elizabeth Timme, whose insights on housing inspired many aspects of this book. Yvette Lopez-Ledesma and Veronica Padilla-Campos. My family members, including my dad, my stepmother, Barbi Leifert, my aunts Esther and Paula, my uncle Melvin, my cousin Miriam, and my mother- and father-in-law, Amelia and John, who provided so many stories that inspired many of the insights found in this book. Anthony Garrett for his early guidance on this project. The entire team at Beacon Press, including Beth Collins, Susan Lumenello, and Raquel Pidal. My brilliant editor, Catherine Tung, whose invaluable feedback helped me refine the various drafts. My two sons, who (sometimes) let Daddy work. My mother, who is responsible for all my good qualities except for my teeth. My wife, Sarah, whose creativity and work ethic inspired me to take on this project.

NOTES

INTRODUCTION

1. Kaid Benfield, Sarah Zhang, and Elizabeth King, "Where Cities Are Growing Faster than Suburbs," *Bloomberg CityLab* (blog), *Bloomberg*, June 29, 2012, https://www.bloomberg.com/news/articles/2012–06–29/why-cities-are-growing -faster-than-their-suburbs, accessed June 3, 2019.

2. Campbell Gibson, "Population of the 100 Largest Cities and Other Urban Places in the United States: 1790 to 1990," US Census Bureau, June 1998, retrieved July 10, 2016, https://www.census.gov/library/working-papers/1998/demo/POP -twps0027.html.

3. US Census Bureau QuickFacts: Boston, https://www.census.gov/quickfacts /fact/table/bostoncitymassachusetts,losangelescitycalifornia/PST045222, accessed June 26, 2023.

4. US Census Bureau QuickFacts: Portland, https://www.census.gov/quickfacts /portlandcityoregon, accessed June 26, 2023.

5. US Census Bureau QuickFacts: New York, https://www.census.gov/quickfacts /newyorkcitynewyork, accessed June 26, 2023.

6. Diana Olick, "A City's Walkability Drives Real Estate Values," *CNBC* (blog), NBC News, June 17, 2014, https://www.cnbc.com/2014/06/17/a-citys -walkability-drives-real-estate-values.html.

7. Sarah Goodyear, "Making the Real Estate Case for 'Walkable Urban Places,'" *Bloomberg CityLab* (blog), *Bloomberg*, June 18, 2014, https://www.bloomberg.com /news/articles/2014–06–18/making-the-real-estate-case-for-walkable-urban-places.

8. Sarah Min, "Average Americans Can't Afford a Home in 70 Percent of the Country," *CBS News* (blog), CBS, March 28, 2019, https://www.cbsnews.com/news /housing-market-2019-americans-cant-afford-a-home-in-70-percent-of-the -country/; Tracy Jan, "A Minimum-Wage Worker Can't Afford a 2-Bedroom Apartment Anywhere in the U.S.," *Washington Post*, January 13, 2018, https:// www.washingtonpost.com/news/wonk/wp/2018/06/13/a-minimum-wage-worker -cant-afford-a-2-bedroom-apartment-anywhere-in-the-u-s.

9. Ronda Kaysen, "A Housing Market Hangover," *New York Times*, December 30, 2022.

10. Roger Vincent, "You'll Share This Apartment with a Stranger—But Don't Dare Call It a Dorm," *Los Angeles Times*, January 6, 2019.

11. Patrick McGeehan, "When the Real Estate Mogul Tried to Supersize His $8 Million Brownstone," *New York Times*, June 7, 2019.

12. California Housing Partnership and the Southern California Association of Non-Profit Housing, "Los Angeles County's Housing Emergency Update," May 2019, https://static1.squarespace.com/static/58793de5f7e0abe551062b38/t /5ce2fc70af9ae10001c74987/1558379634095/Los+Angeles+HNR+2019.pdf.

13. Sam Reed, "Hollywood Homes Threatened by Skirball Fire," *Hollywood Reporter*, December 6, 2017.

14. David Owen, "The Greenest Place in the U.S. May Not Be Where You Think," *Yale E360* (blog), Yale School of the Environment, October 29, 2009, https://e360.yale.edu/features/greenest_place_in_the_us_its_not_where_you _think.

15. Maanvi Singh and Oliver Milman, "Denser Cities Could Be a Climate Boon—but Nimbyism Stands in the Way," *Grist* (blog), August 27, 2021, https:// grist.org/buildings/denser-cities-could-be-a-climate-boon-but-nimbyism-stands -in-the-way.

16. Emily Orminski, "Your Zip Code Is More Important Than Your Genetic Code," *National Community Reinvestment Coalition* (blog), June 30, 2021, https:// ncrc.org/your-zip-code-is-more-important-than-your-genetic-code.

17. Staff, "Since 2010 California Has Added More Jobs than Homes," *Lassen County Times*, December 1, 2021.

CHAPTER 1: PHILADELPHIA ROW HOUSE

1. *In Penn's Shadow (1680–1720): Philadelphia: The Great Experiment*, directed by Andrew Ferrett, written by Devon McReynolds, Nathaniel Popkin, and Andrew Ferrett (History Making Productions: September 4, 2014), YouTube, https:// www.youtube.com/watch?v=-31IitsBAho.

2. Hans Fantel, *William Penn: Apostle of Dissent* (New York: W. Morrow & Co., 1974), 54.

3. Fantel, *William Penn*, 154.

4. George Bishop Tatum, foreword by Theo B. White, *Penn's Great Town: 250 Years of Philadelphia Architecture Illustrated in Prints and Drawings* (Philadelphia: University of Pennsylvania Press, 1961), 18.

5. R. F. Weigley, *Philadelphia: A 300-Year History* (New York: W.W. Norton & Company, 1982), 1.

6. Weigley, *Philadelphia: A 300-Year History*, 20.

7. *Philadelphia: The Great Experiment*, directed by Ferrett.

8. Weigley, *Philadelphia: A 300-Year History*, 16.

9. Weigley, *Philadelphia: A 300-Year History*, 99.

10. Weigley, *Philadelphia: A 300-Year History*, 21.

11. Henry Glassie, *Vernacular Architecture* (Bloomington: Indiana University Press, 2000), 84.

12. Stefan Muthesius, *The English Terraced House* (New Haven, CT: Yale University Press, 1990), 7.

13. Tatum, *Penn's Great Town*, 23.

14. Muthesius, *The English Terraced House*.

15. Weigley, *Philadelphia: A 300-Year History*, 10.

16. Weigley, *Philadelphia: A 300-Year History*, 23; Steven Parissien, *The Georgian House in America and Britain* (New York: Rizzoli, 2008), 19.

17. William John Murtagh, "The Philadelphia Row House," *Journal of the Society of Architectural Historians* 16, no. 4 (1957): 8–13, https://doi.org/10.2307/987872.

18. Murtagh, "The Philadelphia Row House."

19. National Park Service, "Franklin Court," U.S. Department of the Interior, version last updated May 23, 2017, https://www.nps.gov/inde/learn/historyculture/places-franklincourt.htm.

20. Weigley, *Philadelphia: A 300-Year History*, 220.

21. Weigley, *Philadelphia: A 300-Year History*, 175.

22. Donna J. Rilling, *Making Houses, Crafting Capitalism: Builders in Philadelphia, 1790–1850* (Philadelphia: University of Pennsylvania Press, 2001), 11.

23. Rilling, *Making Houses, Crafting Capitalism*, viii.

24. Kanti Bharat, "Vitruvius's *de Architectura*," COVE Studio, February 3, 2020, https://editions.covecollective.org/content/vitruviuss-de-architectura.

25. Mary Ellen Hayward and Charles Belfoure, *The Baltimore Rowhouse* (New York: Princeton Architectural Press, 2001), 25.

26. Kenneth Ames, "Robert Mills and the Philadelphia Row House," *Journal of the Society of Architectural Historians* 27, no. 2 (May 1968): 140–46, https://doi.org/10.2307/988472.

27. Gwendolyn Wright, *Moralism and the Model Home: Domestic Architecture and Cultural Conflict in Chicago, 1873–1913* (Chicago: University of Chicago Press, 1980), 49.

28. Weigley, *Philadelphia: A 300-Year History*, 220.

29. Baldwin-Lima-Hamilton Corporation, *History of the Baldwin Locomotive Works* (Milwaukee: Old Lind Publishers, 1971), 7.

30. Rilling, *Making Houses, Crafting Capitalism*, 166.

31. Tatum, *Penn's Great Town*, 20.

32. Rilling, *Making Houses, Crafting Capitalism*, 163.

33. Weigley, *Philadelphia: A 300-Year History*, 374.

34. Lynn Miriam Alpert, "Philadelphia Corner Stores: Their History, Use, and Preservation," master's thesis, University of Pennsylvania, 2012, https://repository.upenn.edu/hp_theses/184.

35. Weigley, *Philadelphia: A 300-Year History*, 363.

36. Hayward and Belfoure, *The Baltimore Rowhouse*, 81.

37. Quoted in Suleiman Osman, *The Invention of Brownstone Brooklyn: Gentrification and the Search for Authenticity in Postwar New York* (New York: Oxford University Press, 2012), 30.

38. Weigley, *Philadelphia: A 300-Year History*, 535.

39. Elizabeth McKellar, *The Birth of Modern London: The Development and Design of the City 1660–1720* (Manchester: Manchester University Press, 2001), 43–45.

40. Sir Anthony Seldon, "History: 10 Downing Street," GOV.UK, https://www.gov.uk/government/history/10-downing-street, accessed November 21, 2022.

41. Helen L. Parrish, "One Million People in Small Houses," *National Housing Association*, no. 7 (1911).

42. John F. Sutherland, "The Origins of Philadelphia's Octavia Hull Association: Social Reform in the 'Contented City,'" *Pennsylvania Magazine of History and Biography*, April 1975.

43. Gwendolyn Wright, *Building the Dream: A Social History of Housing in America* (Cambridge, MA: MIT Press, 1981), 100.

44. Weigley, *Philadelphia: A 300-Year History*, 495.

45. Hayward and Belfoure, *The Baltimore Rowhouse*, 126.

46. W. E. B. Du Bois, *The Philadelphia Negro: A Social Study*, reprint ed. (Philadelphia: University of Pennsylvania Press, 1995), 296.

47. Elizabeth Hawes, *New York, New York: How the Apartment House Transformed the Life of the City (1869–1930)* (New York: Knopf, 1993), 77.

48. Weigley, *Philadelphia: A 300-Year History*, 532.

49. Hayward and Belfoure, *The Baltimore Rowhouse*, 151.

50. Dan Hanson, "The 10 Richest Neighborhoods in Philadelphia," *Money Inc.*, April 19, 2021.

51. Meredith Glaser et al., eds., *The City at Eye Level: Lessons for Street Plinths* (Utrecht, The Netherlands: Eburon Academic Publishers, 2012).

52. Susan Warner, *Philadelphia's Changing Middle Class: After Decades of Decline, Prospects for Growth* (Philadelphia: Pew Charitable Trusts, February 2014), https://www.pewtrusts.org/-/media/legacy/uploadedfiles/wwwpewtrustsorg/reports/philadelphia_research_initiative/priphiladelphiachangingmiddleclassreportfebruary2014pdf.pdf.

CHAPTER 2: NEW YORK CITY TENEMENT

1. US Census Bureau QuickFacts: New York City, New York, March 23, 2023, https://www.census.gov/quickfacts/newyorkcitynewyork; US Census Bureau QuickFacts: Chicago, Illinois, March 18, 2023, https://www.census.gov/quickfacts/newyorkcitynewyork; US Census Bureau QuickFacts: Los Angeles, California, March 18, 2023, https://www.census.gov/quickfacts/newyorkcitynewyork.

2. Gerard T. Koeppel, *City on a Grid: How New York Became New York* (Boston: Da Capo Press, 2017), 131.

3. Edwin G. Burrows and Mike Wallace, *Gotham: A History of New York City to 1898* (New York: Oxford University Press, 2006), 576.

4. Burrows and Wallace, *Gotham*, 579.

5. Charles Lockwood, Patrick W. Ciccone, Jonathan D. Taylor, Fran Leadon, and Dylan Chandler, *Bricks & Brownstone: The New York Row House* (New York: Rizzoli, 2019), 25.

6. Lockwood et al., *Bricks & Brownstone*, 197–98.

7. Lockwood et al., *Bricks & Brownstone*, 20–76.

8. R. F. Weigley, *Philadelphia: A 300-Year History* (New York: W. W. Norton, 1982), 309.

9. James Brown House, "A Dump with Dignity," The Ear Inn," James Brown House: A Landmark of the City of New York on the National Register of Historic Buildings website, August 12, 2006, http://www.jamesbrownhouse.com/history -earinn.htm.

10. Koeppel, *City on a Grid*, 173.

11. Jacob A. Riis, *How the Other Half Lives: Studies Among the Tenements of New York* (New York: Charles Scribner's Sons, 1890), 14.

12. Morton White and Lucia White, *The Intellectual Versus the City: From Thomas Jefferson to Frank Lloyd White* (Cambridge, MA: Mentor Books, 1962), 25.

13. Zachary J. Violette, "The Decorated Tenement: Working-Class Housing in Boston and New York, 1860–1910," doctoral dissertation, Boston University, 2014, https://open.bu.edu/handle/2144/15106.

14. Bernard L. Herman, *Town House Architecture and Material Life in the Early American City, 1780–1830* (Chapel Hill: University of North Carolina Press, 2012), 238.

15. Violette, "The Decorated Tenement."

16. Violette, "The Decorated Tenement."

17. Elizabeth Blackmar, *Manhattan for Rent: 1785–1850* (Ithaca, NY: Cornell University Press, 1991), 207.

18. Violette, "The Decorated Tenement."

19. Andrew Dolkart, *Biography of a Tenement House in New York City: An Architectural History of 97 Orchard Street* (Charlottesville: University of Virginia Press, 2017), 82.

20. Burrows and Wallace, *Gotham*, 790.

21. Robert W. De Forest, "Tenement House Regulation—the Reasons for It—Its Proper Limitations," *ANNALS of the American Academy of Political and Social Science* 20, no. 1 (July 1902): 83–95, https://doi.org/10.1177/000271620202 000107.

22. Burrows and Wallace, *Gotham*, 790.

23. Lockwood et al., *Bricks & Brownstone*, 101.

24. Burrows and Wallace, *Gotham*, 790.

25. Richard Plunz, *A History of Housing in New York City*, rev. ed. (New York: Columbia University Press, 2016), 22.

26. Burrows and Wallace, *Gotham*, 588.

27. Luc Sante, *Low Life: Lures and Snares of Old New York* (New York: Farrar, Straus and Giroux, 2003), 55.

28. Blackmar, *Manhattan for Rent*, 70.

29. Tom Buk-Swienty, *The Other Half: The Life of Jacob Riis and the World of Immigrant America* (New York: W. W. Norton, 2008), 162.

30. Burrows and Wallace, *Gotham*, 745; The Peopling of New York City Irish Communities RSS Users, "History and Demographics of the Irish Coming to America," Macaulay Honors College at CUNY, April 27, 2009, https://macaulay

.cuny.edu/seminars/gardner-irish/articles/h/i/s/History_and_Demographics_of
_the_Irish_Coming_to_America_248e.html.

31. Bonnie Yochelson and Daniel Czitrom, *Rediscovering Jacob Riis: Exposure Journalism and Photography in Turn-of-the-Century New York*, reprint ed. (Chicago: University of Chicago Press, 2014), 47.

32. Riis, *How the Other Half Lives*, 22.

33. Buk-Swienty, *The Other Half*, 198.

34. Axel Madsen, *John Jacob Astor: America's First Multimillionaire* (New York: Wiley, 2001), 274.

35. Jared Day, *Urban Castles: Tenement Housing and Landlord Activism, New York City 1890–1943* (New York: Columbia University Press, 1999), 51.

36. Day, *Urban Castles*, 24

37. Day, *Urban Castles*, 24.

38. Buk-Swienty, *The Other Half*, 145.

39. Plunz, *A History of Housing in New York City*, 33.

40. Plunz, *A History of Housing in New York City*, 24.

41. Violette, "The Decorated Tenement."

42. Yochelson and Czitrom, *Rediscovering Jacob Riis*, 47.

43. Parrish, "One Million People in Small Houses."

44. Buk-Swienty, *The Other Half*, 192.

45. Harry L. Watson and William M. Rohe, *Chasing the American Dream: New Perspectives on Affordable Homeownership* (Ithaca, NY: Cornell University Press, 2007), 18.

46. Jacob Riis, "The Tenement House Blight," *The Atlantic Monthly*, June 1899.

47. Violette, "The Decorated Tenement."

48. Allison Elizabeth Kelsey, "How the Other Nine-Tenths Lived: Interpreting the Working Class Experience in Philadelphia, 1870–1900," master's thesis, Weitzman School of Design, University of Pennsylvania, 1997, 445, https://repository.upenn.edu/hp_theses/445.

49. Plunz, *A History of Housing in New York City*, 93.

50. Day, *Urban Castles*, 37.

51. Violette, "The Decorated Tenement."

52. No author, "Joseph Durst, 92, Real Estate Man," *New York Times*, January 2, 1974.

53. Dennis Hevesi, "Robert Tishman, Real Estate Developer, Dies at 94," *New York Times*, October 12, 2010.

54. Day, *Urban Castles*, 44.

55. Day, *Urban Castles*, 48–50.

56. Martin Scorsese, "'Can a Person Change?': Martin Scorsese on Gangsters, Death, and Redemption," interview by Terry Gross, *Fresh Air*, WHYY, January 16, 2020.

57. Violette, "The Decorated Tenement."

58. Elizabeth Hawes, *New York, New York: How the Apartment House Transformed the Life of the City (1869–1930)* (New York: Knopf, 1993), 26.

59. Violette, "The Decorated Tenement."

60. Plunz, *A History of Housing in New York City*, 37.

61. Buk-Swienty, *The Other Half*, 69.

62. Buk-Swienty, *The Other Half*, 254–55.

63. Day, *Urban Castles*, 69.

64. Violette, "The Decorated Tenement."

65. Day, *Urban Castles*, 172.

66. David Netto, "Meet the Mastermind of the World's Most Valuable Apartment," *Architectural Digest*, May 14, 2018.

67. Phillipe Martin Chatelain, "Bronx's Grand Concourse: 'The Park Ave. of the Middle Class,'" *Untapped New York*, September 18, 2013, https://untappedcities.com/2013/09/18/history-of-nyc-streets-grand-concourse-20th-century-attempt-bronx-more-like-paris.

68. Day, *Urban Castles*, 172.

69. Dolkart, *Biography of a Tenement House in New York City*, 112.

70. Day, *Urban Castles*, 175.

71. *Rare Iggy Pop Documentary by Bram Van Splunteren (1993)*, directed by Bram Van Splunteren (Acclaim Magazine, May 22, 2013), YouTube, https://www.youtube.com/watch?v=JKGeh4cVRZE.

72. Ross MacWhinney and Omri Klagsbald, *Inventory of New York City Greenhouse Gas Emissions* (New York: New York City Mayor's Office of Sustainability, December 2017).

73. Day, *Urban Castles*, 214–25.

74. Michael Bodley, "Inside the SF Laundromat Basement Where Two Dozen People Lived," *San Francisco Chronicle*, March 19, 2017.

75. Edith Abbott, *The Tenements of Chicago, 1908–1935* (Chicago: University of Chicago Press, 1936), 164.

CHAPTER 3: NEW ORLEANS SHOTGUN

1. Peirce F. Lewis, *New Orleans. The Making of an Urban Landscape* (Chicago: Center for American Places, 2003), 29.

2. *New Orleans—The Natural History*, created by Walter Williams (Terrebone Parish, July 5, 2012), YouTube, https://www.youtube.com/watch?v=ROXcAO9znIk.

3. Father Claudus Dablon, *Relation of the Voyages, Discoveries, and Death of Father James Marquette and the Subsequent Voyages of Father Claudius Allouez* (New York: Redfield, 1852), 178.

4. Richard Campanella, *Bienville's Dilemma: A Historical Geography of New Orleans* (Baton Rouge: University of Louisiana Press, 2008), 123.

5. Jay D. Edwards, "The Origins of Creole Architecture," *Winterthur Portfolio* 29, no. 2/3 (Summer–Autumn 1994): 155–89.

6. Richard Sexton, *Creole World. Photographs of New Orleans and the Latin Caribbean Sphere* (New Orleans: Historic New Orleans Collection, 2014).

7. Scott S. Ellis, *The Faubourg Marigny of New Orleans: A History* (Baton Rouge: LSU Press, 2018), 20.

8. Ellis, *The Faubourg Marigny of New Orleans*, 21.

9. Dell Upton, *Another City. Urban Life and Urban Spaces in the New American Republic* (New Haven, CT: Yale University Press, 2008), 31.

10. Gary A. Van Zante, *New Orleans 1867: Photographs by Theodore Lilienthal* (London: Merrell, 2008), 254.

11. Campanella, *Bienville's Dilemma*, 264.

12. Upton, *Another City*, 39.

13. Lloyd Vogt, *New Orleans Houses: A House-Watcher's Guide* (New Orleans: Pelican Publishing, 1985), 17.

14. Van Zante, *New Orleans 1867*, 16.

15. Van Zante, *New Orleans 1867*, 160.

16. *Egalité for All: Toussaint Louverture and the Haitian Revolution*, directed by Noland Walker, produced by Patricia Aste and Margaret Koval (ITVS: January 25, 2009), YouTube, https://www.youtube.com/watch?v=pBdlwuEoCCU.

17. John Michael Vlach, "The Shotgun House: An African Architectural Legacy, Part I," *Pioneer America* 8 no. 1 (January 1976): 47–56.

18. Louis P. Nelson, "The Architectures of Black Identity: Buildings, Slavery, and Freedom in the Caribbean and the American South," *Winterthur Portfolio* 45, no. 2/3 (Summer/Autumn 2011): 177–d94, https://doi.org/10.1086/660810.

19. Joshua D. Rothman, "Before the Civil War, New Orleans Was the Center of the US Slave Trade," *Smithsonian Magazine*, April 19, 2021.

20. Campanella, *Bienville's Dilemma*, 156.

21. Campanella, *Bienville's Dilemma*, 157.

22. Lewis, *New Orleans*, 48.

23. Jay D. Edwards, "New Orleans Shotgun: A Historic Cultural Geography," in *Culture After the Hurricanes: Rhetoric and Reinvention on the Gulf Coast*, ed. M. B. Hackler (Jackson: University Press of Mississippi, 2010), 44–90, https://doi.org/10.14325/mississippi/9781604734904.003.0003, accessed November 22, 2022.

24. Edwards, "New Orleans Shotgun."

25. Jay D. Edwards, "Shotgun: The Most Contested House in America," *Buildings & Landscapes: Journal of the Vernacular Architecture Forum* 26, no. 1 (Spring 2009): 62–96.

26. Vlach, "The Shotgun House: An African Architectural Legacy, Part I."

27. Edwards, "Shotgun: The Most Contested House in America."

28. Lewis, *New Orleans*, 47.

29. "TriPod Mythbusters: Quadroon Balls and Plaçage," *TriPod: New Orleans at 300*, WWNO, September 22, 2016.

30. Edwards, "Shotgun: The Most Contested House in America."

31. Edwards, "Shotgun: The Most Contested House in America."

32. Edwards, "Shotgun: The Most Contested House in America."

33. Sheryl G. Tucker, "Reinnovating the African-American Shotgun House [Roots]," *Places* 10, no. 1 (July 15, 1995): 64–71, https://escholarship.org/uc/item/7pk7z3kn.

34. bell hooks, "Black Vernacular: Architecture as Cultural Practice," in *Art on My Mind: Visual Politics* (New York: The New Press, 1995), 145–51.

35. Tucker, "Reinnovating the African-American Shotgun House."

36. Van Zante, *New Orleans 1867*, 59.

37. Van Zante, *New Orleans 1867*, 58.

38. George O. Carney, "Shotgun House," *Encyclopedia of Oklahoma History and Culture*, Oklahoma Historical Society, https://www.okhistory.org/publications/enc/entry.php?entry=SH028, accessed November 22, 2022.

39. Joanne Weeter, "Shotgun Cottages," in *The Encyclopedia of Louisville*, ed. John Kleber (Lexington: University Press of Kentucky, 2001), 819.

40. N. D. B. Connolly, *A World More Concrete: Real Estate and the Remaking of Jim Crow South Florida* (Chicago: University of Chicago Press, 2014), 78.

41. Tucker, "Reinnovating the African-American Shotgun House."

42. Tucker, "Reinnovating the African-American Shotgun House."

43. Ellis, *The Faubourg Marigny of New Orleans*, 40.

44. Campanella, *Bienville's Dilemma*, 187.

45. Van Zante, *New Orleans 1867*, 66.

46. Edwards, "Shotgun: The Most Contested House in America."

47. Sarah M. Broom, *The Yellow House: A Memoir* (New York: Grove Press, 2020), 49.

48. Lewis, *New Orleans*, 154–61.

49. Lewis, *New Orleans*, 89.

50. Lewis, *New Orleans*, 145.

51. Campanella, *Bienville's Dilemma*, 185.

52. Peter Grier, "The Great Katrina Migration," *Christian Science Monitor*, September 12, 2005.

53. Ben Casselman, "Katrina Washed Away New Orleans' Black Middle Class," *FiveThirtyEight*, August 24, 2015.

54. Richard Campanella, *Cityscapes of New Orleans* (Baton Rouge: Louisiana State University Press, 2017), 66.

55. Louisiana Landmarks Society, "'New Orleans Nine' Draws Attention to Endangered Places," *Preservation in Print Magazine*, October 2022, https://prcno.org/new-orleans-nine-2022.

56. All Things New Orleans, "New Orleans' Noise Ordinance: What It Sounds Like Now," New Orleans Public Radio, WWNO, May 13, 2015.

57. Edwards, "Shotgun: The Most Contested House in America."

58. Lolis Elie, "Gentrification Might Kill New Orleans Before Climate Change," *New York Times*, August 27, 2019.

CHAPTER 4: CHICAGO WORKERS COTTAGE

1. Kenneth T. Jackson, *Crabgrass Frontier: The Suburbanization of the United States* (New York: Oxford University Press, 1987), 125.

2. David Herbert Donald, *Lincoln* (New York: Simon & Schuster, 1996), 25.

3. No author, "Seven Grandfather Teachings," Nottawaseppi Huron Band of the Potawatomi, https://nhbp-nsn.gov/seven-grandfather-teachings.

4. Settler Colonial City Project, *Mapping Chicagou/Chicago: A Living Atlas* (Chicago: Chicago Architecture Biennial, 2019).

5. Monica Davey, "Tribute to Chicago Icon and Enigma," *New York Times*, June 25, 2003.

6. William Cronon, *Nature's Metropolis: Chicago and the Great West* (New York: W. W. Norton, 2010), 34.

7. John Lamb, "Illinois and Michigan Canal," Encyclopedia of Chicago, 2004, http://www.encyclopedia.chicagohistory.org/pages/626.html.

8. Settler Colonial City Project, *Mapping Chicagou/Chicago*.

9. Cronon, *Nature's Metropolis*, 29.

10. Joseph C. Bigott, *From Cottage to Bungalow: Houses and the Working Class in Metropolitan Chicago, 1869–1929* (Chicago: University of Chicago Press, 2001), 41.

11. Harold M. Mayer and Richard C. Wade, *Chicago: Growth of a Metropolis* (Chicago: University of Chicago Press, 1973), 32.

12. Mayer and Wade, *Chicago*, 192.

13. Gerard T. Koeppel, *City on a Grid: How New York Became New York* (Boston: Da Capo Press, 2017), 173.

14. Sally Ann McMurry and Annmarie Adams, eds., *People, Power, Places: Perspectives in Vernacular Architecture* (Knoxville: University of Tennessee Press, 2000), 14.

15. Cronon, *Nature's Metropolis*, 179.

16. Mayer and Wade, *Chicago*, 35.

17. Cronon, *Nature's Metropolis*, 70.

18. Cronon, *Nature's Metropolis*, 175.

19. Mayer and Wade, *Chicago*, 22.

20. Cronon, *Nature's Metropolis*, 374.

21. Mayer and Wade, *Chicago*, 20.

22. Gwendolyn Wright, *Moralism and the Model Home: Domestic Architecture and Cultural Conflict in Chicago, 1873–1913* (Chicago: University of Chicago Press, 1980), 82.

23. Jackson, *Crabgrass Frontier*, 114.

24. Mayer and Wade, *Chicago*, 138.

25. Ann Durkin Keating, *Building Chicago: Suburban Developers and the Creation of a Divided Metropolis* (Columbus: Ohio State University Press, 2002), 68.

26. Mayer and Wade, *Chicago*, 138.

27. Mayer and Wade, *Chicago*, 32.

28. Mayer and Wade, *Chicago*, 174.

29. Stephen Ward, *Selling Places: The Marketing and Promotion of Towns and Cities 1850–2000* (London: Routledge, 1998), 109.

30. Hartmut Keil and John B. Jentz, eds., *German Workers in Chicago: A Documentary History of Working-Class Culture from 1850 to World War I* (Champaign: University of Illinois Press, 1988), 129.

31. Ward, *Selling Places*, 108.

32. Mayer and Wade, *Chicago*, 21.

33. Edith Abbott, *The Tenements of Chicago, 1908–1935* (Chicago: University of Chicago, 1936), 21.

34. Abbott, *The Tenements of Chicago*, 21.

35. McMurry and Adams, *People, Power, Places*, 42.

36. Paul Groth, "Worker's-Cottage and Minimal-Bungalow Districts in Oakland and Berkeley, California, 1870–1945," *Urban Morphology* 8, no. 1 (2004): 13–25.

37. Keil and Jentz, *German Workers in Chicago*, 129.

38. Abbott, *The Tenements of Chicago*, 32.

39. Abbott, *The Tenements of Chicago*, 378.

40. Abbott, *The Tenements of Chicago*, 478.

41. Matthew Edel, Elliott D. Sclar, and Daniel Luria, *Shaky Palaces: Home-ownership and Social Mobility in Boston's Surburbanization* (New York: Columbia University Press, 1984), 190.

42. Abbott, *The Tenements of Chicago*, 363.

43. Mayer and Wade, *Chicago*, 226.

44. Abbott, *The Tenements of Chicago*, 104.

45. Keating, *Building Chicago*, 3.

46. Cronon, *Nature's Metropolis*, 347.

47. Andrew Jackson Downing, *Victorian Cottage Residences*, ed. George E. Harney (Mineola, NY: Dover Publications, 2011), 164.

48. Jackson, *Crabgrass Frontier*, 65.

49. Downing, *Victorian Cottage Residences*, xi.

50. Wright, *Moralism and the Model Home*, 10.

51. Morton White and Lucia White, *The Intellectual Versus the City: From Thomas Jefferson to Frank Lloyd Wright* (Oxford: Oxford University Press, 1977), 39.

52. Bigott, *From Cottage to Bungalow*, 153.

53. Mayer and Wade, *Chicago*, 254.

54. Editors of Encyclopedia Britannica, "Chicago Race Riot of 1919," *Encyclopedia Britannica*, August 19, 2020, https://www.britannica.com/event/Chicago-Race-Riot-of-1919.

55. Mayer and Wade, *Chicago*, 316.

56. Mayer and Wade, *Chicago*, 366.

57. *Form, Design, and the City (1962)*, presented by the Reynolds Metals Company with the American Institute of Architects (Philadelphia Department of Records, October 4, 2013), YouTube, https://www.youtube.com/watch?v=1GGqSkDXOSg.

58. Mindy Thompson Fullilove and Rodrick Wallace, "Serial Force Displacement in American Cities, 1916–2010," *Journal of Urban Health* 88, no. 3 (June 2011): 381–89, DOI: 10.1007/s11524-011-9585-2.

59. Vera Hogan, "Urban Renewal, When the Walls Came Tumbling Down," *Tri-County Times*, April 19, 2013.

60. Manny Ramos, "Englewood's Population, Housing, Stock Plummets, 2020 Census Data Shows," *Chicago Sun-Times*, September 26, 2021.

61. No author, "Analyzing Teardowns of Workers Cottages," Chicago Workers Cottage Initiative, https://www.workerscottage.org/teardowndata.html, accessed November 22, 2022.

62. Tom Vlodek and Matt Bergstrom (activists), in conversation with the author, May 5, 2022.

CHAPTER 5: PORTLAND BUNGALOW

1. City of Portland Bureau of Planning and Sustainability, *East Portland Historical Overview and Historic Preservation Study* (Portland: Bureau of Planning and Sustainability, March 2009), https://www.portlandonline.com/portlandplan /index.cfm?a=346260&c=51427.

2. Carl Abbott, *Portland in Three Centuries: The Place and the People* (Corvallis: Oregon State University Press), 20.

3. Abbott, *Portland in Three Centuries*, 56–57.

4. Phil Stanford, *Portland Confidential: The Rise and Fall of Big Jim Elkins* (Lincoln Beach: West Winds Press, 2004), 3.

5. City of Portland, *East Portland Historical Overview and Historic Preservation Study*.

6. City of Portland, *East Portland Historical Overview and Historic Preservation Study*.

7. Gwendolyn Wright, *Moralism and the Model Home: Domestic Architecture and Cultural Conflict in Chicago, 1873–1913* (Chicago: University of Chicago Press, 1980), 40.

8. Virginia McAlester and Lee McAlester, *A Field Guide to American Houses* (New York: Knopf, 1984).

9. *Memories of the Future: William Morris, John Ruskin*, directed by Peter Fuller (Channel 4 England, 1983), YouTube, August 27, 2017, https://www.youtube .com/watch?v=_5IWBdSGECU.

10. Anthony King, *The Bungalow: The Production of a Global Culture* (Oxford: Oxford University Press, 1995), 19.

11. King, *The Bungalow*, 42.

12. King, *The Bungalow*, 114.

13. Ted Bosley, "The House Beautiful: Truth to Nature in the Work of Greene and Greene," lecture, Huntington Museum, San Marino, CA, December 13, 2019.

14. Wright, *Moralism and the Model Home*, 119.

15. King, *The Bungalow*, 130.

16. King, *The Bungalow*, 144.

17. Gwendolyn Wright, *Building the Dream: A Social History of Housing in America* (Cambridge, MA: MIT Press, 1981), 166.

18. Paul Groth, "Worker's-Cottage and Minimal-Bungalow Districts in Oakland and Berkeley, California, 1870–1945," *Urban Morphology* 8, no. 1 (2004): 13–25.

19. Peirce F. Lewis, *New Orleans: The Making of an Urban Landscape*, 2nd ed. (Santa Fe: Center for American Places, 2003), 68.

20. Wright, *Building the Dream*, 163.

21. Thomas C. Hubka, *How the Working-Class Home Became Modern, 1900 to 1940* (Minneapolis: University of Minnesota Press, 2020), 88.

22. Thomas C. Hubka and J. T. Kenny, "Examining the American Dream: Housing Standard and the Emergence of a National Housing Culture, 1900–1930," *Perspectives in Vernacular Architecture* 13, no. 1 (2006): 46–49.

23. City of Portland, *East Portland Historical Overview and Historic Preservation Study*.

24. Wright, *Moralism and the Model Home*, 237.

25. Matthew Edel, Elliott D. Sclar, and Daniel Luria, *Shaky Palaces: Home-ownership and Social Mobility in Boston's Surburbanization* (New York: Columbia University Press, 1984), 281.

26. Carl Abbott, *Portland: Planning, Politics, and Growth in a Twentieth-Century City* (Lincoln: University of Nebraska Press, 1983), 72.

27. Elizabeth Blackmar, *Manhattan for Rent: 1785–1850* (Ithaca: Cornell University Press, 1991), 328.

28. City of Portland, Oregon, "New Research by PSU Grad Student Reveals Racist Covenants Across Portland," *Portland Department of Planning and Sustainability (BPS)* (blog), March 22, 2018, https://www.portland.gov/bps/new/2018/3/22/new-research-psu-grad-student-reveals-racist-covenants-across-portland.

29. Charles Cheney, "Removing Social Barriers by Zoning," *The Survey* 44, no. 11 (May 22, 1920): 275–78.

30. Abbott, *Portland: Planning, Politics and Growth*, 87.

31. Hubka, *How the Working Class Home Became Modern*, 19.

32. Kenneth T. Jackson, *Crabgrass Frontier: The Surburbanization of the United States* (New York: Oxford University Press, 1987), 187.

33. "Homeownership Rates (United States by state, 1900–2000)," US Census Bureau, https://www2.census.gov/programs-surveys/decennial/tables/time-series/coh-owner/owner-tab.txt.

34. Jackson, *Crabgrass Frontier*, 209.

35. Alfred M. Staehli, "They Sure Don't Build Them Like They Used To: Federal Housing Administration Insured Builders' Houses in the Pacific Northwest from 1934 to 1954," master's thesis, Portland State University, 1987, Paper 3799, DOI: 10.15760/etd.5683.

36. Jackson, *Crabgrass Frontier*, 200.

37. Maria Godoy, "In US Cities, The Health Effects of Past Housing Discrimination Are Plain to See," NPR, November 19, 2020.

38. Jackson, *Crabgrass Frontier*, 241.

39. Witold Rybczynski, *Last Harvest: How a Cornfield Became New Daleville: Real Estate Development in America from George Washington to the Builders of the Twenty-First Century, and Why We Live in Houses Anyway* (New York: Scribner, 2007), 83.

40. Abbott, *Portland in Three Centuries*, 123.

41. John Gunther, *Inside U.S.A.*, 50th-ann. ed. (New York: The New Press, 1997), 90.

42. Abbott, *Portland in Three Centuries*, 131.

43. *Mayoral Lessons: Words of Wisdom from Bud Clark and Vera Katz*, City Club of Portland, presented July 25, 2008, YouTube, February 4, 2015, https://www.youtube.com/watch?v=uY8hY9xsT-0.

44. Mitchell S. Jackson, *The Residue Years* (New York: Bloomsbury, 2013), 179.

45. Abbott, *Portland: Planning, Politics, and Growth*, 138.

46. Robert Moses, *Portland Improvement* (New York: William E. Rudge's Sons), November 10, 1943, https://www.portlandmercury.com/images/blogimages /2009/09/30/1254339381-portland_improvement_-_robert_moses_1943.pdf.

47. Abbott, *Portland: Planning, Politics, and Growth*, 188.

48. Sam Roberts, "Vera Katz, Mayor Who Oversaw Portland's Flowering, Dies at 84," *New York Times*, December 13, 2017.

49. Joseph S. Uris, "The Lair Hill Park Neighborhood on Examination of the Phenomenon of Community Creation," master's thesis, Portland State University, 1971, Paper 727, doi: 10.15760/etd.727.

50. Abbott, *Portland: Planning, Politics, and Growth*, 184.

51. Abbott, *Portland in Three Centuries*, 146.

52. Abbott, *Portland: Planning, Politics, and Growth*, 185.

53. City of Portland, *East Portland Historical Overview and Historic Preservation Study*.

54. Abbott, *Portland: Planning, Politics, and Growth*, 245.

55. Abbott, *Portland: Planning, Politics, and Growth*, 251.

56. Carl Abbott, *Greater Portland: Urban Life and Landscape in the Pacific Northwest* (Philadelphia: University of Pennsylvania Press, 2001), 10.

57. Abe Asher, "How Will Oregon Address Its Growing Affordable Housing Crisis?" *Portland Mercury*, November 26, 2021.

58. Janet Eastman, "Cooling Portland Area Home Prices: Median Sales Price Drops $15,000 in a Month," *The Oregonian*, October 21, 2021.

59. Nigel Jaquiss, "The Black Population of Inner North and Northeast Portland Continues to Shrink," *Willamette Week*, August 25, 2021.

60. Edward Glaeser, and Atta Tarki, "California Housing Development Remains Abysmal Despite Reforms. Here's What's Missing," *Los Angeles Times*, February 19, 2023.

CHAPTER 6: BOSTON TRIPLE-DECKER

1. Gwendolyn Wright, *Building the Dream: A Social History of Housing in America* (Cambridge, MA: MIT Press, 1981), 8–9.

2. Matthew Reed Baker, "One Last Question: Are Boston's Streets Really Paved Over Cow Paths?" *Boston Magazine*, March 6, 2018.

3. Bernard L. Herman, *Town House: Architecture and Material Life in the Early American City, 1780–1830* (Chapel Hill: University of North Carolina Press, 2017), 7.

4. Walter Muir Whitehill, *Boston: A Topographical History*, 2nd ed., enlarged (Cambridge, MA: Harvard University Press, 1968), 47.

5. Douglass Shand-Tucci, *Built in Boston: City and Suburb, 1800–2000* (Amherst: University of Massachusetts Press, 2000), 9.

6. Lawrence W. Kennedy, *Planning the City upon a Hill: Boston Since 1630* (Amherst: University of Massachusetts Press, 1992), 58.

7. Whitehill, *Boston*, 111.

8. Morton White and Lucia White, *The Intellectual Versus the City: From Thomas Jefferson to Frank Lloyd White* (Cambridge, MA: Mentor Books, 1962), 38.

9. Matthew Edel, Elliott D. Sclar, and Daniel Luria, *Shaky Palaces: Home-ownership and Social Mobility in Boston's Surburbanization* (New York: Columbia University Press, 1984), 46.

10. Edel, Sclar, and Luria, *Shaky Palaces*, 43.

11. Mona Domosh, *Invented Cities: The Creation of Landscape in Nineteenth-Century New York and Boston* (New Haven, CT: Yale University Press, 1998), 116.

12. Whitehill, *Boston*, 164.

13. *The Race Underground*, directed, written, and produced by Michael Rossi (*American Experience*, November 12, 2019), PBS/WGBH.

14. Sam Bass Warner, *Streetcar Suburbs: The Process of Growth in Boston, 1870–1900*, 2nd ed. (Cambridge, MA: Harvard University Press, 1978), 140.

15. Shand-Tucci, *Built in Boston*, 108.

16. Kingston Wm. Heath, *The Patina of Place: The Cultural Weathering of a New England Industrial Landscape* (Chattanooga: University of Tennessee Press, 2016), 121.

17. Whitehill, *Boston*, 120.

18. Robert Treat Paine, "The Housing Conditions in Boston," *Annals of the American Academy of Political and Social Sciences* 20 (July 1902): 123–36.

19. Warner, *Streetcar Suburbs*, 52–64.

20. Warner, *Streetcar Suburbs*, 140.

21. Arthur J. Krim, *The Three-Deckers of Dorchester: An Architectural Historical Survey* (Boston: Boston Redevelopment Authority, 1977).

22. Lloyd Rodwin, *Housing and Economic Progress* (Cambridge, MA: Harvard University Press, 1961), 36–37.

23. Kennedy, *Planning the City upon a Hill*, 147.

24. Warner, *Streetcar Suburbs*, 129.

25. Lloyd Rodwin, "Studies in Middle Income Housing," *Social Forces* 30, no. 3 (March 1952): 292–99.

26. Howard Husock, "Rediscovering the Three Decker House," *National Affairs* (Winter 1990).

27. Robert A. Woods and A. J. Kennedy, *The Zone of Emergence: Observations of the Lower Middle and Upper Working-Class Communities of Boston, 1905–1914* (Cambridge, MA: MIT Press, 1969), 39.

28. Heath, *The Patina of Place*, 146.

29. Henry Adams, *The Education of Henry Adams: An Autobiography* (New York: Modern Library, 1999), 419.

30. Daniel Okrent, *The Guarded Gate: Bigotry, Eugenics, and the Law That Kept Two Generations of Jews, Italians, and Other European Immigrants Out of America* (New York: Scribner, 2019), 38.

31. Okrent, *The Guarded Gate*, 208.

32. "The Workingman Pays the Heavy Freight," *Providence Magazine*, January 1917.

33. Liberty and Power, "Lawrence Veiller: Progressive Tenement Reformer and Eugenicist," History News Network, Columbian College of Arts and Sciences, June 28, 2014, https://historynewsnetwork.org/blog/153403.

34. Jacob A. Riis, *How the Other Half Lives: Studies Among the Tenements of New York* (New York: Charles Scribner's Sons, 1890), 107.

35. Paine, "The Housing Conditions in Boston."

36. Rodwin, "Studies in Middle Income Housing."

37. Rodwin, "Studies in Middle Income Housing."

38. Paine, "The Housing Conditions in Boston."

39. Husock, "Rediscovering the Three Decker House."

40. *Souvenir Book of the Great Chelsea Fire: April 12, 1908* (Boston: N. E. Paper & Stationery Co., 1908).

41. Kathleen Conti, "When Chelsea Burned," *Boston Globe*, April 10, 2008.

42. William Tucker, "Building Codes, Housing Prices, and the Poor," in *Housing America: Building Out of a Crisis*, ed. Randall Holcombe and Benjamin Powell (Piscataway, NJ: Transaction Publishers, 2009).

43. Richard M. Candee and Greer Hardwicke, "Early Twentieth-Century Reform Housing by Kilham and Hopkins, Architects of Boston," *Winterthur Portfolio* 22, no. 1 (1987): 61, http://www.jstor.org/stable/1181147

44. William C. Ewing, "Merits and Demerits of the Three Decker," *American Contractor* 39 (March 16, 1918).

45. Husock, "Rediscovering the Three Decker House."

46. Madeline Bilis, "The Anatomy of a Three-Decker," *Boston Magazine*, August 10, 2016.

47. Okrent, *The Guarded Gate*, 344–49.

CHAPTER 7: LOS ANGELES DINGBAT

1. *Farm Life in the Early 20th Century: Avoiding Waste*, produced by Iowa Public Television, excerpted from the documentary *The People in the Pictures: Stories from the Wettach Farm Photos* (Iowa PBS, April 28, 2015), YouTube, https://www.youtube.com/watch?v=BtZbB73Pjmk.

2. Robert M. Fogelson, *The Fragmented Metropolis: Los Angeles, 1850–1930* (Berkeley: University of California Press, 1993), 70.

3. Fogelson, *The Fragmented Metropolis*, 80.

4. Carey MacWilliams, *Southern California: An Island on the Land*, 9th ed. (Layton, UT: Gibbs Smith, 2009), 167.

5. Richard W. Longstreth, *City Center to Regional Mall: Architecture, the Automobile, and Retailing in Los Angeles, 1920–1950* (Cambridge, MA: MIT Press, 1998), 6.

6. Fogelson, *The Fragmented Metropolis*, 146

7. Merry Ovnick, *Los Angeles: The End of the Rainbow* (Los Angeles: Balcony Press, 1994), 21.

8. Nathanael West, *Miss Lonelyhearts & The Day of the Locust: Two Novels* (New York: Modern Library, 1998), 132.

9. Austin F. Cross, "Los Angeles Is a City of Hen Coop Architecture," *Ottawa Evening Standard*, March 19, 1935.

10. Ovnick, *Los Angeles*, 79.

11. Nathan Masters, "Seventh & Broadway: Photos of Downtown's Crossroads Through the Decades," KCET, August 1, 2012, https://www.kcet.org/shows/lost-la/seventh-broadway-photos-of-downtowns-crossroads-through-the-decades.

12. Fogelson, *The Fragmented Metropolis*, 148.

13. Longstreth, *City Center to Regional Mall*, 12.

14. City of Portland Bureau of Planning and Sustainability, *East Portland Historical Overview and Historic Preservation Study* (Portland: Bureau of Planning and Sustainability, March 2009), https://www.portlandonline.com/portlandplan/index.cfm?a=346260&c=51427; Fogelson, *The Fragmented Metropolis*, 92.

15. Longstreth, *City Center to Regional Mall*, 66.

16. Fogelson, *The Fragmented Metropolis*, 152.

17. Ovnick, *Los Angeles*, 145.

18. Liz Falletta, *By-Right, By-Design: Housing Development Versus Housing Design in Los Angeles* (London: Routledge, 2020), ebook.

19. Thomas S. Hines, *Irving Gill and the Architecture of Reform: A Study in Modernist Architectural Culture* (New York: Monacelli Press, 2000), 11.

20. Robert Winter, *The California Bungalow* (Santa Monica, CA: Hennessey and Ingalls, 1980), 65.

21. Ovnick, *Los Angeles*, 203.

22. Richard Florida, "America's Truly Densest Metros," *Bloomberg*, October 15, 2012.

23. Fogelson, *The Fragmented Metropolis*, 257.

24. Carl Abbott, *Portland: Planning, Politics, and Growth in a Twentieth-Century City* (Lincoln: University of Nebraska Press, 1983), 83.

25. Falletta, *By-Right, By-Design*.

26. Nick Kotsopoulos, "Zoning Conversation Begins for Former Three-Decker Lots," *Telegram & Gazette*, September 21, 2013.

27. Inga Saffron, "Changing Skyline: New Zoning Code: Toward a More Competitive Livable City," *Philadelphia Inquirer*, August 24, 2012.

28. Thurman Grant and Joshua G. Stein, *Dingbat 2.0: The Iconic Los Angeles Apartment as Projection of a Metropolis* (Los Angeles: DoppelHouse Press, 2016), 64.

29. Falletta, *By-Right, By-Design*.

30. Bob Nero, "The Blooming of the Plastic Hibiscus," *Los Angeles Times*, February 13, 1972.

31. Grant and Stein, *Dingbat 2.0*, 71.

32. Nero, "The Blooming of the Plastic Hibiscus."

33. "Councilman, Builder in Sharp Exchange," *Pomona Progress Bulletin*, October 5, 1954.

34. Longstreth, *City Center to Regional Mall*, 193.

35. Austin F. Cross, "Los Angeles, Meaning Angeles: A Geography Lesson," *Ottawa Evening Citizen*, March 15, 1935.

36. Nero, "The Blooming of the Plastic Hibiscus."

37. Héctor Tobar, "The Assassin Next Door," *New Yorker*, July 22, 2019.

38. Fogelson, *The Fragmented Metropolis*, xvi.

39. William Fulton, *The Reluctant Metropolis: The Politics of Urban Growth in Los Angeles* (Baltimore: Johns Hopkins University Press, 2001).

40. Greg D. Morrow, "The Homeowner Revolution: Democracy, Land Use and the Los Angeles Slow-Growth Movement," PhD diss., University of California, Los Angeles, 2013, https://escholarship.org/uc/item/6k64g20f#main.

41. Morrow, "The Homeowner Revolution."

42. Dana Cuff, Tim Higgins, and Per-Johan Dahl, *Backyard Homes LA* (Los Angeles: cityLAB, UCLA Department of Architecture and Urban Design, 2010), https://static1.squarespace.com/static/58e4e9705016e194dd5cdc43/t/58fb37f83a 041197bb7b1cd6/1492858885878/2010_Backyard_Homes.pdf.

43. Tim Arango, "We Are Forced to Live in These Conditions: In Los Angeles, Virus Ravages Overcrowded Housing," *New York Times*, January 23, 2021.

44. James Rojas, "The Enacted Environment: The Creation of 'Place' by Mexicans and Mexican Americans in East Los Angeles," master's thesis, MIT, 1991, https://dspace.mit.edu/handle/1721.1/13918.

45. Justin Fox, "Why America's New Apartment Buildings All Look the Same," *Bloomberg*, February 13, 2019.

46. Michael Maltzan, Hilary Sample, Níall McLaughlin, Florian Idenburg, Amale Andraos, and James Graham, *Social Transparency: Projects on Housing* (New York: Columbia Books on Architecture and the City, 2016), 93.

47. Andrew Khouri, "LA Developers Grapple with Affordable Housing Measure," *Los Angeles Times*, November 10, 2016.

48. Los Angeles Department of City Planning, "Housing Progress Reports," (2018 and 2019), retrieved, May 14, 2022, https://planning.lacity.org/resources /housing-reports.

49. Ron Galperin, "The Problems and Progress of Prop. HHH: Reviewing L.A.'s Performance over the First Five Years," Ron Galperin, LA City Controller website, February 23, 2022, https://storymaps.arcgis.com/stories/bc84be5b5f794 fc7a1c6e81bc5ef0104.

50. Alan Durning, "Apartment Blockers: Parking Rules Raise Your Rent," Sightline Institute, August 22, 2013, https://www.sightline.org/2013/08/22 /apartment-blockers.

CHAPTER 8: VANCOUVER POINT TOWER

1. Ray Spaxman, A. McAfee, L. Beasley, and B. Toderian, "Future and Past: Planners and Planning in the City of Vancouver," presentation, Simon Fraser University City Program, Vancouver, October 29, 2015.

2. Anthony King, *The Bungalow: The Production of a Global Culture* (Oxford: Oxford University Press, 1995), 152.

3. Michael A. Goldberg and John Mercer, *The Myth of the North American City: Continentalism Challenged* (Vancouver: UBC Press, 1986), 154.

4. Goldberg and Mercer, *The Myth of the North American City*, 24.

5. Michael Harcourt, Ken Cameron, and Sean Rossiter, *City Making in Paradise: Nine Decisions That Saved Vancouver* (Vancouver: Douglas & McIntyre, 2007), 40.

6. City of Vancouver, "West End Community Plan," Vancouver City Council, November 20, 2013, https://guidelines.vancouver.ca/policy-plan-west-end.pdf.

7. Robert M. Walsh, "The Origins of Vancouverism: A Historical Inquiry into the Architecture and Urban Form of Vancouver, British Columbia," doctoral thesis, University of Michigan, 2013, https://deepblue.lib.umich.edu/handle/2027.42/97802.

8. John Mackie, "The Week in History: 1959: A New Wave of High-Rises Transforms the West End," *Vancouver Sun*, November 22, 2019.

9. Lance Berelowitz, *Dream City: Vancouver and the Global Imagination* (Vancouver: Douglas & McIntyre), 2010.

10. Walsh, "The Origins of Vancouverism."

11. *West End 66 (excerpts), B&W, 1966*, produced by CBUT, CBC Vancouver, February 2016, YouTube, https://www.youtube.com/watch?v=TYjxfmG95NE.

12. John Punter, *The Vancouver Achievement: Urban Planning and Design*, new ed. (Vancouver: UBC Press, 2004), 37.

13. Punter, *The Vancouver Achievement*, 92.

14. *Homes by Design*, TV series, Sound Vision International, 1999–2001.

15. Harcourt, Cameron, and Rossiter, *City Making in Paradise*, 5.

16. Harcourt, Cameron, and Rossiter, *City Making in Paradise*, 98.

17. Stuart McNish, "Vancouver Forever Changed by Expo '86," KCTS 9, July 29, 2016.

18. Harcourt, Cameron, and Rossiter, *City Making in Paradise*, 86.

19. Greater Vancouver Regional District, "The Livable Region: 1976/1986: Proposals to Manage the Growth of Greater Vancouver," Greater Vancouver Regional District Planning Committee, March 26, 1975, http://www.metrovancouver.org/about/library/HarryLashLibraryPublications/Livable-Region-1976-1986-Proposals-to-Manage-the-Growth-of-Greater-Vancouver.pdf.

20. City of Burnaby Planning and Development Committee, "Burnaby Transportation Plan Update," City of Burnaby, July 2017, https://pub-burnaby.escribemeetings.com/filestream.ashx?DocumentId=38647.

21. TransLink, "TransLink: 2017 Transit Service Performance Review," Translink.ca, https://www.translink.ca/-/media/translink/documents/plans-and-projects/managing-the-transit-network/tspr/2017_tspr_summary.pdf.

22. Trevor Brody, "False Creek, Dubai," *BC Business*, September 1, 2006.

23. Dennis Lynch, "Onni Group Adds to Downtown Portfolio with 60-Story Residential Tower," *The Real Deal,* April 13, 2018.

24. Brian Libby, "Vancouver, Portland's Point-Tower Role Model, Embraces Mid-Rise Housing for Olympics," *Portland Architecture*, February 19, 2010.

25. "City of Vancouver in Middle of the Pack When it Comes to Density," *CBC News*, January 9, 2018.

26. Jennifer Saltman, "2016 Census: Transit Use Increases Among Metro Vancouver Commuters," *Vancouver Sun*, November 29, 2017.

27. Metro 2040 Dashboard website, http://www.metrovancouver.org/metro 2040, accessed June 6, 2023.

28. Ian Mulgrew, "Vancouver's Expo '86 May Fall on Its Face—As Its Mascot Did," *Christian Science Monitor*, September 26, 1985.

29. Jason Proctor, "Deal of the Century: Expo 86 Land Purchase Changed Vancouver," CBC, May 4, 2016.

30. Taras Grescoe, "The Best Asian Food in North America? Try British Columbia," *New York Times*, June 4, 2018.

31. Mathew Campbell and Natalie Obiko Pearson, "The City That Had Too Much Money," *Bloomberg Businessweek*, October 20, 2018.

32. Campbell and Pearson, "The City That Had Too Much Money."

33. Norimitsu Onishi, "In Vancouver, Indigenous Communities Get Prime Land, and Power," *New York Times*, August 23, 2022.

34. Justin McElroy, "One Chart Shows How Unprecedented Vancouver's Real Estate Situation Is," *Global News*, August 4, 2016.

35. Darryl Dyke, "At Vancouver's 'Cold Harbour' a Neighborhood Hollows Out," *Globe and Mail*, May 3, 2013.

36. Oliver Bullough, *Moneyland: The Inside Story of the Crooks and Kleptocrats Who Rule the World* (New York: St. Martin's Press, 2018).

37. Kenneth Chan, "61% of Vancouver Resident's Considering Leaving Region Due to Housing Affordability: Survey," Daily Hive, September 9, 2022.

38. Michael Kaminer, "Do You Want to Buy a House in Canada? Not So Fast," *New York Times*, December 29, 2022.

39. Paul Goldberger, "Too Rich, Too Thin, Too Tall?" *Vanity Fair*, May 2014.

40. McElroy, "One Chart Shows How Unprecedented Vancouver's Real Estate Situation Is."

41. Dan Bertolet, "Vancouver's New Plan to Allow Homes of All Shapes and Sizes," Sightline Institute, August 14, 2018.

42. Tracey Lindeman, "New Taxes and Higher Density Aren't Fixing Vancouver's Housing Problem," CityLab, May 7, 2019.

CHAPTER 9: HOUSTON TOWNHOUSE

1. Stephen L. Klineberg, *Prophetic City: Houston on the Cusp of a Changing America* (New York: Avid Reader Press, 2021), 11.

2. Robert Wooster and Christine Moor Sanders, "Spindletop Oilfield," Texas State Historical Association, April 2, 2019. https://www.tshaonline.org/handbook/entries/spindletop-oilfield.

3. Barrie Scardino Bradley, *Improbable Metropolis: Houston's Architectural and Urban History* (Austin: University of Texas Press, 2020), 14.

4. George M. Baily, "Early Morning Observations," *Houston Post*, November 10, 1921.

5. Klineberg, *Prophetic City*, 28.

6. Bradley, *Improbable Metropolis*, 159.

7. Bradley, *Improbable Metropolis*, 159.

8. Bradley, *Improbable Metropolis*, 211.

9. Matthew Lasner, *High Life: Condo Living in the Suburban Century* (New Haven, CT: Yale University Press, 2012), 204.

10. William G. Salter, "Housing Development Process," master's thesis, Rice University, 1975, https://scholarship.rice.edu/bitstream/handle/1911/104872/RICE 2518.pdf?sequence=1&isAllowed=y.

11. Stephen Fox, "The Houston Townhouse," *Cite: The Architecture and Design Review of Houston* 49 (Fall 2000): 19–23, https://offcite.rice.edu/2010/03/The HoustonTownhouse_Fox_Cite49.pdf.

12. Salter, "Housing Development Process."

13. Fox, "The Houston Townhouse."

14. Salter, "Housing Development Process."

15. Cyndy Severson, "The House that Art Built," *Texas Monthly*, September 1977.

16. Bradley, *Improbable Metropolis*, 230.

17. Jake Wegmann, "Bayou City Townhouse Boom: Does Houston Have Something to Teach Us About Pro-Climate Transformation?" *Platform*, October 2020.

18. Wegmann, "Bayou City Townhouse Boom."

19. Dylan McGuinness, "New Houston District Aims to Preserve Last Remnant of History Near Rice Military," *Houston Chronicle*, January 26, 2022.

20. NuNu Chang, "Planning the Houston Way, Part II: Special Minimum Lot Size," *Rice Design Alliance* (blog), March 21, 2018.

21. Bradley, *Improbable Metropolis*, 135.

22. Donovan Adesoro (real estate developer), in conversation with the author, July 2022.

23. Russell Redman, "H-E-B Opens First Store in Mixed Use Development," *Supermarket News*, October 9, 2019.

24. Walkable Places Committee, "City of Houston Users' Guide for Walkable Places and Transit-Oriented Development," Planning and Development Department, City of Houston, 2020, https://www.houstontx.gov/planning/docs_pdfs /User's%20Guide%20for%20WP%20and%20TOD%20report_2020-10-01.pdf.

25. William Fulton, urban planner, in conversation with the author, April 2022.

26. Mark J. Perry, "New US Homes Today Are 1,000 Square Feet Larger Than in 1973 and Living Space Per Person Has Nearly Doubled," American Enterprise Institute, June 5, 2016.

27. Timothy Egan, "In Portland Houses Are Friendly or Else," *New York Times*, April 20, 2000.

28. Steven Litt, "Critics Want Cleveland to Replace Zoning Code Allowing Controversial, Oversized Townhouses, 'Slot Houses,'" Cleveland.com, March 28, 2021.

29. David Netto, "Is Roman Abramovich's Controversial New York City Mansion the Future of Manhattan Real Estate?" *Town and Country*, January 30, 2019.

30. Rachel Holliday Smith, "NYC's Wealthy Enclaves Lost Housing in Past Decade as Combining of Apartments Outpaced New Construction," TheCity.NYC, February 8, 2021. https://www.thecity.nyc/housing/2021/2/8/22273634/nycs -wealthy-enclaves-lost-housing-in-past-decade

31. Sarah Freishtat, "Chicago's Two-, Three-, and Four-Flats are Disappearing, Changing Communities and Who Can Afford to Live in Them," *Chicago Tribune*, May 13, 2021.

32. Corinne Ruff, "St. Louis Is Losing Multifamily Units. Some Aldermen Want to Charge a Conversion Fee," St. Louis Public Radio, November 15, 2021.

33. Marissa Gluck, "In L.A., a Cheaply Constructed Pop-Up Bar That's a Work of Art," *New York Times*, August 27, 2015.

34. Walkable Places Committee, *City of Houston Users' Guide for Walkable Places and Transit-Oriented Development*.

CONCLUSION: THE TINY TOWER

1. Jonathan Tate, architect, in conversation with the author, August 2022.

2. Brian Phillips, architect, in conversation with the author, July 2022.

3. Jonathan Tate, architect, in conversation with the author, August 2022.

4. Justin Fox, "What Happened When Minneapolis Ended Single-Family Zoning," *Bloomberg*, August 20, 2022.

5. Ian Carlton, David Garcia, Kate MacFarlane, and Ben Metcalf, *Will Allowing Duplexes and Lot Splits on Parcels Zoned for Single-Family Create New Homes?* Terner Center for Housing Innovation, UC Berkeley, July 2021, https://terner center.berkeley.edu/wp-content/uploads/2021/07/SB-9-Brief-July-2021-Final.pdf.

6. Senator Toni G. Atkins, "SB 9 (Atkins): California HOME (Housing Opportunity & More Efficiency) Act," fact sheet, April 2021, https://cayimby.org /wp-content/uploads/2021/04/SB-9-Atkins-Factsheet-4.5.pdf.

7. Chris Arnold et al., "There's a Massive Housing Shortage Across the U.S. Here's How Bad It Is Where You Live," NPR, July 14, 2022.

IMAGE CREDITS

1. House diagram with architectural terms: Max Podemski
2. A Philadelphia row house: Max Podemski
3. Narrow lots in Philadelphia: Max Podemski
4. Three centuries of Philadelphia row homes: Max Podemski
5. 65 Mott Street: Max Podemski
6. Tenements drenched in ornamentation: Max Podemski
7. Diagram from an 1895 report on tenement house conditions: Courtesy of the NYC Municipal Library
8. A New Orleans double shotgun: Max Podemski
9. The evolution of the shotgun: in Haiti: Max Podemski
10. A Chicago workers cottage: Max Podemski
11. Evolution of a workers cottage: Max Podemski
12. Aerial photo from 1901 of Chicago's Near West Side: Robert Hunter, *Tenement Conditions in Chicago: Report by the Investigating Committee of the City Homes Association* (1901).
13. Chicago became plastered in ads: Courtesy of Chicago History Museum, ICHi-006577. The image on the left is from 1891; the image on the right is from 1883.
14. A Portland bungalow: Max Podemski
15. The evolution of the Portland bungalow: Max Podemski
16. Aerial photo of Levittown, 1959: Public Domain, via Wikimedia Commons
17. Aerial view of downtown Portland: ©Historic Photo Archive
18. A Boston triple-decker. Max Podemski
19. The evolution of a Boston streetcar suburb: Max Podemski
20. The evolution of urban housing in Boston: Max Podemski
21. A Los Angeles dingbat. Max Podemski
22. Horatio West Court: Max Podemski
23. Boulevard transformation: Max Podemski
24. Los Angeles architecture firms and podium buildings: Here and Now Agency

25. 888 Beach Avenue: Max Podemski

26. West End of Vancouver in the 1950s and '60s: Max Podemski

27. Floor plans of two buildings: Max Podemski

28. Metrotown: Courtesy of iStock/Overflightstock Ltd.

29. A Houston town home: Max Podemski

30. Three eras of Houston town homes: Max Podemski

31. Tiny Tower in Philadelphia: Sam Oberter

32. 3106 St. Thomas Street: Courtesy of Will Crocker

INDEX